DanielNotes

An Inspirational Commentary
on the Book of Daniel

DanielNotes

An Inspirational Commentary
on the Book of Daniel

Greg Hinnant

CREATION
HOUSE PRESS®

DANIELNOTES by Greg Hinnant
Published by Creation House Press
A part of Strang Communications Company
600 Rinehart Road
Lake Mary, Florida 32746
www.creationhouse.com

Unless otherwise noted, all Scripture quotations are from *The New Scofield Study Bible*, authorized King James Version (New York: Oxford University Press, 1967).

Scripture quotations marked AMP are from the Amplified Bible. Old Testament copyright © 1965, 1967 by the Zondervan Corporation. The Amplified New Testament copyright © 1954, 1958, 1987 by the Lockman Foundation. Used by permission.

Scripture quotations marked KJV are from the King James Version of the Bible.

Scripture quotations marked MODERN LANGUAGE BIBLE are from the *New Berkeley Version in Modern English*, revised edition, copyright © 1945, 1959, 1969 by Zondervan Publishing House. Used by permission.

Scripture quotations marked NAS are from the New American Standard Bible. Copyright © 1960, 1962, 1963, 1968, 1971, 1972, 1973, 1975, 1977 by the Lockman Foundation. Used by permission. (www.Lockman.org)

Scripture quotations marked NKJV are from the New King James Version of the Bible. Copyright © 1979, 1980, 1982 by Thomas Nelson, Inc., publishers. Used by permission.

Scripture quotations marked PHILLIPS are from *The New Testament in Modern English*, revised edition. Copyright © 1958, 1960, 1972 by J. B. Phillips. Macmillan Publishing Company. Used by permission.

Scripture quotations marked TLB are from *The Living Bible*. Copyright © 1971. Used by permission of Tyndale House Publishers, Inc., Wheaton, IL 60189. All rights reserved.

Words that are set off by vertical lines are words in *The New Scofield Study Bible* that differ from the authorized King James Version. These differences are slight, but the reader who is very familiar with the King James Version would notice them.

Cover design by Terry Clifton
Interior design by David Bilby
Scroll art by Sarah Hinnant

Library of Congress Catalog Card Number: 2002117087
International Standard Book Number: 1-59185-169-6

03 04 05 06 07 — 8 7 6 5 4 3 2 1
Printed in the United States of America

To Oswald Chambers,
whose broad-ranging, deep Bible teachings
inspired me to build an altar of steadfast Bible
study in my life...

To A.W. Tozer,
whose uncompromising, laser-sharp writings
stirred me to place the wood of studious
contemplation and the sacrifice of prayerful
writing on that altar...

To Walter H. Beuttler,
whose insightful, passionate messages enflamed
my heart-altar with a burning passion "to
minister and to give" to others every truth that
has been given to me.

ACKNOWLEDGMENTS

With a heart full of praise to God and thanksgiving to His people, I want to acknowledge the individuals who ceaselessly and selflessly assist me in the work of this ministry. Without their faithful help, I would not be able to pass on to the body of Christ these truths from the Book of Daniel. Many, many thanks to:

Alice W. Bosworth
Jean Brock
Suzanne Hinnant
John J. McHugh, Jr.
Virginia G. McHugh
Kathleen E. McHugh

Phyllis H. McNeill
Mary Ann Mowery
Chris D. Smith
Melissa N. Smith
Evelyn A. Ward

I also gratefully acknowledge the staff of Creation House Press for their willing investment in this work. Their prayers, thoughts, and skillful labors have helped polish and present this message. My hearty appreciation to:

Rev. Dr. Allen Quain, Manager
Amy Condiff, Administrative Assistant
Deborah Poulalion, Editor
Deborah Moss, Copyeditor
Terry Clifton, Graphic Design
David Bilby, Interior Design

Furthermore, I wish to recognize the following individuals for taking the time to review this manuscript prior to its publication:

Dr. Ian Bond, Christian Life School of Theology
Dr. William C. Suttles, Raleigh Institute of Biblical Studies

Finally, I lovingly thank my daughter, whose sketch of the ancient scroll shown on the back cover of this book appears on the title page of each chapter:

Sarah Hinnant

Contents

PREFACE

For many years, my workday mornings have been given largely to systematic, prayerful Bible study and annotation. A few years ago, the Lord prompted me to better organize the insights He was giving me. After arranging these commentaries in a much more publishable format, I sent excerpts to Dr. Judson Cornwall, who encouraged me to publish them. Sensing God's will, I began seeking to publish the first of these commentaries, *DanielNotes*.

Doubtless its prime contribution will not be merely more academic information. Nor will it add significantly to the massive amount of prophetic data now pervading the Church. Rather, its value lies chiefly in the practical spiritual lessons it sets forth. By design, this work is more insightful than academic, more inspirational than informational. It will present to every reader just what I have repeatedly asked God to give me in study: not merely the letter but the spirit of the Word. By studying these spiritual principles extracted from Daniel's scroll, you will discover to your delight many things the Spirit is saying to the Church today. Then you have only to put them to use.

If you are a minister or Bible teacher, you will find here much sermonic material. Use it freely to enlighten, comfort, and challenge the Lord's sheep under your care. For simplicity, the chapters of this commentary are numbered to correspond to the chapters in the Book of Daniel. Every entry is prefaced by the exact chapter and verse(s) it discusses. The chief spiritual lessons in most entries are stated succinctly at their close. Many entries are cross-referenced to link, and further exposit, similar entries. Numerous biblical references are also given at the close of most entries to help better illustrate the points presented. They also serve as illustrations for teaching. For greater variation in building sermons taken from this commentary, you may want to occasionally use one of the biblical references as your main text, rather than repeatedly using the texts taken from the Book of Daniel. In this way, you will not seem to draw only from Daniel's well of biblical water.

If you are a Bible student, this commentary will help you understand not only the literary work it examines but also the larger truths of overcoming Christianity it proffers, which are so desperately needed in this final and perilous hour of Church history.

And for every reader, may I suggest you read the Bible verses or portions referenced before their corresponding entries. Or you may want to read by chapter—a chapter of the Book of Daniel, then a chapter of commentary. Whatever your preference, I pray the Holy Spirit will abundantly reward you as you obey His great command, "Study to show thyself approved unto God…" (2 Tim. 2:15).

—GREG HINNANT

INTRODUCTION

DANIEL: THE MAN AND HIS MESSAGE

To fully understand a man's message, we must understand the man. And yet, to fully understand the man, we must also understand his message. To truly discover the character and Book of Daniel, therefore, let's ponder *Daniel—the man and his message.*

Daniel—the Man

#5 Born into Judean nobility in 621 B.C., Daniel was deported to Babylon as a teenager (approximately sixteen years old). Once there, he quickly displayed what would become his most prominent character trait: uncompromising loyalty to God's Word. (See chapter 1.) For Daniel's special devotion, God gave him special gifts of the Spirit of God, which rendered Daniel a scholar of gifted intellect, an astute counselor, a proficient administrator, an accurate interpreter of dreams, and an exceptionally far-seeing prophet. These gifts led to Daniel's promotion to high government office, first during Babylonian supremacy

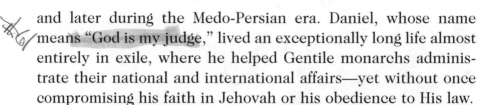

and later during the Medo-Persian era. Daniel, whose name means "God is my judge," lived an exceptionally long life almost entirely in exile, where he helped Gentile monarchs administrate their national and international affairs—yet without once compromising his faith in Jehovah or his obedience to His law. For a long period late in his life (over twenty years, 561–539 B.C.), Daniel was out of public service. Two facts reveal this. First, Daniel was not a member of King Belshazzar's court when the famous "handwriting on the wall" appeared at the king's dinner party. (See chapter 5.) Second, his previously renowned wisdom had been long forgotten. Only the king's mother remembered him on that fateful evening, and Belshazzar summoned Daniel only after her high and urgent recommendation (Dan. 5:10–12). After Belshazzar's subsequent death, Daniel's giftedness was immediately recognized by Darius the Mede, who served under Cyrus, king of Persia, and Daniel was appointed to a very high government position in yet another Gentile kingdom (Dan. 5:30–6:3). *The Spirit-Filled Life Bible* notes that Daniel's writings cover the reign of two Gentile kingdoms (Babylon and Medo-Persia) and four kings (Nebuchadnezzar, Belshazzar, Darius and Cyrus; p. 1230). *The New Analytical Bible* adds, "With the exception of Joseph, no other member of his race held such positions of honor and influence in foreign states" (p. 1008). *The Wycliffe Bible Encyclopedia* states that he served "until the third year of Cyrus (536 B.C.), being perhaps ninety years of age and still active" (p. 422).

Indeed, Daniel's was a long and prolific ministry, his own hand testifying that he began training for service in 605 B.C. and was still serving effectively in 536 B.C., some sixty-nine years later (Dan. 10:1). Though officially he never held the prophetic office and is therefore not categorized by Hebrew theologians as a major prophet (the Book of Daniel is part of the Writings, not the Prophets, in the Hebrew Old Testament), Daniel's upright, disciplined character and amazing, far-reaching prophecies serve as major inspirations to both Jew and Christian alike. As to his authenticity as a prophet, the definitive answer to this question is found in the words of Christ, who in His Olivet Discourse referred to him as "Daniel *the prophet*" (Matt. 24:15, emphasis added). With these passing words the prime biblical authority confirms that, indeed, Daniel was a true prophet of God. End of controversy.

Also most noteworthy is the Book of Daniel's disclosure that Daniel—a man of impeccable character, courageous faith, and remarkable spiritual insight—was one of God's favorite children. Three times angels declared him to be "greatly beloved" by God (Dan. 9:23; 10:11, 19). *Of no other Bible character is such a lofty inspired commendation ascribed.* Furthermore, God Himself testified to Daniel's holy character elsewhere in Scripture by mentioning him in company with such indisputably great characters as Noah and Job. (See Ezek. 14:14, 20.)

The Book of Daniel— Its Themes

The central theme of this book is the sovereignty of God. The introduction to *The Living Bible* states:

> Daniel's major theme is the sovereignty of God. God rules over the affairs of men, directing the course of history toward his own ends, working in and through the acts of men. The kingdoms of men rise and fall but God remains forever... (p. 896)

The *Spirit-Filled Life Bible* states:

> The purpose is to show that the God of Israel, the only God, is in control of the destiny of all nations. (p. 1229)

Daniel's writings describe how God went to great lengths to show King Nebuchadnezzar, the first Gentile monarch to rule over Israel and the known world, that He, not Nebuchadnezzar, was in ultimate control. Then God apparently ordered Nebuchadnezzar to write his lesson as a testimonial to all posterity (see Dan. 4:1–3), so all future heads of state might walk humbly before Him. Daniel's book also reveals that the sequence of temporal Gentile kingdoms

will lead up, and ultimately give way to, the eternal kingdom of
Christ. Thus, from beginning to end, God is sovereign—in unchal-
lengeable control of the affairs of nations. Nothing happens without His permission, and He intervenes whenever, wherever, and
however He wills to alter the course of history according to His
predetermined plan of redemption.

Other very prominent themes in this book are the testing
of the righteous, divine chastening, divine judgment, and
prophecy. The series of increasingly severe tests experienced by
Daniel and his three friends reveals God's intent to test the
righteous. The chastisement of King Nebuchadnezzar demonstrates divine chastening in its most severe form and is a warning to all Christians and non-Christians alike of the dangers of
pride, arrogance, and unresponsiveness to divine instruction
and mercy. The sudden capital judgment of King Belshazzar
(chapter 5) reveals the wrath of God against all who presump-
tuously blaspheme Him, His people, or holy things. And the rest
of the book is given largely to prophecy.

Primarily, the prophecies of this book are addressed to the
Jews, for God withheld the revelation of the Church from Daniel.
Also, God reveals the future of the Gentile world solely as it
relates to the Hebrew people: their nation, Israel; their capital,
Jerusalem; their center of worship, the temple; their worst
enemy, the "prince that shall come" (Dan. 9:26); and their most
honorable Son and divine Savior, "Messiah, the Prince" (Dan.
9:25). For Christians, however, these prophecies are just as vital.
Without the prophetic information they add, clarify, or set in
order, we could not clearly see the glorious and edifying picture
God has revealed in His jigsaw puzzle of End-Time prophecy, the
pieces of which are found scattered throughout the prophets,
Gospels, and Epistles, as well as the Book of Revelation.

The Book of Daniel—
Revealing Christ

The revelation of Jesus is the central theme unifying every book in the Bible (Rev. 19:10). Accordingly, the Book of Daniel reveals Jesus in three different perspectives.

First, Jesus is revealed walking with Shadrach, Meshach, and Abednego in Nebuchadnezzar's fire (Dan. 3:25). Second, Daniel sees Him returning to earth to overthrow Israel's enemies and liberate her captive people (7:13–14, 21–22, 24–27). (This is the same incident in which He will fulfill the "smiting stone" prophecy of chapter two; see 2:31–35.) Third, Daniel records his personal vision of Christ in His eternal glory (10:5–6), comparable to what the apostles witnessed on the mount and John witnessed on Patmos.

In these three portrayals the Book of Daniel reveals three truths about Jesus. He is:

1. Our comforting Companion in great trouble

2. Our faithful Deliverer from (and the smiting Stone of) all oppressors

3. Fully God in fullest glory

The Book of Daniel— Its Style and Purpose

This book, particularly its final half, is an apocalypse, or unveiling. *The New Scofield Study Bible* states that this literary form "uses many figures and symbols"; also, that when evil seemed to be triumphing in the world, God gave apocalyptic writing "to show the real situation behind that which was apparent, and to indicate the eventual victory of righteousness upon the earth" (p. 896). Thus the Book of Daniel, as other apocalyptic writings, serves the vital purpose of giving understanding and hope to God's people in their darkest hours of despair.

Other apocalyptic writings are the Book of Revelation, the Book of Zechariah, and four chapters of the Book of Isaiah (Isa. 24–27).

The Book of Daniel—
Foreshadowings of Israel's End

The New Scofield Study Bible states:

> The historical events in Daniel, occurring at the begin-
> ning of the times of the Gentiles, illustrate events
> prophetically set forth in the book as taking place at the
> end of this period and culminating catastrophically in
> the termination of Gentile world rule at the return of
> Christ…Thus, the persecution of the children of God
> in chapters 3 and 6 foreshadows the more severe and
> universal persecution of God's people to take place at
> the end of this age… (p. 896)

Indeed, in His infinite wisdom and power, God providen-
tially shaped the historical events recorded in the Book of
Daniel to foreshadow Israel's future. Nebuchadnezzar's idol, his
institution of enforced state religion, his order to execute all
who refused to worship—these events paint a clear and detailed
typological portrait of Antichrist's blasphemous idolatry and
murderous tyranny. The three Hebrew boys' defiance of
Nebuchadnezzar's worship order and their subsequent trial in
his furnace illustrate the Jewish remnant's uncompromising
obedience to God in the Great Tribulation. And, in a subtler
way, Belshazzar's and Babylon's sudden judgment (Dan.
5:30–31) foreshadows the sudden, catastrophic end of
Antichrist and his worldwide kingdom.

Understand also that because Daniel knew nothing of the
Church, these foreshadowings of fiery trials to come speak of
Israel's end, not the Church's. That they so plainly point to the
tribulation period shows us that *this fixed period of special testing is divinely designed for Israel, not the Church*. The Church
must and will be fully tested by fire in this present age *before* the
Holy Spirit is taken out of this world at the Rapture (see 2 Thess.
2:6–7; 1 Thess. 5:9–10) with the purified, proven bride of Christ—
the object of His sacred mission—in tow. (See Gen. 24:61–67.)

The Book of Daniel—
Its General Lessons

Here are four general spiritual lessons we may draw from the Book of Daniel:

1. God reveals the end from the beginning.

Through Daniel's interpretations and visions, God revealed the ultimate collapse of Gentile world power to Israel at the beginning of her long seventy-year Babylonian captivity, and at the beginning of the much longer "times of the Gentiles"—the yet-unfinished, multi-century period in which God has permitted Gentiles to rule His world, and more particularly Jerusalem and the Jewish people. (Though its national sovereignty was restored in 1948, Israel is far from the peaceful, secure state it will be in the Day of the Lord. Daily it is strongly challenged, influenced, or limited by the will of Gentile nations, both friendly and hostile, and must yet suffer one final, full captivity to Antichrist's regime during the Great Tribulation.) So God revealed the end of these lengthy adversities from their beginning. (See Isa. 46:9–10.)

2. Ultimately, God and His people always succeed.

Daniel's interpretation of Nebuchadnezzar's dream (chapter 2) and his vision of Antichrist's rise and fall (chapters 7–8) revealed that, despite Israel's present horrific exile, God would yet raise His people to rule the world under Him. So Daniel saw *through* the long day of Gentile rule all the way to the coming Day of the Lord. This vision of victory was good news to Jews, who at the time were utterly defeated—without homeland, nation, temple, king, prophet, respect, and hope. Hence, they could say with Job, "Though He slay us, yet shall we trust in Him" (see Job 13:15); and with Christ, "'Though we are dead, yet shall we live' and prosper in Messiah's everlasting kingdom" (see John 11:25; Dan. 7:27). So Daniel foresaw that God and the Jews would ultimately succeed.

3. Successful testing prepares us for the fulfillment of prophecy.

The order in which the Book of Daniel presents its subject matter is revealing. In the first six chapters, the Holy Spirit occupies the reader primarily with the intensive and extensive testing of the uncompromisingly righteous—Daniel and his three friends (see chapters 1–3, 6). In the final six chapters, He turns to address prophecy almost exclusively (see chapters 7–12). Thus the subjects addressed are first testing, then prophecy.

By doing this the Spirit has sent us a subtle message: "Testing comes first, not prophecy. Heed and believe prophecy, but don't consider it more important than the central issues over which God is presently testing you. First learn your lessons and pass your tests, as Daniel and company did. This will prepare you, as it did them, to understand, share, and face future events."

4. God gives wisdom and prophetic understanding to those who obey Him uncompromisingly.

The order of the information presented in the first chapter of the Book of Daniel illustrates another key truth. The Inspirer of Scripture first draws the reader's attention to the uncompromising obedience of Daniel and his three peers. (See Dan. 1:5, 8–16.) Then He describes how subsequently all four youths were given exceptional wisdom and how Daniel received an especially clear and full understanding of prophecy (Dan. 1:17). (Meanwhile, it is implied that the other Jewish youths who compromised their faith by defiling themselves with the king's diet were *not* similarly gifted; see Dan. 8:27c.) So first we are informed of the uncompromising obedience of the "faithful four," then of their special gifts of wisdom and prophetic understanding.

Thus the Spirit reveals that God gives special wisdom and understanding of prophecy to believers who, like Daniel and friends, obey Him uncompromisingly. Christ's promise, "He will show you things to come" (John 16:13), belongs rightly to them.

The Book of Daniel—
Its Divisions

The Book of Daniel may be outlined as follows:

1. The testing of the righteous (chapters 1–3, 6)
2. Divine chastening (chapter 4)
3. Divine judgment (chapter 5)
4. Prophecy (chapters 2, 7–12)

The Book of Daniel—
Its Languages

Six of the first seven chapters of the Book of Daniel are written in Aramaic (2:4 to 7:28), the official language of Babylon, which Daniel learned in the king's college (see 1:4) and used throughout his lifetime of public service. The first and last five chapters of the book are written in Daniel's native tongue, Hebrew.

PART ONE

OVERCOMERS IN ACTION

Besides being the repository of Daniel's extraordinary prophetic visions, the Book of Daniel is a vital source of inspiration for overcoming Christians. Note how often its chapters portray Daniel, Shadrach, Meshach, and Abednego—God's "faithful four"—courageously facing and conquering various challenges to their faith.

In chapter 1, all are tried over their loyalty to God's law; in chapter 2, by a sudden crisis resolvable only by fervent prayer and faith; in chapter 3, Shadrach, Meshach, and Abednego are again tempted to compromise God's law; in chapter 4, Daniel bravely delivers a most unpleasant message to a most arrogant and volatile king; in chapter 5, he conquers life "on the shelf" and shows himself a master of spiritual readiness; in chapter 6, he refuses to compromise his devotional fellowship with God, even at the cost of breaking Persian law and being thrown to the lions; and in chapter 10, when faced with apparent unanswered prayer, he proves himself a very persistent and successful petitioner of heaven. Thus, seven times Daniel and company overcame their trials of faith.

As if a distant biblical echo of their resounding victories, Jesus challenges us seven times in His messages to the Church age to overcome every challenge to our faith: "To him that overcometh will I give…" (Rev. 2:7, 11, 17, 26–28; 3:5, 12, 21). To become overcomers, we must understand overcomers. For that, God has given us the Book of Daniel.

So let's study this, His inspiring record of *overcomers in action*.

CHAPTER ONE

UNCOMPROMISING!

1:1–2 IN THE BEGINNING. Daniel's inspired description of his life, times, and works begins with the first of three major deportations of Judean Jews by the Babylonians. The year was approximately 605 B.C. Daniel was only a "youth" (Dan. 1:4; approximately sixteen years old), and "Nebuchadnezzar, king of Babylon" (v. 1), who was approximately Daniel's age, was in fact, not the sitting monarch but the crown prince of Babylon. Daniel apparently referred to Nebuchadnezzar as king because He ascended to the throne only one and a half months later, after the death of his father, King Nabopolassar. Nebuchadnezzar's immediate entrance into the story is fitting since he soon becomes a very central figure in Daniel's inspiring autobiography.

1:1–2 Sacrilege. After taking Judah, Prince Nebuchadnezzar committed sacrilege by destroying God's holy temple and taking "part" (v. 2) of its utensils, which were also holy, to display as the spoils of war in the shrine of his god Nebo. *The Ryrie Study Bible* claims he confiscated these utensils "as a prize and as proof of the power of Nebuchadnezzar's gods" (p. 1306). These "vessels" were further desecrated many years later by Nebuchadnezzar's grandson King Belshazzar during his blasphemous dinner party. (See chapter 5.)

Simply defined, sacrilege is *temple robbing*. It is dishonoring the shrine and holy things of a purported deity, or the "violation or profanation of anything sacred or held sacred" (*Webster's Encyclopedic Unabridged Dictionary of the English Language*). Sacrilege was the highest crime a conquering people could commit against their vanquished foes. It crushed their very spirit by spoiling their faith in their greatest hope, their all-important god. Hence, they were left totally disconsolate, with nothing to hope in—except, perhaps, the so-called god who had conquered their god. Such were the reasons sacrilege was practiced in antiquity.

As men of uncompromising faith, Daniel and his three friends were not fooled by this false show of Nebo's superiority. They held fast their confidence in Jehovah, although to the unspiritual minds of their day everything looked as if Jehovah were powerless and Nebo peerless. (See Hab. 3:17–19.) Knowing and believing God's law, they recognized the Babylonian victory and deportation for what it was: not a failure of their God but a successful fulfillment of His plain warning. In His law, God had promised to bring ruthless foreign invaders against His people if they rebelled (see Lev. 26:32–39; Deut. 28:49–68), and now He had done it. Hence, Nebo had not defeated Jehovah. Jehovah had only *used* Nebo's servants to chasten His own disobedient children and was still to be worshiped as the absolute Sovereign He was and is.

Other great temple robbers are Antiochus IV (Epiphanes; see Dan. 8:13; 11:31) and Antichrist (see Dan. 9:27; 12:11; Matt. 24:15).

1:2 The Giver of victory. "And the Lord gave Jehoiakim... into his hand" (Dan. 1:2). Here, strangely, God gave victory to the Gentiles rather than to His own people. Why? Because this too is one of His ways.

Just as the Bible repeatedly informs us that God "gave" His people's enemies into their hands in the days of their righteous leadership and national obedience, it also records that when sin and idolatry were rampant among them He did precisely the opposite: He gave victory to the heathen kings and peoples who defied them. In this case, He gave victory to Nebuchadnezzar to chasten Judah for its past and ongoing national idolatry and for King Jehoiakim's personal wickedness (2 Chron. 36:5–6). In these and many other biblical examples of battles and conflicts, this lesson stands out: Victory is given by the Lord.

Truly, God alone is the ultimate decider of every conflict involving His people. Usually He gives victory to His children, provided they walk in uprightness and humble trust. At times, however, He gives victories to their enemies, either to chasten His people for their willful sins or to afford them with the ultimate test of their loyalty and faith (Dan. 7:21–22; Luke 22:53).

Nebuchadnezzar's victory over Jehoiakim marked the beginning of two prominent eras in Israel's history:

1. The captivity (approximately seventy years)

2. The times of the Gentiles (from the captivity to the kingdom of Christ)

Further along in his writings, Daniel described two other times in which God would give a heathen king victory over Israel. First, the Syrian desolater, Antiochus IV (Epiphanes), will defeat the Israelis (see Dan. 8:9–14); second, the final and worst of heathen kings, Antichrist, will attack and defeat Israel at the mid-point of the tribulation period (see Dan. 7:20–22, 24–25; 8:23–24; Rev. 13:7). Unlike their defeat in Daniel's day, Israel's final captivity will be for righteousness' sake; at that time "all Israel" (Rom. 11:26) will have at last turned to Jesus as their Messiah.

It is vital that we have the kind of faith that realizes God Himself personally determines whether we or our opponents win in every power struggle (Prov. 21:31); that, if we "do evil in

the sight of the Lord," He may indeed justly punish us by hand-
ing us over to our enemies; and, conversely, if we walk in
uncompromising obedience to Him, He will always give us ultimate victory—even if he ordains the temporary triumphing of
the wicked as the ultimate test of our faith, loyalty, and
endurance. Whatever His reason, always, God is the Giver of
victory.

Will you acknowledge and thank the Lord for giving you
victory? And will you also acknowledge that your defeats come
from His hand? (See Job 1:21b; 2:10b.) If so, the Spirit will
establish in you the kind of humility and faith that can with-
stand any storm and ultimately win every battle.

See John 19:11; 2 Chronicles 36:5–6; Judges 2:11–15;
3:7–8; Proverbs 21:31; 2 Chronicles 25:7–8; Job 1:21b; 2:10b.

*Lesson: Whether His people are given victory or given
into their enemies' hands, God is always the
Giver of victory.*

1:1–2 Daniel—a star in the night. The opening of the Book
of Daniel describes the darkest hour in Israel's national history
to date. Not since the Hebrews' bitter Egyptian slavery had they
been fully subjected to the tyranny of a Gentile monarch. Yet it
was in this black, hopeless midnight that God placed one of His
brightest stars, Daniel.

So God does to this day. He still reserves His brightest servants for His people's darkest times: periods of apostasy and
idolatry; the triumphing of the wicked; or other seasons of trouble, confusion, or oppression. As dark as it is today on the world's
horizon, we should be looking for the rising of God's new stars.

In this we see the unfailing faithfulness of God and the inex-
haustible sufficiency of His grace. No matter how low His people
get, no matter how bad their times, no matter how complete the
victory of evildoers may seem, God is still present, faithfully
sending light-bearers to give hope and strength to sustain His
covenant people. In *Paths to Power*, A. W. Tozer wrote:

> Invariably where daring faith is struggling to advance
> against hopeless odds, there is God sending "help from
> the sanctuary." (p. 36)

Indeed, Daniel's person, passion, and prophecies were a mighty "help from the sanctuary" above (Ps. 20:2), a great, guiding spiritual lodestar, to God's downtrodden, confused people, then and now.

The Light of the world has ordained that every believer be a light-bearer to this world. Are we preparing ourselves to be stars in the night, seeking, obeying, and sharing the illuminating Word of God in the thick darkness of this midnight hour?

See Exodus 2:2; Acts 26:16–18; Matthew 5:15–16; Philippians 2:15–16.

Lesson: God reserves His brightest servants for His people's darkest hours.

1:1–2; 1:21 From the alpha to the omega. This chapter opens with the beginning of Judah's captivity (Dan. 1:1–2) and closes with a reference to its end (the "first year of King Cyrus," v. 21). Furthermore, it states that Daniel continued to serve in high government positions until the year the Jews' captivity ended (v. 21). What is the Spirit saying here?

As stars shine throughout the night, so Daniel—God's brightest witness—shone all the way through the long darkness of the captivity. He rose and began radiating the knowledge of the one true God at the start of the captivity (vv. 1–20) and continued shining until the darkness of judgment gave way to the dawn of a new day of restoration (v. 21). God still does the same today.

His overcomers are His witness throughout this present Church age, and they will not stop shining until this age ends in the Rapture. Then in the tribulation that follows, God will still have His light-bearers, the 144,000 during the first half of that period (Rev. 7:1–8) and the "two witnesses" during its latter half (Rev. 11:3–12). So, from alpha to omega, the darkness of this Church age and the gross darkness of the tribulation will

be dotted with God's faithful light-bearers, containing, com-
mending, and communicating His truths in a world darkened by
unbelief. Like Christ, His overcomers will endure unto the end.

Daniel endured as God's faithful witness from the beginning
to the end of the darkness of the captivity. Are we enduring to
the end of our trials, or is our devotion growing weaker and our
witness dimmer by the day?

See Isaiah 43:10–12; Acts 1:8.

*Lesson: From the beginning to the end of every age, God's
servants bear witness to eternal truth amid the
universal darkness of unbelief.*

1:6–7 The remnant. These verses introduce the four principle characters in the Book of Daniel. The balance of Daniel's
writings reveals that their spiritual state stands in sharp contrast to that of their Jewish peers. While their nation was utterly
corrupt, Daniel, Hananiah, Mishael, and Azariah were utterly
incorruptible. They were as godly as the typical Jews of their
day were ungodly. In Daniel and his three friends, therefore, we
see the law of the remnant: Even in the worst times, God
always has His remnant of true, uncompromising believers.

A remnant is "a small remaining portion taken from a much
larger original whole." It is also "a residue" or "the substance
remaining after a fire or chemical reaction." Spiritually, a remnant is a small group of uncompromisingly faithful believers in
the midst of a larger, unfaithful body of religious professors.
After the "chemical reaction" of trial by fire, these alone will
remain fully devoted, firmly believing, and faithfully serving.
The New Scofield Study Bible describes Israel's remnant as, "a
spiritual Israel within the national Israel" (p. 1225). It further
states:

> Two things characterize the believing remnant
> always—loyalty to the Word of God, and separation
> from those who mock at that Word. (p. 786)

This law of the remnant holds equally true in the present

Church age. In every generation, the Church's remnant is the comparatively small company of wholly surrendered, uncompromising "disciples indeed" (John 8:31) who continue walking closely with Jesus while the majority of their professing Christian peers live in spiritual lukewarmness or full-blown apostasy.

Historically, the Scriptures reveal other members of the remnant during the captivity and post-captivity periods. They were Jeremiah, Baruch, Ebed-melech, Ezekiel, Mordecai, Esther, Ezra, and Nehemiah. In the gospel era, John the Baptist, Anna, Simeon, Elisabeth and Zacharias, and the apostles were all part of Israel's remnant. In the churches at Thyatira and Sardis, and the periods of Church history to which they correspond, there were faithful remnants existing in otherwise deceived, spiritually dead congregations. (See Rev. 2:24; 3:4.)

Prophetically, Daniel and his three friends foreshadow the faithful remnant of Christian Jews during the latter half of the tribulation period who will choose martyrdom or flight rather than worship the Antichrist. (See Rev. 13:15–17; 12:17.) They are referred to as a remnant, not because Israel will be apostate, but because they will be the only surviving believers on earth. (The 144,000 witnesses and their Jewish and Gentile converts will have been translated at or near the mid-point; see Rev. 7:9–17.)

Presently, Daniel and the three Hebrew boys are role models for the Christian remnant of this Laodicean era. Jesus' own words verified that, despite the prevailing lukewarmness, this age has in it those who will answer His call to full devotion and overcoming discipleship. It is these whom He calls to buy "gold, tried in the fire" of testing (Rev. 3:18, 20–22). As stated above, implicit in the concept of God's remnant is the willingness to be separate from the ungodly majority in times of spiritual declension. Are you willing to gather with God's faithful few if necessary, or are you determined to run with the religious herd wherever it goes? Your answer will reveal if you have in you what Daniel and his three friends had in them—and if you're in the remnant Jesus is calling in these last days.

See Romans 9:27; 11:5; 1 Kings 19:18; Isaiah 1:9; Luke 2:38; Revelation 11:13; 12:17; Ezra 9:8; Nehemiah 1:3; Isaiah 11:11, 16; 37:4, 31–32; Jeremiah 15:11; Ezekiel 6:8; Zephaniah 2:9; Haggai 1:12, 14.

Lesson: *Even in the worst times, God always has a remnant of uncompromisingly righteous believers.*

1:5 A changing of the guard. "...that, at the end of them, they might stand before the king." After being coronated king of Babylon (v. 3), Nebuchadnezzar selected prime captive youths for special training, hoping to find among them skilled administrators to fill his royal cabinet. Thus we see, as with many historical books of the Bible, a changing of the guard described on the opening page of Daniel's record. For the new time subsequently described (the captivity), new leaders are selected and installed in leadership.

Though the changing of Israel's civil rulers (kings) and religious leaders (priests, prophets) is noted in many biblical introductions (see Exod. 1:8; Josh. 1:1–7; 2 Chron. 1:1), Daniel called our attention to the change in the ruling secular government of Babylon. Thus with the first few strokes of his anointed pen, he informed us there was to be a new king and new counselors for the new time ahead. The old king had passed, and a new king, whom heaven would teach significant lessons (see chapter 4), had arisen. The old counselors (steeped in the heathenisms of sorcery and astrology) remained, yet they now would give way to the counsel of a spiritually minded and divinely sensitive superior, Daniel. (See Dan. 1:20; 2:48.) Thus God ensured that, though Gentiles would rule His people, He would overrule their leaders. If they ignored His will, He would chasten them (see Dan. 4:1–33); if they defied and blasphemed Him, He would remove them (see Dan. 5:18–31); and if they would walk humbly, respect His will, and favor His people, He would bless them (see Dan. 4:34–36; Gen. 41:47–49; Isa. 45:1–4).

It is a great day for us when we realize that a change of guard is not a change of God. Political, judicial, and religious leaders, good and bad, come and go in this fallen world, but God remains ever Ruler of all. Are you fretting at the existing guard or trusting in the sovereign rulership and faithful interventions of God?

See Exodus 1:6–8; Joshua 1:1–2; Judges 1:1; 1 Samuel 2:34–35; 2 Samuel 1:1; 1 Kings 1:1, 13, 30.

Lesson: *God provides new political and religious leadership at the outset of every new season among His people and among the nations—yet remains Ruler over all.*

1:3–5 The king's college. Once crowned, King Nebuchadnezzar decided to use the brightest of his conquered subjects to help govern his vast empire. But before he could use them, he had to educate and examine them. So the best young men were selected—the royals, the nobles, the most intelligent, gifted, responsible, good-looking, and hard-working youths—and placed in Babylonia's top academic institution, where for three years its most distinguished wise men gave them special instruction in Babylonian language (Aramaic), knowledge, culture, and ways. Thus, thoroughly "Babylonianized," these foreign nationals would be ready for use in the king's administration. That is, if they passed their examinations. Those dreaded tests came in the form of an interview by the king himself, who alone determined their fitness for his court (Dan. 1:18–19). It was at this interview that the superiority of Daniel, Hananiah, Mishael, and Azariah's God-given wisdom was first evident. Hence, they were given posts on the king's cabinet of advisers.

Nebuchadnezzar's actions here parallel those of Jesus, the King of kings. Jesus understands that potential must be educated and tested if it is to be discovered, developed, and used. Hence, He does with believers precisely what Nebuchadnezzar did with the faithful four: Jesus enrolls us in various "colleges" to instruct and examine us. First, He allows us to study and grow in the knowledge of His Word. Then, after a sufficient time, He tests us in the experiences of life to see if we are fit for further development and use as His servants. Do we discern the vision of heaven's king to use us in His future kingdom and His hand in our present "college"?

Currently, ours may be a college of devotion, in which we learn to seek the Lord early every day, pray, and prayerfully study the Bible to show ourselves approved unto God. Or we may be in a college of humility and grace, where daily we must learn to think spiritually and react graciously to ungracious people. Or we may be in a college of patience, where we must wait to have the things we need or desire. Perhaps we may be in a college of labor, where we must do unnoticed work willingly and diligently. Maybe ours is a college of suffering, where we must learn to be misunderstood and rejected for Christ's sake. Or ours may be a college of submission, in which we must learn to consistently cooperate with the human authorities God has placed over us in the home, school, workplace, or church.

Scripture reveals that our King's college has many campuses: Jesus was trained at the Nazareth campus; the apostle Paul studied first in Gamaliel's Bible college (Jerusalem), then in Arabia, and completed his internship in Tarsus; Moses received his undergraduate education in Egypt, then did extensive research in Midian and Sinai, recording the sum of his findings in his grand thesis, the Pentateuch; Elijah matriculated first at the Cherith campus and later completed his degree at Zarephath. Where is your current campus?

Wherever our school of the Spirit, one thing is sure: the biblical principles and godly ways we consistently obey will determine our performance when the King tests us. And that season of testing alone will determine if and when we become "a vessel unto honor," like Daniel, "sanctified, and |fit| for the master's use, and prepared unto every good work" (2 Tim. 2:21).

See 2 Timothy 2:15, 20–21; Luke 2:51–52; 1 Kings 17:2–7,

8–24; Acts 7:22–32; Galatians 1:15–18; Acts 9:26–30 (Acts 22:3).

Lesson: *Jesus places us in circumstantial schools of the Spirit, to teach us His Word and test our obedience, that we may be fit to rule with Him in time and eternity.*

1:3–17 Sanctified students in a secular system. The experience of Daniel and his three friends in Nebuchadnezzar's college also gives hope to Christians whose children must attend public schools (when church or home schooling is not possible). What God has done before, He can do again.

When Daniel and his three friends were required to attend institutions of learning that had neither knowledge of, or respect for, their God, they chose to continue walking in obedience to God's Word among the heathen. Hence, they lived holy lives among the unholy, studying Babylon's language and fields of knowledge but refusing to deny their God by worshiping Babylon's gods or indulging in its sins. So they sanctified themselves in the midst of a very secular educational system. For this, God rewarded them with special gifts of wisdom and personally blessed their personal education despite its heathen setting: "God gave them knowledge and skill in all learning and wisdom" (Dan. 1:17). And in the end He used them to show that His wisdom far excels that of fallen mankind (vv. 19–20).

He will do the same today with Christians who voluntarily live sanctified lives in secular educational systems. They too will receive "knowledge and skill in all learning and wisdom" (v. 17) and eventually rise to the top of their class.

If your children must attend a Babylonian school, remember to do two things: First, don't defile yourself or your children by forsaking biblical standards; second, ask God to give your little captive exiles "knowledge and skill in all learning and wisdom."

Lesson: *God will bless His people's children even in a secular educational system, if they will abide sanctified.*

1:4,17 Don't limit the Teacher. Observe that God gave Hananiah, Mishael, and Azariah knowledge and skill in *"all* learning and wisdom" (Dan. 1:17, emphasis added), not only in biblical studies. The fields of study in Nebuchadnezzar's college were exclusively Babylonian: "wisdom…knowledge…science…the learning and the tongue of the Chaldeans" (v. 4). Obviously, such a curriculum did not include the Hebrew law and prophets. Yet God still gave them knowledge and skill in all their studies. Why?

Because the heavenly Teacher is not limited to spiritual subjects. Jesus taught us that the Holy Spirit would "teach you *all* things" (John 14:26, emphasis added); also that He would "guide you into *all* truth" (John 16:13, emphasis added; see 16:15). "All things" includes more than the knowledge of God, His Word, and His ways. It also includes every acceptable field of human knowledge and worldly wisdom. All human knowledge has been given by God (see James 1:17) for the material betterment of man's world and the blessing of God's redeemed ones while here. Hence, the Holy Spirit will give us wisdom in the studies, disciplines, technologies, sciences, crafts, arts, trades, and occupations of this present world—if with humility and faith we ask Him to do so. Too often we limit the Teacher by expecting His help only in studying the Bible and other distinctly Christian subjects or endeavors. As long as we are in the body, the all-knowing Spirit will help us learn anything and everything we need to know to help us on our journey through our "Babylon."

Are you limiting the Teacher, or by believing prayer are you loosing Him to help you in whatever you do?

See John 14:26; 16:13, 15; James 1:17; Colossians 3:23; Exodus 31:1–7; Acts 18:3.

Lesson: The Holy Spirit teaches us "all things"—human knowledge as well as spiritual knowledge.

1:6–7 "Babylonianization." In a thinly veiled attempt to make Babylonians out of Daniel and his three friends,

Ashpenaz, the chief eunuch who oversaw their training, assigned them Babylonian names. (Joseph and Hadassah were also given Gentile names while in captivity; see Gen. 41:45; Esther 2:7.) As their Hebrew names had praised the God of Israel, so their new Babylonian names would now bring honor to the gods of Babylon. The *Modern Language Bible* notes, "The new names were intended to discard remembrance of God and to replace Him by Bel, Marduk and Nebo" (p. 872). (It further notes that Daniel's new name, Belteshazzar, meant "Bel, protect his life," whereas the similarly spelled name of Nebuchadnezzar's royal grandson, Belshazzar, meant, "Bel, protect the king" [p. 877].) So Ashpenaz hoped to make Bel-worshiping Babylonians of Daniel and his three friends.

But his hopes soon proved false. Time and again Daniel's writings prove that these name changes were nothing more than elaborate misnomers. Unlike the new names God assigned to signify vital changes in His chosen servants' characters (see Gen. 32:28; Acts 13:9), the faithful four's new titles induced no changes in their characters. Their hearts and their faith remained beautifully unchanged (Dan. 3:16–18; 6:10). Never "Babylonianized," they remained in the world but not of it. Though the shocking fall of Jerusalem made their God appear powerless before the gods of Babylon, they held fast their faith.

Their immutability is a subtle challenge to us. Whatever the achievements, honors, promotions, or prosperity we receive while in this present Babylon, we must never submit to Babylonianization. Whatever our "Babylonian" titles, offices, credentials, or distinctions, we must strive to remain as unchanged as the faithful four—humble and utterly committed to God's Word and ways in our heart and conduct. If the Lord were to appear today, would He find you sanctified or "Babylonianized"?

Lesson: We must not allow our worldly achievements, titles, credentials, or distinctions to change our inner beliefs, values, and personal ways of living.

1:8–20 The dilemma of godly ones in a godless land.
Daniel and his three friends were as godly as Babylon—the first
Gentile world system to rule Judah—was godless. Hence, the
faithful four symbolize godly Christians, and Babylon symbolizes this unbelieving world in which we presently live.

As soon as they arrived in Babylon, the faithful four ran
headlong into a dilemma. Their initial trial may be outlined as
follows:

1. The dilemma (v. 5)
2. The decision (v. 8)
3. The test (vv. 11–15)
4. The reward (v. 17)
5. The results (vv. 18–20)

The dilemma

The problem here was simply that the righteous could not
obey both God and king. Nebuchadnezzar had ordered a diet for
his new pupils of his very own royal meats and wines, which were
previously offered to Babylon's idol-gods, Nebo, Bel, or Marduk. In
addition, the meats included those deemed unclean in God's law.
God's law forbade that they consume these foods. (See Lev.
11:1–47; Exod. 34:15; Num. 25:2–3, 5; 1 Cor. 10:20–21.) To dine
on foods offered to a deity was to worship and commune—be at
one—with that deity. Hence, their obedience to the first and second commandments (see Exod. 20:1–5) was put to the test. The
dilemma was that one or the other, God or the king, had to be disobeyed, and neither could be disobeyed without dire consequences. Disobedience to God's law would bring the curse, so
recently impressed upon Daniel's mind by his own deportation.
And disobedience to the command of a Gentile tyrant would
surely bring swift capital punishment, as the chief eunuch
urgently reminded Daniel (Dan. 1:10). Hence, forced to choose
between two undesirable alternatives, they found themselves
caught in a bona fide dilemma.

The decision

Simply yet wisely, Daniel and friends decided to obey God's Word (the Mosaic law) and trust Him to deliver them from the adverse consequences of their obedience. Thus they cast their burden entirely on Him. He had commanded in His Word, He had constrained them into their circumstances, so He was responsible to help them once they fully committed themselves to the path of obedience. (See Ps. 37:5; 55:22; 1 Pet. 5:7.)

The test

Once announced, Daniel's brave decision immediately drew fire. Fearing for his own life, Ashpenaz, the chief eunuch, shot down Daniel's initial request for a change of diet (Dan. 1:10). He favored Daniel, but he favored something else even more: his head remaining on his shoulders. Undaunted, Daniel persisted, turning then to Melzar, the eunuch whom Ashpenaz had appointed to look after Daniel and his friends, and proposing that he grant them a ten-day trial run (vv. 11–14). This would either confirm or deny Ashpenaz's fears that the faithful four would suffer malnutrition. Comfortable with this, Melzar agreed to give it a try (v. 14). But Melzar's peace of mind was not the only reason for the faithful four's ten-day test (v. 15).

It was their make-or-break point: It would either prove the reality or destroy the essence of their faith. By trial's end, their faces were healthier in appearance than their peers who had feasted on the king's rich fare. That they even gained weight ("fatter in flesh," v. 15) reveals that God had miraculously intervened. After they obeyed Him, He supernaturally prospered their physical health and growth in ten days (see Ps. 43:5). And that's not all. The miracle continued throughout their three-year enrollment in the king's college. How do we know this? If at any time during their education they had appeared ill-fed, especially when the king interviewed them (Dan 1:18), Ashpenaz's and Melzar's heads would have rolled (vv. 3, 10–11, 18). But they didn't. After three years, everything was still intact—the Jews' faith and the eunuchs' heads.

The reward

For the loyalty, trust, and holy fear they rendered, the faithful four were rewarded by God with special intellectual abilities (v. 17). With these, they mastered all the fields of current Babylonian knowledge. A special gift of interpreting visions and dreams was given to Daniel, who used it freely throughout his lengthy prophetic ministry. So God rewarded His faithful ones.

Their special abilities represent the gifts of the Spirit, which God *gives* all Christians who are Spirit-baptized and which He *activates* in those who by their obedience in trial put their loyalty to Him and His Word first. Thus today He continues to reward godly ones in a godless land.

The results

God-honoring results issued from these God-given rewards. When the king interviewed the faithful four, he found them by far the brightest students in his program, so they were graduated with highest honors from his college and promptly appointed to his advisory council (vv. 18–19). Subsequently, their advice proved consistently to be far better than that rendered by any other member of His council (v. 20). Thus by their honorable graduation from the king's college, their appointment to his council, and their shining on that council, these four godly Jews glorified Jehovah, who had given them wisdom (v. 17) and favor (vv. 9, 19).

As soon as we become true Christians in "Babylon," we too find ourselves in uncomfortable dilemmas that force us to choose between loyal obedience to God's Word and conformity to the sins and ways of this ungodly world. Have we made the elementary yet profound decision to obey God and trust Him to help us through the consequences, or are we compromising the Word to avoid conflicts? Our answers will determine if we are godly ones in a godless land—and if we qualify for God to fully activate the gifts of the Spirit in our lives unto His fullest glory.

See "Daniel chapter two outlined," chapter 2; "The dilemma of godly ones in a godless land...again!" chapter 3; "The king's purpose will not be changed," chapter 6.

See Psalm 34:19; 2 Timothy 3:12.

Lesson: In this godless world, godly Christians will inevitably face spiritual or moral dilemmas. If in these tests we decide to obey God's Word uncompromisingly and trust Him to help us overcome the consequences, He will reward us with gifts that will glorify Him.

1:8–20 A model test—and sign of things to come. Note the similar spiritual pattern seen in this, the faithful four's first test, and that seen in their subsequent tests. In chapters 2, 3, and 6, they followed essentially the same spiritual course they charted in chapter 1: They faced a dilemma (or crisis), made a brave decision, endured a test, received rewards, and, as a result, honored God. Hence, this chapter is a model test and a sign of things to come.

1:20 The superiority of the Spirit. Observe that the king's other counselors, who competed with the faithful four for his favor, were "magicians and astrologers" (Dan. 1:20). That is, they sought to obtain vital information, especially knowledge of future events, by occult means. The faithful four's abilities, conversely, were given by God (see verse 17). Hence, *The Spirit-Filled Life Bible* notes, "The occult forces were no match for the Spirit of God" (p. 1234). Indeed, the wisdom of God's Spirit is superior to that acquired from all other secular sources, including the occult. (See Dan. 2:27–28.)

See "The superiority of the Spirit" entries, chapters 2, 4, 5.

Lesson: The wisdom and gifts of the Holy Spirit are superior to those of occultism.

1:8 Determined or defiled? *The Amplified Bible* translates

Daniel 1:8: "But Daniel determined in his heart that he would not defile himself..." Thus it records that Daniel made a fixed decision that under no circumstances would he break God's law and jeopardize his relationship with Him. It was this holy determination—his zeal for God's holiness and need of His favor—that kept him from not only ceremonial but, more importantly, spiritual defilement. Conversely, spiritual defilement will keep us from having zeal for the holiness and favor of God. These two spiritual forces—godly determination and ungodly defilement—are mutually exclusive. When one enters, the other must leave; hence, where one is, the other is not. Why is it so important that Daniel determined in his heart to be holy?

Because every blessing that follows in this book—Daniel's gifts, his friends' gifts, their joint rise to prominence in Babylon, Daniel's supervision of the renowned Chaldean wise men, his three friends' appointments to high government posts, their victory over Nebuchadnezzar's idol and furnace, Nebuchadnezzar's royal decree honoring their faith and their God, Daniel's deliverance from the den of lions, and Jehovah's subsequent praise and honor—results from this great initial decision to be holy. Furthermore, all the informative and inspiring prophecies recorded in this book—revealing the order of the successive Gentile world governments; the tyranny of King Antiochus IV (Epiphanes); the first advent and rejection of Messiah; the tribulation period; the rise and reign of Antichrist; the return, triumph, and kingdom of Messiah, and thus Israel's ultimate, permanent victory over gentilism—sprang from this one brave and righteous pledge, entered jointly by Daniel and his three companions (Dan. 3:18, 28).

Where do you stand in light of Daniel's great decision of heart? Are you determined or defiled, purposed or polluted, in your thoughts, behavior, and associations? Just think what may happen if, following Daniel's example, we determine to be holy, as individuals, families, prayer meetings, Bible study groups, churches, ministries, and ministerial associations. There can be only one result: Again, many blessings and revelations will flow!

See Psalm 45:7; Hebrews 1:9; Numbers 25:11–13; Deuteronomy 33:8–11; John 2:13–17; Psalms 15:1–5; 101:1–7; 1 Peter 1:15–16; Hebrews 12:14; Colossians 3:2.

Lesson: Determined holiness will keep us from spiritual defilement, and vice versa.

Lesson: Determined holiness brings many blessings and revelations.

1:11–16 Helping those who help His people. The faithful four's brave decision to refuse the king's fare put not only themselves but also Melzar, their Babylonian overseer, at risk. Hence, by blessing Daniel's vegetable diet plan for three years, God not only delivered the faithful four, but also Melzar, who had allowed the plan to proceed. Remember, Melzar could have refused Daniel's request, or worse, reported their noncompliance to the king and requested their expulsion from the king's college. But he did not. Hence, God helped him for helping His uncompromising children. The pattern of divine action here is: God protects and delivers not only His overcomers but also those who assist them.

So don't fret when those who support your work, ministry, or church meet opposition from others because of their support. Pray for them and rest, knowing God will help them because they are helping you do His will.

See Genesis 12:3; Exodus 1:17–21; Joshua 6:25; 1 Kings 2:7 (2 Samuel 17:27–29; 19:31–40); Jeremiah 39:15–18; Matthew 25:40; 2 Timothy 1:16–18.

Lesson: God protects not only His overcomers but also those who help them.

CHAPTER TWO

POWER AND PROSPERITY—BY COURAGE, NOT COMPROMISE

2:1–49 DANIEL CHAPTER TWO OUTLINED. Chapter two breaks down as follows:

1. The crisis (vv. 1–13)
2. The decision (vv. 14–18)
3. The trial (vv. 19–45)
4. The reward (vv. 48–49)
5. The results (vv. 46–47)

King Nebuchadnezzar's forgotten dream and rash execution order created the *crisis* that tried the faith of the faithful four. The *decision* was Daniel's brave choice to, again, lean entirely on God, this time through prayer. The *trial* lasted for at least two days: On the first, Daniel and friends prayed and received their answer from God that night; the next day Daniel went before Nebuchadnezzar and gave him the word of the Lord. The *reward* consisted of great honor, rewards, and authority for Daniel and his friends. The *result* was that, once more, God was greatly honored by the faith and loyalty of His servants.

2:4–7:28 Messages to the Gentiles. "Then spoke the Chaldeans to the king in |Aramaic|..." (2:4). From this verse until the end of chapter 7 (v. 28), Daniel writes his message in Aramaic, the official language of Babylon, the first Gentile nation to rule the world in the "times of the Gentiles" (Luke 21:24). Why would Daniel, a loyal Jew, use this language rather than his own beloved and native Hebrew? Because he wrote as God's oracle, and *God was sending messages to the Gentiles*. Always, God prompts His servants to speak or write in the language of those to whom He (and they) wish to speak. (See Acts 21:37, 40; 22:2; 2:11; 1 Cor. 9:22.) That these central chapters of Daniel's scroll were written in the primary Gentile language of the day reveals that God wanted these truths understood not only by the Jews but also by the Gentile kings and peoples of Daniel's time and their successors throughout the long day of the "times of the Gentiles."

Indeed, the inspired record of God's dealings with the first Gentiles to overrule the chosen nation is more than mere history. The principles and patterns set forth therein—God's responses to Gentile attitudes and actions—constitute God's voice sending vital messages to all subsequent Gentile rulers and their populations. Here is what the Spirit saith unto the Gentiles:

1. Your rulership of My earth and My people is only temporary. Though your successive world-ruling kingdoms seem gloriously impressive to you and undefeatably strong, I will one day end all your kingdoms and establish My eternal kingdom. (See Daniel 2, especially 2:31–35; 7:21–27.)

2. Don't persecute My people for their uncompromising obedience to My Word; if you do, I will ultimately deliver them and punish you. (See Daniel chapters 3, 6.)

3. Regardless of your wisdom and strength, never take credit for the size and splendor of your nation-kingdom.

You rule, but I overrule, always. If you become vain, I can and will remove you from power. (See Daniel chapters 4, 5.) Let one of your own, King Nebuchadnezzar, bear witness; surely you will believe him. (See Daniel 4:1–3, 4–37.)

4. Don't dishonor, mock, or abuse holy things—My Word, name, temple, or people. If you do, I can and will replace you with another head of state, or put your nation down and raise another to prominence in its stead. (See Daniel chapter 5.)

5. Learn from history. Observe My judgments of kings, dictators, presidents, and nations in times past, and humbly follow the precedents I establish. (See Daniel 5:18–22.)

6. The savage and ruthless way in which you gain and retain power (by eliminating your rivals, militarily, politically, commercially), your contentment with mere fleshly gratifications, and your failure to acknowledge, seek to know and commune with Me render you bestial in My sight. (See Daniel 7:1–8, 17, 23; also Ps. 53:1–4.)

Generalizing, God warns national and international leaders to govern humbly, in constant recognition of His all-powerful grace, and to retain great respect for Him, His holy Word (standards of righteousness), His covenant people (Jews and Christians), and their faith.

Oh, how these lessons have been neglected! So many leaders and nations have not heeded them: Emperor Hirohito and the Japanese people; Stalin and the people of the former Soviet Union; the Caesars and the citizens of Rome; Napoleon and his French subjects; Hitler and Germans who supported Nazism. But that was then and this is now, right?

Have no illusions, my fellow believer. This nation's historic preference for Christianity aside, America is in dire trouble today largely due to disbelief and defiance of these very truths.

2:1–23 Deliverance from unreasonable superiors. By any

standard, Nebuchadnezzar's demand that his wise men remember and interpret his dream was highly unreasonable. But when they pointed this out to him (vv. 10–11), their royal boss stubbornly denied the obvious and continued demanding the impossible. Suddenly, his subordinates found themselves in big trouble, for death was the penalty for non-compliance. And suddenly, the faithful four found themselves in big trouble, for they too were among those scheduled for execution (v. 13b). So once more, as at the Red Sea, the stakes were high and the odds impossible for God's children: there was no way out. Yet, again, through their prayers (v. 18), faith (v. 16), and patience ("give him time," v. 16), God made a way of escape, and His overcomers survived.

Their survival is good news for Christian employees with unreasonable, obstinate, or obsessively driven superiors. Nebuchadnezzar was obsessively driven. It was most likely fear—the terrifying urge to know the potentially ominous meaning of his dream—that drove Nebuchadnezzar to his folly, for we read that "his spirit was troubled" (v. 1). Hence, his unreasonable demand to know the unknowable. When impossible (or seemingly impossible) demands are made of us, we may take comfort in remembering that, like the faithful four, we still have a faithful and reasonable God to help us get along with unfaithful, unreasonable superiors. He is the same today as He was when He saved Daniel and his friends from their boss's murderous rage. How will He save us? Exactly as He did the faithful four: by acceptance, prayer, faith, and patience.

> 1. ACCEPTANCE. First, Daniel neither panicked nor rebelled but accepted the unfairness of the situation God had permitted. Without this attitude of accepting adversities as coming directly from the heavenly Father's hand to test and mature us (submission to God's permissive will; see Job 2:10), he would not have kept his spiritual composure and subsequently overcome.

2. PRAYER. Accepting his unacceptable situation, Daniel then turned to prayer, not reason, as his means of extrication. For additional empowerment, he wisely called on his believing friends to pray the prayer of agreement with him (Dan. 2:17–18; see Matt. 18:19–20; Acts 12:5, 12).

3. FAITH. Knowing well the impotency of faithless prayer however desperate, Daniel distinctly chose to believe that God heard their petition and would help before it was too late. (The king had imposed a time limit; see Dan. 2:16.)

4. PATIENCE. After prayer, Daniel and his friends retained their composure by letting patience have "her perfect work" (James 1:4; see Ps. 27:13–14). So they trusted; so they endured; so they overcame…until God came to them (Dan. 2:19).

Thus they were delivered from the tyranny of their unreasonable superior. Theirs is a pattern the Scriptures compel us to follow.

Didn't Jesus teach us to pray, "Deliver us from [the] evil [one, or ones]" (Matt. 6:13)? And didn't Paul pray for deliverance from "unreasonable and wicked men" (2 Thess. 3:2) and later testify that God had delivered him from "the mouth of the lion" (2 Tim. 4:17b) and would always deliver him from "every evil work" (2 Tim. 4:18)? If we assume Daniel's attitude—humbly accepting temporary injustice as part of God's plan to test us—and follow his example, God will come to us as He did to Daniel. (See 1 Cor. 10:13.)

The alternative is that we handle our unfairness as people do who don't know God—complaining, contending, threatening, and rebelling—and we let the lion devour our spiritual life and future fruitfulness for God. Isn't Daniel's way better?

See Job 2:10; Matthew 6:13; 1 Corinthians 10:13; 2 Thessalonians 3:2–3; 2 Timothy 4:17–18; Colossians 3:22–24; Titus 2:9–10; James 1:4; Psalm 27:13–14.

Lesson: *When unreasonable or evil superiors make seem-*
ingly impossible demands of us, God will faithfully
make us a way of escape if we will call on Him in
a spirit of acceptance, faith, and patience.

2:10 The Chaldeans. The word *Chaldeans* has two mean-
ings. First, it applies to people from the ancient Mesopotamian
country of Chaldea, of which Babylon was the capital. Second, it
refers to a special and renowned class of wise men in Chaldea
who were exceptionally knowledgeable and hence typically
served as royal counselors. These Babylonian wise men are the
"Chaldeans" Daniel describes in this verse.

Without modern equal, these enigmatic members of the
Babylonian intelligentsia were a unique combination of
occultism, scholarship, priesthood, and experience. Part magi-
cian, scientific researcher, religious leader, and elder sage, their
expertise was fourfold:

1. As magicians, they sought supernatural knowledge
   (real or purported) by use of astrology and the magi-
   cal arts, including magic and sorcery.

2. As astronomers, they diligently "studied the stars and
   the planets" (*The Modern Language Bible*, p. 873).
   The Zondervan Pictorial Bible Dictionary adds,
   "Astrology was...inextricably mixed with astronomy" in ancient times (p. 896).

3. As priests, they were religious leaders who "special-
   ized in astronomy and mathematics (the science of
   which originated in Babylonia) or used these sciences
   for astrology, horoscopes, or other omen practices"
   (*The Wycliffe Bible Encyclopedia*, p. 321). *The Ryrie
   Study Bible* calls them "a class of wise men priests"
   (p. 1308).

4. As elder sages, they were older men experienced in
   the adversities of life, who were also highly studious,
   sensitive, and thoughtful. Hence, they possessed an

abundance of academic knowledge, worldly wisdom, and experiential know-how. They were the pundits, the great thinkers and experts of the ancient world (though part of their knowledge was gained by methods highly dubious by modern standards).

As it is today, it was common practice in the ancient world for kings to have at their immediate call the wisest men in the nation. (See Gen. 41:8; Exod. 7:11; Esther 1:13.) The Chaldeans, who were "reputedly the wisest men of ancient times" (*The New Scofield Study Bible*, p. 897), were the Babylonian version of such sage courts. Hence, as the top advisers of the king of Babylon, they were immediately summoned when urgent problems arose, such as Nebuchadnezzar's forgotten dream.

Thus we see what a miracle it was for the embarrassingly youthful faithful four to be given a seat on the prestigious court of the Chaldeans (Dan. 1:19) and what an even greater miracle it was that subsequently their counsel proved "ten times better" (v. 20) than the Chaldeans, whom Daniel eventually superintended as Babylon's unofficial "Secretary of Wisdom and Knowledge." (See Dan. 2:48; 5:11.) (Though long professionally associated with the Chaldeans, the faithful four neither condoned nor practiced their occult methods of discovery. Their uncompromisingly righteous characters, as seen in their tests involving the king's diet [Dan. 1], the king's idol [Dan. 3], and the Persian prayer ban [Dan. 6] make this exceedingly clear.)

2:17–18,23 Calling on friends for prayer. Though a man of exceptionally strong faith, Daniel felt a need for his believing friends to add their faith and prayers to his in the crisis they faced. After hearing of the impending execution of all the king's advisors—including himself and his three friends—and begging time from the king, Daniel went straight home to ask Hananiah, Mishael, and Azariah to pray with him (vv. 17–18). *The Modern Language Bible* notes, "Again they joined forces as believers in God" (p. 873). And after receiving God's answer that night,

Daniel acknowledged the joint nature of their prayers ("we… us," v. 23). That someone of Daniel's faith asked his friends to agree with him in prayer, and that God honored their efforts, shows us that asking others to pray with us is no evidence of lack of faith but rather a way of wisdom that God will honor. Indeed, it is particularly wise to ask others to pray with us about our needs when we are in crises, as Daniel was. Jesus taught, and so called us to practice, the prayer of agreement. (See Matt. 18:19–20.) Many before us have answered His call.

King Jehoshaphat brought all Judah together for prayer when Jerusalem was suddenly threatened by an imminent, large-scale attack (2 Chron. 20:4). In his epistles, Paul openly solicited the assistance of praying Christians (Eph. 6:19; Col. 4:2–3; 2 Cor. 1:11). Queen Esther requested that "all the Jews" in Shushan, along with her maidens, fast (and by implication pray) with her before she went in boldly before the king (Esther 4:16). When surrounded by Sennacherib's murderous hordes, King Hezekiah asked the prophet Isaiah to join him in prayer for deliverance (2 Chron. 32:20). Church leaders decided to meet the crisis of Peter's sudden arrest and imprisonment with round-the-clock corporate prayer (Acts 12:5, 12). This calling on the saints for prayer is also portrayed symbolically in other biblical references.

When advised that a Samaritan assault on Jerusalem was imminent, Nehemiah ordered his trumpeter to blow the *shofar* (ram's horn trumpet) wherever the enemy attacked, so the Jews might gather there and repel the enemy (Neh. 4:19–20). Thus the strength of many would meet the need of the few who were under attack. We do the same spiritually when a prayer-call goes forth (by telephone, fax, or e-mail) and the saints cluster their prayers together for those who are under a special, direct attack from the enemy. Nothing can prevent God from answering such prayers—except our failure to pray because of unbelief, carnal reasoning, or religious pride (fearing some will misjudge our prayer request as evidence of panic or weak faith).

When critical prayer needs arise, will you call on your

friends to join you in the prayer of agreement? Or do you have more faith and wisdom than Daniel?

See 2 Chronicles 20:4; 32:20; Matthew 18:19–20; Ephesians 6:18–19; Colossians 4:2–3; 2 Corinthians 1:11; Esther 4:16; Acts 12:5, 12; Nehemiah 4:19–20.

Lesson: *It is wise and effective to call on believing friends to pray with us concerning our needs in times of crisis.*

2:12 The folly of fury. According to Daniel, when the Chaldeans informed King Nebuchadnezzar that they simply could not recall his dream, he flew into a rage: "The king was angry and very furious" (v. 12). Observe, it was in this highly agitated emotional state that he decided to kill all his wise men and hastily issued a royal decree to that effect (vv. 12b–13). His acts illustrate the utter foolishness and haste of anger.

Like Nebuchadnezzar, when we are angry, all our good sense goes from us, and, until we cool off, everything we decide, say, or do is likely to be unkind, unwise, or blatantly self-opposing. In this case, had Nebuchadnezzar's order been executed, he would have slain the very men upon whom he relied most for counsel in time of trouble. If war had visited, he would have found himself without the vital guidance of an able war cabinet—all because, to put it in rural Southern slang, "he threw a fit and fell in it." Furthermore, he would have been guilty of killing God's prime spokesman (Daniel) and three of His most outstanding servants (Shadrach, Meshach, and Abednego) in the slaughter (vv. 12, 18)—a tragic error sure to have silenced the voice of God (who spoke to him through Daniel; see 2:31–35; 4:19–27) in his personal life and brought divine wrath upon his servants, the people of Babylon. Why? Having sown folly, he would have had to reap it.

Truly, when fury rests upon us, folly rules over us. Why do we oppose ourselves when we think, speak, or act in anger? Because unforsaken anger gives place to Satan in our souls (see

Eph. 4:26–27), and once he enters, he always immediately seeks to harm us. Thus through rage we ruin ourselves: "For wrath killeth the foolish man" (Job 5:2). Nebuchadnezzar's folly bids us, when furious, to quickly step back and cool down before making decisions, speaking, or taking actions.

Are you walking in the folly of fury or the wisdom of self-control?

See "The folly of fury…again!" chapter 3.

See Daniel 3:13, 19; Ecclesiastes 7:9; Ephesians 4:26–27; Psalm 37:1, 8–9; Proverbs 12:16; especially 14:29; 16:32; 19:11; 19:19; 29:20; 2 Chronicles 16:10; 2 Kings 5:11–13; James 1:19–20; Esther 7:7; 2 Timothy 2:24–26; 1 Samuel 25:13; 2 Samuel 13:22.

Lesson: *When angry, immediately "cease from anger, and forsake wrath" (Ps. 37:8) before making decisions, speaking, or acting. If you don't, everything you think, say, or do is likely to be unkind, unwise, or blatantly self-opposing.*

2:14–15 Sanctified employees in a secular job. These verses reveal that when Arioch, the king's chief executioner, arrested Daniel and whisked him away to the palace for execution, Daniel had no idea what was going on. Only after asking, "Why the hurry?" was he informed of the king's frightening dream and his counselors' failure to recall and interpret it and of the resultant execution order. (See Dan. 2:15.) Obviously, then, Daniel was not in the select group of magicians, sorcerers, and Chaldeans whom the king initially summoned (vv. 2–12). There is a subtle but sound implication here: The Hebrew counselors, who didn't practice any form of astrology, occultism, or idolatry, kept themselves and their counsel separate from the Chaldeans. Yet because they were also on the king's larger board of advisers, they too had been slated for execution (vv. 12–13).

This suggests that the faithful four lived as they had been educated—separated unto God. In the king's college, they had

learned to accept a separated lifestyle, eating separately for
three years to avoid defilement at the king's table. Now, as his
adult employees, they retained that same vital Christlike separation they had learned in their youth. (See Heb. 7:26; Titus
2:11–12.) They were sanctified employees in a secular government, laboring side by side with the worshipers of Bel, Nebo,
and Marduk by day, and no doubt praying for them, but not
chumming or socializing with them by night or seeking their
favor.

Further inspired evidence indicates that, indeed, they
walked a path apart. When Shadrach, Meshach, and Abednego
refused to bow to Nebuchadnezzar's image, it was the
"Chaldeans" (Dan. 3:8), their fellow royal counselors, who
reported their insubordination—hardly something close friends
would have done. And years later, Daniel's administrative peers
targeted his religion as a means of trapping him in the den of lions
(Dan. 6:5, 10). No one close to Daniel would have treated him and
his faith with such murderous contempt. Obviously, as zealous
Jews, the faithful four were still somewhat social pariahs despite
their high positions. This should not surprise us. Every sanctified
Christian should realize that without this godly separation, the
faithful four could not have retained the high degree of divine
favor they enjoyed. To compromise with sin or join closely with
sinners is to forfeit the presence and favor of the Holy One. If they
had pleased man, they could not have been the servants of Christ.
(See Gal. 1:10.)

That Daniel and his three companions lived separated lives
while successfully employed by Babylonia refutes the idea that
Christians cannot work in a secular government (or business)
and at the same time maintain a godly, separated lifestyle. If the
faithful four did it, so can we.

Are you a sanctified servant or compromised employee in
your secular job?

See "Sanctified students in a secular system," chapter 1.

See Psalm 1:1; 2 Corinthians 6:14–7:1; 2 Timothy 2:19–22;
Titus 2:11–12; Hebrews 7:26; Galatians 1:10.

Lesson: *Christian employees should strive to live sancti-*
fied lives despite their secular employment in
government or business.

2:24–30 The highest for the humblest. Having discovered
Daniel's signature characteristics—loyalty to God's Word, faith,
courage, and prayerfulness—we now behold the beautiful
humility of the man. Though he is the recipient of a remarkable
gift of interpretation and has now received a rare message from
God for the most powerful man in the world, Daniel isn't puffed
up. He still sees himself soberly, others rightly, and God highly.
This wasn't a rare, fleeting moment of meekness. It was Daniel's
lifelong attitude.

Many years later, Daniel responded similarly when he was
suddenly called before King Belshazzar to interpret the handwriting on the wall. (See chapter 5.) When Belshazzar praised
his giftedness (Dan. 5:16), Daniel didn't even respond to the
king's compliment, turning instead to the sober business at
hand: again, interpreting a vital message from God to a sitting
monarch (vv. 18–28). All business and no boast, Daniel was the
embodiment of godly humility. And it was to him that God
imparted the highest gifts and callings.

In Daniel's life, as in Joseph's, we see that God invariably gives
the loftiest gifts and positions to those with the humblest attitudes.
This is also evident in the lives of Moses and David, whom God
thoroughly humbled before raising them to the highest places and
purposes. (Other anointed ones, such as King Saul, became proud
after their divine promotion, but to a man they were humble when
God first imparted His gifts and fulfilled His callings in their lives.
See 1 Sam. 9:21 and 15:17.)

Do you want God to impart spiritual gifts to you and raise
you up to a new plane of usefulness? Of course you do—how else
can you bless His people, build His kingdom, and honor Him?
Then let me ask you: Are you growing in humility or haughti-
ness? Christlike self-denial or worldly self-promotion? Business-
like obedience or shameless religious ambition?

See Proverbs 18:12; 15:33; James 4:6; Exodus 3:11; Numbers 12:3; Luke 10:21; 1 Samuel 18:23; 25:41–42; 9:21; 15:17; Acts 3:12–16; 1 Peter 5:5–6; Proverbs 3:34; Matthew 23:12; Luke 14:7–11; Philippians 2:8–16.

Lesson: *God invariably reserves the highest gifts and positions for Christians with the humblest attitudes.*

2:24–30 Shades of Joseph. Daniel's interview before Nebuchadnezzar is strikingly similar to Joseph's first meeting with Pharaoh (Gen. 41:1–57). Compare these points:

- In both cases, God's servants have identical gifts— interpretation of dreams and administrative skill—and hold similarly high positions in prominent foreign governments. (Compare Gen. 41:15, 40–41 and Dan. 2:36, 48.)

- They are both hastily brought in before the most powerful Gentile king of their generation in the midst of great crises. (Compare Gen. 41:14 and Dan. 2:25.)

- With the Holy Spirit's help, they succeed where renowned occultists have failed. (Compare Gen. 41:8, 15 and Dan. 2:27–28.)

- Humbly, they refuse to take personal credit and openly acknowledge that special revelation has been given them by God, not that they might be honored but that God might show key leaders things to come and thus deliver, or preserve, many innocent people from harm. They understood that their messages were more important than they were. God was communicating with kings; they were just His messengers. (Compare Gen. 41:16, 25, 36 and Dan. 2:30.)

  - In Joseph's case, God had two objectives: 1) Pharaoh must understand a great famine is coming so Egypt can fully prepare for it and, along with other nations, survive. 2) God's chosen people, the children of Israel, who would one day give the world a Savior, must have a place of refuge (Gen. 45:5–7).

- In Daniel's case, God's purpose was also twofold: 1) Nebuchadnezzar and all future Gentile world rulers must understand that one day God will supercede their kingdoms with His own. 2) Nebuchadnezzar's wise men and God's faithful four must be delivered from the king's rash execution order (Dan. 2:28).

- Finally, both Joseph and Daniel were highly honored, richly rewarded in material gifts, and given great authority. (Compare Gen. 41:40–45, 50–52 and Dan. 2:46–49.)

Hence in gifts, position, character, and attitude, Daniel and Joseph were very similar.

2:27–29 The superiority of the Spirit...again! While Daniel carefully disclaims having any special wisdom or ability to discover undisclosed things, he pointedly declares that his God's knowledge is superior to the wisdom of witchcraft in all its varied forms, specifically, astrology, magic, sorcery, and for-tune-telling (Dan. 2:27–29).

What is the Bible saying to us in this passage? Clearly it declares that the wisdom of God's Spirit is superior to the dark revelations of occultism. Why would any Christian, armed with the infallible wisdom of Scripture and timely insights given by the Holy Spirit in response to prayer, seek after psychics? Only because they believe a lie—that occultism offers something superior to the wisdom of the Spirit of Christianity. Daniel shows us repeatedly that it does not.

The Book of Acts enlarges Daniel's revelation by repeatedly showing that God's *power* is also superior to that of occultism. Whenever the gospel spread into new regions of the world, the first thing God did was expose and soundly defeat the power of witchcraft—the "power of Satan" (Acts 26:18)—that previously bound that region. (See Acts 8:5–13; 13:6–13; 16:16–18; 19:11–20.)

See "The Superiority of the Spirit," entries, chapters 1, 4, 5. See Daniel 1:20; 4:7–8.

Lesson: *The wisdom and power of God's Spirit are superior to those of all forms of occultism.*

**2:31–45 The times of the Gentiles: The Gentile image/
smiting Stone vision**. Just as God chose to reveal the coming
famine to Pharaoh in Joseph's day, so He decided to reveal the
future to King Nebuchadnezzar in Daniel's time. In
Nebuchadnezzar's dream—one of two visions in the Book of
Daniel describing "the times of the Gentiles" (Luke 21:24)—
there are two central objects:

> 1. An impressive metallic image of a man (an idol)
> 2. A great Stone

There are also three major events foreseen:

> 1. The creation of the Stone "without hands"
>
> 2. The destruction of the image by the Stone (a final vio-
>   lent clash)
>
> 3. The transformation of the Stone into a great moun-
>   tain (a final great kingdom)

The Great Gentile Image

The image Nebuchadnezzar saw was a representation of the
glory of Gentile rule. It was large, "a great [large] image. This
great [large] image" (Dan. 2:31). It shined brightly with its own
glory, "whose brightness was excellent" (v. 31). It was imposing,
or awe-inspiring: "It was terrible" (v. 31). Thus the spirit of
worldwide gentilism materialized before Nebuchadnezzar's
stunned eyes. Since it assumed the form of a *body*, we may
rightly call it the body of gentilism, or the body of secularism.

From head to foot, its body parts reveal in chronological
sequence the rise of four great world-ruling Gentile empires—
Babylonia, Media-Persia, Greece, and Rome—with the fourth
appearing in two forms, near (two legs, two feet) and distant
(ten toes). Note that every metal is *less refined* and less valuable

than the one preceding it. The first is likened to "fine" gold (v. 32); hence it alone has been refined (no other is called "fine"). This represents the diminishing moral and cultural standards of each successive Gentile kingdom, each being baser and more corrupt than its predecessor (due to the increasing corruption of universal sin). Daniel's use of the adjective "inferior" (v. 39) confirms this.

Observe also that each metal represented is *stronger* than the one before it. Silver is stronger than gold; bronze is stronger than silver; and iron is stronger than bronze, silver, and gold. The description of the fourth kingdom points out that its strength is far superior to any preceding kingdom: "And the fourth kingdom shall be strong as iron...[it] breaketh all these [other metals]... [it shall] break in pieces and bruise" (v. 40). This represents the increasing military power of each coming kingdom; each is more warlike and effective at imposing its will by use of deadly force. The eventual split in the fourth, or Roman, kingdom, resulting in Western (Rome) and Eastern (Constantinople) capitals, is foretold in Daniel 2:41: "The [fourth] kingdom shall be divided."

See also the *place* where this image of Gentile rule is smitten: upon its feet and ten toes (vv. 34, 41–44). This reveals the precise time at which the Stone (Jesus) will shatter Gentile rule and establish His own eternal kingdom, namely, in the days of the revived, or final, form of the fourth world kingdom: "And in the days of these kings [ten kings of Antichrist's kingdom] shall the God of heaven set up a kingdom, which shall never be destroyed" (v. 44; see Rev. 17:12–13). That final form is depicted as ten toes (nations and their respective heads of state), part of iron and part of potter's clay (Dan. 2:41–43). This odd admixture of metal and potter's clay represents *a union between unsaved Gentiles and apostate Jews and Christians*. The unsaved are likened to iron (totally hardened and unresponsive to God) and are referred to as the "seed of men" (v. 43), while the apostates are likened to potter's clay (now hardened but originally soft and "miry" [v. 41]), and are described as "they" who "mingle themselves" (join in unequal unions) with the "seed of men" (v. 43). Though originally soft and "miry," the clay is now hardened into the shape of a toe (as clay that is only bisque fired, not finished and fit for the Master's use) and is so used to help *support* the Gentile system, albeit without the strength of iron. (The clay toes must be hard, for the Gentile image stands on them.)

Why do these toes of hardened clay symbolize apostates? Because God describes His people as soft clay in His, the heavenly Potter's, hands. (See Jer. 18:1–6; Isa. 64:8; Rom. 9:20–23.) If His people respond to His dealings in faith and obedience, He shapes and makes them into vessels of honor. But if they refuse to trust and obey Him, and fall back into the unbelief and sins of the world, they eventually become dry and rigid (without the softening effect of the Spirit of humility and truth). No longer "miry" (soft and responsive to the Potter and fit for His use), they are now hardened in rebellion through the deceitfulness of pride and sin. (See Heb. 3:7–8, 13; Dan. 5:20; Ps. 95:7–8.) It is in this backslidden, defiant state that apostate Jews (who continue rejecting Jesus despite the impact of the Rapture and the subsequent worldwide revival that sweeps Israel) and apostate Christians (left behind and still unrepentant!) will join the emerging, impressive Gentile system and resist Christ's surviving people and imminent return to rule the earth. It is these who "shall mingle themselves with the seed of men" (Dan. 2:43), seeking strength through alliances with the ungodly, just as Judah sought help from Egypt during its pre-exile apostasy. (See Isa. 30:1–7.) But, though united, they will never truly become one. God declares, "They shall not |adhere| one to another" (Dan. 2:43). Why? Because of their fundamentally different spiritual makeups. Those who have known God and turned away can never truly be one with those who have never known Him. Forever changed at heart, born-again Christians can never return to their pre-conversion state of being—no matter how earnest their efforts are to revisit their old ways. So, as ten united toes supporting the final body of gentilism, unbelieving Jews and apostate Christians (as part of the final unfaithful church system, an alliance of all religions headed by the Roman

Catholic church) will labor alongside Antichrist's followers to hasten his rise to power, but they will never be truly one with them.

Such an unequal yoking is not without precedent in New Testament times. Pilate, Herod (Antipas), and the apostate Jewish leaders never became one, yet they worked in perfect unity to rid the world of Jesus of Nazareth. Later, in the fourth century A.D., Christianity and Romanism merged during the reign of Constantine, the first Roman emperor to convert to Christianity and give full legal status to the faith (A.D. 324). In its beliefs and practices, the Church was from that time forward somewhat a mixture of iron and clay (paganism and Christianity, false and true doctrine, professed and real believers) and continued to be so until the time of the Reformation (A.D. 1517), when God began dividing His true Church body from the body of traditional Roman Christianity. Prophetically, Jesus addressed this early period of ecclesiastical mixture in His message to the Church at Pergamum (see Rev. 2:12–17), which He described as dwelling "where Satan's |throne| is" (Rev. 2:13). *The New Scofield Study Bible* says Jesus' words here are "suggestive of the church mixing with the world" (p. 1353). This initial linkup of apostate Christians and pagans foreshadows things to come in the latter days, when the truth-rejecting church system and Christ-rejecting Jews (see John 5:43) unite with all the religions of the world to support Antichrist during his three-and-a-half-year rise to world domination (the first half of the tribulation period).

Ironically, it was a cooperative effort of two united yet fundamentally different peoples—the Romans (represented by Pilate) and apostate Jews and Christians (represented by the Pharisees and Judas respectively)—that smote the divinely conceived Stone (Jesus) when He first appeared. It is only fitting, then, that when the Stone returns, He will smite another union of latter-day Romans and apostate Jews and Christians. Thus the spiritual children of Pilate, Judas, and the Pharisees will reap what they and their spiritual forebears have each willfully sown. And the body of gentilism will cease to exist.

Consider the completeness of Nebuchadnezzar's vision. God showed him everything about the times of the Gentiles: its beginning, with his kingship and the Babylonian empire; its early stages, in the successive Medo-Persian, Greek, and Roman empires; its final form, in a ten-ruler (nation) federation; its end, with a sudden, irrecoverable blow; and its ultimate replacement, the eternal kingdom of the Stone—the Rock of Ages, Jesus Christ (Dan. 2:44–45). Graciously, God has given the Gentile world full prophetic disclosure.

The Greater Smiting Stone

The origin and nature of the Stone Nebuchadnezzar sees is most important. By revelation he senses and relates to us that it was made "without hands" (Dan. 2:34, 45), meaning without the work of *human* hands. Hence, the Stone was a purely divine creation, a work of God alone (see Dan. 8:25). This describes Jesus' first coming. Divinely conceived in the womb of Mary by the power of the Spirit (see Luke 1:35), Jesus of Nazareth was not born of the will of the flesh. Nor was He trained by, and hence a product of, the existing religious system in Israel. (See Luke 2:47; John 7:15.) He was neither a scribe, Pharisee, or Sadducee, nor a student of Gamaliel. His life, understanding of God, spiritual power, and phenomenal ministry were entirely the work of God by the power of His Spirit. No human "hand" (crafting, training, wisdom) produced the God-man, Jesus of Nazareth, the Christ.

The actions of the Stone are also revealing. First, it suddenly smites the great Gentile image, utterly destroying and scattering it (Dan. 2:34–35). This represents Jesus' second coming, specifically His return to earth at the Battle of Armageddon. Second, the Stone then transforms itself into a great "mountain" (kingdom) and fills the whole earth. (See Hab. 2:14.) This portrays the inauguration and establishment of Christ's thousand-year kingdom on this present earth. Thus the Stone completely and permanently replaces the great Gentile image.

Understand, however, that this vision does not represent the coverage of the earth by the *gospel*, but rather the worldwide implementation of the *actual, visible governmental authority and glory* of Jesus Christ. The gospel is to fill the earth now in these last days before the Rapture "for a witness" (Matt. 24:14); that is, that individuals everywhere may have an opportunity to personally believe and obey the Lord, not to establish Christ's governance over all the nations. To the contrary, Daniel 2 strongly establishes that Christ will not rule all nations until *after* the sudden and total destruction of Gentile rule as foreseen in this vision.

The New Scofield Study Bible notes:

> The Smiting Stone (2:34–35) destroys the Gentile world system (in its final form) by a sudden and irremediable blow, not by the gradual processes of conversion and assimilation; and then and not before, does the Stone become a mountain which fills "the whole earth" (cp. Dan. 7:26–27). Such a destruction of the Gentile monarchy system did not occur at the first advent of Christ. On the contrary, He was put to death by the sentence of an officer of the fourth empire, which was then at the zenith of its power...It is important to observe that (1) Gentile world power is to end in a sudden catastrophic judgment...and (2) it is immediately to be followed by the kingdom of heaven. The God of the heavens will not set up His kingdom until after the destruction of the Gentile world system... (pp. 898–899)

See "The times of the Gentiles," chapter 7.

See Psalm 118:22; Isaiah 28:16; Matthew 21:42; Acts 4:11; Ephesians 2:20; 1 Corinthians 3:11; 1 Peter 2:6–8.

Lesson: *At His return to earth (Armageddon), Jesus will first destroy Gentile rule and then establish His everlasting kingdom. His earthly government over the nations will not be established before this, His great and epochal return.*

2:31–45 World empires foretold—and limited. In this vision, God not only foretells but also authorizes which Gentile empires He will permit to rule His earth; His covenant people, Israel; and their covenant land, Palestine. He even authorizes the order in which they will appear, including the eventual split in the fourth, or Roman Empire ("the kingdom shall be divided," Dan. 2:41). By authorizing only these four kingdoms, God and the Book of Daniel imply that no other Gentile kingdoms will successfully rule the world until the appearance of the final form of the Roman kingdom: Antichrist's ten-nation federation. Why is this? Because God has not "given" (see vv. 37–38) any other despotic ruler and government permission to temporarily rule His world.

This explains why, despite their formidable military forces, Napoleon, Hitler, and Stalin failed to achieve their vision of world domination: Heaven limited the number of Gentile empires it would permit, and they weren't in that number.

Have recent distresses, collapses, and wars among nations shaken your confidence in God's omnipotence? "Be still, and know" that He's still controlling and has fully predestined the course of world history.

See Psalm 46:1–11, esp. verse 10.

Lesson: God is controlling—and has fully predestined—
 the course of world history.

2:31 The great Gentile image—foreshadowing the tribulation. "Thou, O king, sawest, and behold a great *image*" (Dan. 2:31, emphasis added). The Aramaic word here rendered "image" is also used and so rendered in Daniel 3:1: "Nebuchadnezzar, the king, made an *image* of gold" (emphasis added). This word *tselem* means "an idolatrous figure." Hence Nebuchadnezzar's visionary (Dan. 2:31) and public idols (Dan. 3:1) are linked not only contextually (both disclosed in the Book of Daniel) but linguistically (the Spirit using the same language and word to describe each image). This linkage is not incidental but typological: Both images foreshadow the work of the coming Antichrist. Once invested with total power, Antichrist will erect an "image" to himself in the reconstructed Jewish temple and demand that all people worship it. (See Rev. 13:14–15.) *The New Scofield Study Bible* states, "It is noteworthy that Gentile world dominion begins and ends with a great image" (p. 899).

Let's consider the symbolism implicit in Nebuchadnezzar's visionary and physical images.

The glory (worship) of man

The image Nebuchadnezzar envisioned was a representation of a *man*. Bright, shining, and impressive, it represents the glory of man. Thus subtly the Scripture reveals that Gentile rulers and populaces generally glory in *man*—the wisdom, strength, ways, and achievements of fallen, unredeemed mankind united in independence and hence defiance of God. Notice that this image stands independently in its own strength, needing nothing but itself: "This great image...*stood* before thee" (Dan. 2:31, emphasis added). This posture depicts "the pride of life" (1 John 2:16), which manifested originally at Babel, where unredeemed mankind united to reach and possess (or at least more closely view) heaven on its own power and by its own merit. (See Gen. 11:1–9.) Still today, by its persisting independence and self-satisfaction, unredeemed mankind looks up to the Creator and says, "Look how good and wise and successful we are, God. We can stand on our own two feet...without any help from You!"

The amazing advances of the twentieth century in science, medicine, travel, communication, space exploration, and other technologies (foretold by God in Daniel's writings; see Dan. 12:4) have greatly increased mankind's infatuation with this most impressive "image" of its glory. Only one goal—lasting world peace—has eluded Adam's race in its age-old quest for independent greatness. This too will be attained under Antichrist. But not for long. Vain humanism always brings divine judgment, as it did originally at Babel. Consequently, in the latter half of the tribulation, God's trumpet and bowl judgments will fully and finally purge the world of this spirit of the glory of man.

Because it was a portrayal of a man, Nebuchadnezzar's image also encourages the worship of *men*—exceptionally wise, rich, gifted, powerful, or successful people. Refusing to acknowledge that God graciously *gives* knowledge, gifts, discoveries, skill, etc., to mankind for its betterment (see James 1:17; John 3:27; Dan. 2:21–22; 4:17; Gen. 41:16; 1 Cor. 4:7), it gives all credit instead to acclaimed (and often inflated) individuals. Ubiquitous, this evil attitude has even manifested in the Church. When Christians glory too much in Church leaders—whether the Pope or evangelical or charismatic preachers—rather than in the Lord Jesus alone from whom all mercies flow, they worship flesh (man) in lieu of the Immortal Spirit (see 1 Cor. 3:3–4; John 4:24; Rev. 19:10). Wisely, the early Church maintained a steady watch against the worship of man. (See Acts 10:25–26; 13:11–15; 1 Cor. 3:5, 21; 2 Cor. 12:6.) Are we learning to do the same?

Have you felt yourself caught up lately with foolish pride in the goodness, wisdom, or achievements of any person, minister, ministry, or nation, or of humanity?

See 1 Corinthians 1:29, 31; 3:21; James 1:17; Daniel 2:20–22.

The glory (worship) of self

By divine design, Nebuchadnezzar envisioned himself at the head of the Gentile image. Daniel told him, "Thou art this head of gold" (Dan. 2:38). Hence, his vision spoke not only of the glory of mankind but of the glory of himself, Nebuchadnezzar. Daniel pointed out Nebuchadnezzar's greatness as a man, that he was indeed a special king (a "king of kings," v. 37), that his kingdom ranked first among all others (v. 38), and that all kings and kingdoms that followed would be "inferior to thee" (v. 39). To Nebuchadnezzar, then, this was a most flattering vision in its initial aspect. In a very real sense, he saw the glory of his *self*.

So today the Antichrist spirit that pervades modern civilization bids people to live for self-realization—"What do you want to do with your life?"—rather than for Christ-realization, the holy determination to fully know Jesus and do His pleasure in this life He has given you (finishing the course *He* sets before you; see 2 Tim. 4:7). If we seek the glory of self, we will never know or seek the glory of God.

To which image will you bow—the image of your successful self or the image of God's successful Son, Jesus? Do you see Jesus as merely the means of helping you be successful in life or yourself as His means of bringing honor to His name?

Lesson: *In the Great Tribulation, the world will worship the image of gentilism and the man of sin who heads it.*

Lesson: *In this fallen world, mankind and great men are worshiped.*

Lesson: *In this fallen world, self-realization is worshiped.*

2:31–35 How do you see the system? In the Book of Daniel, God gives two separate visions of man's system of worldwide rule. They tell the same basic story but with very different symbols. God gives Nebuchadnezzar, the ultimate man of the world, the worldly perspective on the coming Gentile system: He sees the Gentile kingdoms as unredeemed men see them (Dan. 2:31–35). But to Daniel, a superlatively spiritual man, God grants the divine or spiritual perspective: He sees the successive Gentile kingdoms as God sees them (Dan. 7:1–8, 11).

From Nebuchadnezzar's viewpoint (Dan. 2:31–35), the Gentile world system is: Very important, or "great" (v. 31); very good, or "excellent" (v. 31); radiantly impressive, emanating "brightness" (v. 31); imposingly strong, or "terrible" (v. 31); and pricelessly valuable, or comprised of the most precious metals. Thus Nebuchadnezzar idolizes these godless world empires because, as others who have never beheld the glory of God, he knows of nothing more glorious. But those who know God or have seen His glory (Dan. 10:5–8; Isa. 6:1–5; Ezek. 1:1; Rev. 1:12–17; 4:2–11; Matt. 17:1–8) can no longer glory in flesh, even the best of redeemed flesh, such as Moses and Elijah (see Matt. 17:3–5). Once dazzled by the Glory, they henceforth "see no man, save Jesus only." Never again can they stand in awe of mankind, any person, or themselves.

Consequently, from Daniel's enlightened perspective the Gentile nations (and system) are most inglorious, like wild animals attacking and devouring one another (see Dan. 7:1–8, 11). They are not best but bestial—unspiritual, unaware of God, and incapable of communion with Him. They are not wondrous but wild—violent and cannibalistic, devouring one another in their greed and lust for possessions, position, power, and honor in this world. This is God's perspective of this present world system. It explains why He transformed King Nebuchadnezzar into a beast, not a beauty, and why He calls the man of sin, who is the *best* product of the Gentile system and world spirit, simply "the beast" (Rev. 13:4, 17–18).

What about you? How do you see the Gentile nations and their world system? Is your perspective Nebuchadnezzar's or Daniel's? Are you considering the present Gentile system through the eyes of human pride or through the eyes of the Holy Spirit?

See "Do you want to be a beast?" chapter 4, and "Two men, two visions, two perspectives—one message," chapter 7.

Lesson: Unspiritual souls view the Gentile nations and present world system with worshipful wonder, while those who know God see its underlying bestial spirit.

2:34–35 Jesus—the destroyer of every proud image. In Nebuchadnezzar's dream, the image of Gentile pride was at last destroyed by God: "Thou sawest until a stone…smote the image…[it was] broken to pieces" (Dan. 2:34–35). If God destroyed one proud image, will He not destroy all proud images? (Remember, pride sits first on His list of "most hated" sins; see Prov. 6:16–19.) Absolutely, for God is no respecter of persons—or images. Indeed, every time an evildoer lifts up himself, and especially if he defies and oppresses God's humble servants (as did the Gentile rulers depicted by this image), he will end in this manner—suddenly and utterly broken by the Stone, who is the eternal defender of His humble disciples. And the Spirit's message doesn't stop there. Subtly, Nebuchadnezzar's vision implies that not one image of personal pride—non-Christian or Christian—will survive when Jesus returns. He is the destroyer of every proud image. Thus saith the Bible.

Throughout, the Scriptures make nearly everything of character and nearly nothing of public image. Today Western culture does just the opposite: It makes nearly everything of image and very little of character. Joseph P. Kennedy, patriarch of the most popular family in modern American culture, unashamedly taught his children, "It's not what you are that counts, but what people think you are." Thus he encapsulated his personal political philosophy and that of the modern American public. Indeed, everywhere Americans (and far too many Christians) give endless time, money, and energy to build up their social, professional, or political "image"—perceived public persona—while caring little for what they really are in private. So the disciples of Madison Avenue ride easily down the national highway in their stretch limos, while proponents of reality, humility, and character are forced to stand aside and watch.

As we watch this endless parade of proud images, we do well to remember our roots. We Christians follow a man whose personal philosophy and lifestyle was the antithesis of the elder Kennedy's motto. Jesus made integrity everything and image nothing. He taught what matters most is not what people think we are but what God thinks we are. He taught us to seek to please our heavenly Father "who seeth in secret," and He rebuked the Pharisees for seeking to "be seen of men" (see Matt. 6:5–6), rather than to be approved of God (see Matt. 23:25–28).

Christian, what are you earnestly building—a public image or a pure character? If you build an image of and for yourself, know this: God will one day destroy it; the shattered image of proud gentilism is proof enough of that. But if you build a pure character by steady submission to God in private and public life, God will raise you up and use you for His glory.

See 1 Corinthians 1:29, 31; Daniel 4:37b; 5:22–23, 30; James 5:1–6, 9; Matthew 23:12; 2 Timothy 2:15.

Lesson: Jesus will ultimately crush every image of pride.

2:34–35 God's "big bang." In full defiance of God's account of creation as recorded in the Book of Genesis, secular scientists theorize that the universe began with a stupendous explosion of original matter (supposedly compressed into a few millimeters, or some say within the confines of a single atomic nucleus!) some fifteen billion years ago. From this incomprehensibly huge and violent primal action, all the matter in the universe gradually assumed its current status. While offering no explanation for the creation of matter prior to this theorized explosion, or the cause of the explosion, this theory, known as the "big bang" is widely accepted as fact in lieu of biblical revelation. (For the biblical account of the original creation of matter, see Heb. 11:3.) While having utmost respect for scientific fact, I find the big bang scientific fiction—and a most blasphemous denial of God's creatorship! And I don't think God likes it either!

For Daniel sees an event yet to come that may well be God's long-delayed response to the gospel of the big bang. But this stupendous future event won't be theoretical but real and verifiable when it occurs. When the heavenly Father sends Jesus (the Stone) and heaven's armies to smash Gentile rule (the image) on His earth, Antichrist's one-world system of government (which fervently embraces Darwinian and big bang theory), will suddenly go *bang!*...and never again exist on earth: "Thou sawest until a stone was cut out without hands, which *smote* the image...[and it was] broken to pieces together" (Dan. 2:34–35, emphasis added). For further details of God's big bang, study Revelation 19:11–21.

Thank God, Daniel gives us a "big bang" worth believing in, one that will create a new world indeed.

2:37–38 Given from above. Through Daniel's interpretation, God informed Nebuchadnezzar twice that He had "given" him his great political authority over many nations (see Dan. 2:37–38). This agreed wholly with Jeremiah's repeated assertions (see Jer. 25:9; 27:6; 28:14). But Nebuchadnezzar didn't hear, or acknowledge, what God was saying—that God, not he, was due all credit for the vast kingdom he had acquired. If he had, his severe chastisement for his pride (see chapter 4) would never have been necessary.

What about us? Have we heeded Nebuchadnezzar's failure to heed God? Do we realize that whatever we have has been "given" us by God (see John 3:27)? If we believe this, we will never again be puffed up by pride when we receive favors or blessings. Why? We will know God has graciously *given* them to us. On the other hand, when favor and blessings are denied us, we will not be offended with people. Why? We will realize God has withheld them from us. If we consistently choose to think this way, we'll stay humble, and God will never chasten us for pride as He did Nebuchadnezzar.

See John 3:27; James 1:17; Deuteronomy 8:18; Daniel 2:20–22; Genesis 41:16; Exodus 24:12; Psalm 68:11; 2 Timothy 3:16; 2 Peter 3:15; Ephesians 6:19; 1 Samuel 30:23; 1 Corinthians 12:7–8; 1 Thessalonians 4:8; 2 Corinthians 5:18; John 17:2, 9, 11, 22, 24.

Lesson: Every good thing we have has been given us by God.

2:46–49 The rewards and results of successful trial. Daniel 2:46–49 records the rewards and results of the faithful four's test of the king's dream. Their rewards were twofold: gifts and positions.

1. VALUABLE GIFTS. Daniel receives undisclosed gifts from King Nebuchadnezzar. That these were given by

the king of Babylon—one of the world's richest men—implies they were of highest quality and immensely valuable; hence, Daniel calls them "great gifts" (Dan. 2:48). They were also given in quantity: "*many* great gifts" (v. 48, emphasis added). Thus Daniel received what amounted to a material fortune, as did Joseph centuries earlier. (See Gen. 41:42–43.)

2. HIGH POSITIONS. Initially, Nebuchadnezzar assigned Daniel two key posts in his administration, (unofficially) Ruler of Babylonia and Secretary of Wisdom and Knowledge (or Chief of Wise Men; see Dan. 2:48). Then, at Daniel's request, the king reassigned Daniel's post as Ruler of Babylonia to his three friends. Apparently, Daniel's friends discharged the many administrative duties of ruling the home province and reported to Daniel, who sat in the king's gate as one of his most honored and trusted officials (v. 49). Thus all four shared the responsibilities and rewards of high office.

The result of all this was simply that, again, God was glorified.

Though at first glance it appeared an idolatrous act, Nebuchadnezzar's impromptu prostration before Daniel (v. 46) was not that. Rather, it was his heathen way of showing homage to Daniel's God. *The Amplified Bible* translates that he "paid homage to Daniel [as a great prophet of the highest God]" (v. 46). This is evident from Nebuchadnezzar's own words, which praised not Daniel but his God: "Of a truth it is that your God is [the] God of gods, and [the] Lord of kings" (v. 47). Apparently, Nebuchadnezzar was responding to Daniel's earlier testimony that God, not he, was responsible for revealing the king's secret (vv. 28–29). So God was highly honored by His overcomers' victories.

The faithful four here are but types of Christians who overcome severe tests (theirs was severe). If we endure to the end, God rewards us richly, and we honor Him greatly.

See Psalm 50:15; Daniel 3:29–30; 5:29; 6:1–2, 25–28; Acts 28:10; Genesis 41:42–43.

Lesson: *After overcoming severe trials of our faith, we are richly rewarded and God is highly honored.*

2:46–47 Another win for the Lord. Insightfully, *The Modern Language Bible* notes, "Nebuchadnezzar at the feet of Daniel represents the Gentile powers humbled before Israel's God" (p. 875). And in a deeper sense still, Nebuchadnezzar's obeisance suggests his spiritual head, Satan, humbled before Daniel's Lord, Jehovah. Thus God won another battle and received yet another honor in the ongoing war between heaven and hell over the souls of men.

Similarly, the outcome of each of our trials either honors God or Satan. If we stand fast until the Lord delivers us, our faith honors God. He then duly reports our victory and His honor to the enemy: "Hast thou considered my servant, Job?...Still he holdeth fast his integrity" (Job 2:3). Conversely, if we compromise with our persecutors, or panic and faint in the day of adversity, they win the contest for their lord, Satan. Such was the case when the Philistines enslaved Samson and later killed King Saul: On earth the righteous lay prostrate before their enemies, and in heaven Satan gloated before the Lord (see 2 Sam. 12:14) and returned to his dark kingdom boasting of his victory.

The next time you're so vexed with your adversary that you're considering disobeying God, quickly do two things: Visualize Nebuchadnezzar prostrate before Daniel; then consider well the consequences of your actions. Do you want to make Satan bow low before God—or to enable Satan to reproach Him? The power to create either scenario is in your hands.

See Job 2:3; 2 Samuel 12:14; 19:18; 1 Kings 1:53; Psalm 110:1; Genesis 50:18; Revelation 3:9.

Lesson: *Our spiritual victories force Satan to bow low before God; our defeats enable him to boast and reproach the Lord.*

2:28–30,46–48 The Lord gets—and shares—the victory.
Before revealing and interpreting Nebuchadnezzar's dream
(Dan. 2:28–29), Daniel carefully gave all credit to God and
denied having any special personal wisdom (v. 30). Therefore,
God received all the glory, honor, and praise for Daniel's won-
drous message.

As stated above, Nebuchadnezzar's first words to Daniel
reveal that, indeed, he gave all glory to the Lord. Nebuchadnezzar
spoke not of Daniel's wisdom and gifts but of the omniscience and
supremacy of Daniel's God (v. 47). Deeply moved, he openly pro-
fessed faith that Daniel's God was:

1. The greatest God, greater than any other purported
   deity, including his (Nebo)

2. The greatest Ruler of all kings, including himself

3. The greatest Revealer of hidden knowledge (greater
   than occultists from whom he previously sought to
   discover secret things)

Nebuchadnezzar's public acclamation, which honored God
throughout all Babylon, was a great victory for God. Yet God's
response was most gracious. By all accounts—Daniel's,
Nebuchadnezzar's, Babylon's—the lone Victor, God, chose to
share His victory with His overcomer, Daniel. Though unwrit-
ten, it was surely God who put it in Nebuchadnezzar's heart to
honor, enrich, and promote Daniel to high office. How gracious!
How Christlike!

A type of Christ, Joshua demonstrated the same graciousness
when he let Israel's captains share the honor of his victory over the
five kings of Canaan. (See Josh. 10:24–25.) Thus he foreshadowed
Jesus who, though He will win victory at Armageddon by His
power alone, will graciously allow us, His saints, to participate in
the great battle and share in the rewards that follow.

Throughout its pages the Bible reveals that "the battle is
the LORD'S" (1 Sam. 17:47). Daniel's experience adds the
thought, "And the victory is His also!" Yet, gracious as He is, the

Lord Jesus delights to share His victories and rich rewards with us, His overcoming servants. Daniel learned to say thank you. (See Dan. 2:19–23.) Have we?

See 1 Samuel 17:47; 2 Chronicles 20:15, 17; Exodus 14:13–14; Revelation 2:26–27; 3:20–21.

Lesson: Though our spiritual victories are the Lord's, He graciously shares them and their rewards with us, His overcomers.

2:49 Christlike loyalty—remembering friends and helpers. In the hour of his personal promotion, Daniel didn't forget his loyal friends and helpers. Instead, he sought their promotion by asking the king to let his three friends govern the province of Babylon in his stead. Thus the grace shown him was manifested in him and he proved he was "like his Lord" (Matt. 10:24–25). Daniel's Christlike loyalty reminds us that Jesus is "not unrighteous to forget" (Heb. 6:10) the loyal friendship and assistance we render Him. Other Bible characters also demonstrated the grace of Christlike loyalty.

Elisha, a strong type of Christ, remembered the Shunammite woman who had built his "prophets' quarters" onto her home. (See 2 Kings 4:12–17.) David, another clear type of Christ, remembered the people who helped him survive his many trials. He remembered Jonathan's caring loyalty by caring for his crippled son after Jonathan's death (2 Sam. 9:1–13). He remembered Barzillai's sustaining gifts by sustaining his son after Barzillai's death (2 Sam. 17:27–29; 19:31–40). He remembered the elders of Judah, who helped him live victoriously in the wilderness, by sharing with them the spoils of his victory over the Amalekites (1 Sam. 30:26–31). And he remembered Abigail, who gave him wise counsel in his time of need, by taking her into his home in her time of need (1 Sam. 25:31, 39–42).

And as the types, so is the Antitype. Consider these ways in which Jesus remembered His disciples:

- He explicitly promised to repay anyone who gave any

assistance to His disciples for His name's sake (Matt. 10:42).

- At the Last Supper, He praised their faithfulness to Him and promised they would help administrate His coming kingdom (Luke 22:28–30).

- At His Ascension, He vowed to remain with them "always, even unto the end of the [age]" (Matt. 28:19–20).

- On the Day of Pentecost, He empowered them with the Holy Spirit (Acts 2:33) and afterward gave them great favor and fruitfulness in Jerusalem (Acts 2:47).

- After Pentecost, He honored their prayers, granting mighty miracles (Acts 4:29–30, 33; 5:12–16).

- He halted and humbled their most livid and lethal enemy and relentless persecutor, Saul of Tarsus (Acts 9:1–4).

- He promised that when He returned He would remember all those who had shown faith and loyalty to Him by protecting and assisting His brethren, the believing Jews (Matt. 25:34–40). (He also promised to remember the *disloyal*; see Matt. 25:41–46.)

Thus He proved He is "not unrighteous to forget" His loyal friends and helpers.

Where are we in relation to this grace of Christlike loyalty? Do we remember those who help us? Are we loyal to those who have been loyal to us for Christ's sake? Like Jesus and those who typify Him in Scripture (like Daniel), we should share the honors, rewards, and blessings we receive with our loyal Christian friends and helpers.

See "The Lord gets—and shares—the victory," chapter 2.

See Hebrews 6:10; Philippians 4:14–19; 2 Timothy 1:16–18; 2 Kings 4:12–17; Luke 7:4–5; 1 Samuel 25:31, 39–42; 30:26–31; 2 Samuel 17:27–29; 19:31–40; 9:1–13; Joshua 6:22–25; Esther 8:1; Matthew 10:42; 25:34–40; Luke 22:28–30; Psalm 41:1–3; Proverbs 19:17.

Lesson: *We should remember in success those who have helped us in distress.*

2:46–47 Converting belligerents into believers. In this chapter, and again in chapter 3, the loyal faith and obedience of God's servants during severe trials converted their enemy to faith in Jehovah. In both instances, Nebuchadnezzar—who was at best belligerent and at worst blasphemous—issued a public confession of faith (Dan. 2:47; 3:29). These were not the only biblical examples of belligerents being converted into believers.

Jesus promised to do the same for the Philadelphian Christians by vowing to make their most vocal detractors (the local Jewish congregation, whom He wryly dubbed the "synagogue of Satan") "come and worship [Jesus] before thy feet" (Rev. 3:9). Plainly, He was saying that because the Philadelphians had uncompromisingly, persistently, and patiently kept His Word (see Rev. 3:10), He would convert their enemies to the faith and bring them into their assembly, henceforth obedient to Him.

This is encouraging news to every persecuted Christian. If we persistently trust and obey God in our trials, He will one day utterly break the hostile spirits of our worst enemies and convert them to faith in Him. Are we ready to receive our repentant enemies and henceforth teach and lead them in the Word and ways of Christ?

See "When adversaries become advocates," chapter 3.

See Revelation 3:9; Acts 1:14 (cp. John 7:1–5); Acts 8:13; 6:7b; 9:1–9, 20–22 (cp. Gal. 1:23); Acts 18:12–17 (cp. 1 Cor. 1:1); 2 Samuel 3:6–21; Genesis 50:18–21.

Lesson: *If we persistently trust and obey God, He will one day convert our enemies into believers.*

2:48–49 Converting foes into "footstools." By issuing his rash execution order, which would have meant death for the faithful four, Nebuchadnezzar suddenly became their worst enemy. As stated above, because Daniel and his friends trusted God and prayed, God made their enemy a believer of sorts and hence their friend. But the divine miracle didn't stop there.

God went on to make the Babylonian monarch their "footstool" (Ps. 110:1). A footstool is "something that serves, supports, helps, and gives rest." Notice that the king gave them wonderful—even the best—jobs in his administration (see Dan. 2:48–49). Thus he did more than stop opposing them and politely agree with their religious faith; he actively sought their welfare, served their best interest, and tangibly improved their quality of life (Dan. 3:30). So, helped by their new supporter, the faithful four rested.

Are you ready for those who previously burdened you to now get in the yoke with you and pull and pull and *pull*...making your load lighter? No, it's not too good to be true; it's too good *not* to be true. Focus your faith on this thought: God can convert your hinderers into helpers.

See Psalm 110:1; Proverbs 16:7; Ezra 6:6–10; Acts 18:12–17 (cp. 1 Cor. 1:1); Philemon 10–11.

Lesson: *If we persistently trust and obey God, He will one day turn our spoilers into supporters.*

2:48–49 Power and prosperity—by courage or compromise? Fittingly, this episode, which began in terrorizing trouble, ends in satisfying success: "Daniel sat in the gate of the king" (Dan. 2:49). What is the significance of this verse?

In antiquity, the king's gate was *the* most important place in the entire kingdom. In that royal portal to the city the king held court, received important guests, transacted state business, inquired of his counselors, formulated law, issued decrees, and maintained vital personal contact with his subjects. Daniel sitting in Nebuchadnezzar's gate, endowed with great gifts and high office by the reigning monarch of the greatest nation on earth, is an example of the highest power and prosperity attainable in this present world. Daniel was indisputably a man of power, wealth, and prominence. As such, he presents his readers with an important contrast to another redeemed one who attained power and prosperity: Lot.

Like Daniel, Lot also sat in the gate of a prominent city, Sodom. Regarding Daniel 2:49, *The New Scofield Study Bible* notes:

> Compare Gen. 19:1, Lot, the compromiser with Daniel, the resolute. To sit in the gate of the king was to be in the place of authority (p. 900).

Truly, both Daniel and Lot attained great political power but by totally different means. Daniel (like Joseph) followed the path of the will of God without compromising God's Word or ways. He was ready to give up everything, if necessary, to retain God's approval and fellowship (see Dan. 1:8). Lot, conversely, followed the path of self-interest and consistently compromised God's standards of righteousness in order to gain material wealth, social influence, and political power. He was all too ready to give up God's favor and fellowship to have the things of this world. And time and again, when his tests arose, he did just that.

Most significant are the very different ends to which each man eventually came. After passing through some severe initial tests, Daniel (like Joseph) rose to power and prosperity and remained there for the duration of his life, still "[fit] for the Master's use" (2 Tim. 2:21) in his nineties. Thus the blessings he attained by walking with God uncompromisingly were never taken from him. Lot, however, who became a leader (perhaps mayor) in Sodom by undisclosed means, had all his power and prosperity suddenly stripped away when God visited Sodom in righteous judgment—thus he lost the worldly life he so cleverly gained and earnestly hoped to retain.

Which road are we traveling on today—the way of courageous, uncompromising obedience or the way of compromise? Daniel and Lot set before us the inevitable ultimate ends of these two ways (see Matt. 10:39).

See "Promotion and prosperity—God's way," chapter 6.

See Genesis 13:10–13; 14:16; 19:1; Daniel 1:8; 6:10, 16; Genesis 39:7–9; Matthew 10:39.

Lesson: *The power and prosperity God gives His uncompromising servants will remain, while that gained by spiritual and moral compromise will be lost.*

CHAPTER THREE

TRIAL BY FIRE!

**3:1–30 THE DILEMMA OF GODLY ONES IN A GODLESS LAND...
AGAIN!** Some sixteen years after the events of Daniel 2:46–49,
Nebuchadnezzar erected a golden image in the plain of Dura and
called an international convocation at which it was to be dedicated, with a full orchestral accompaniment. We know certain
things about this image: that it was an idol (Nebuchadnezzar's
words in Dan. 3:28 confirm that he considered his image to be a
"god"), that it was made of gold (probably overlaying wood), that
it was ninety feet in height and nine feet in width, and that
Nebuchadnezzar intended for all his subjects to worship it. We do
not know, however, if it was a likeness of Nebuchadnezzar or of
one of his idol-gods, such as Bel, or possibly even his attempt to
make an icon of Babylon in the form of the great head of gold he
had seen in his earlier vision (see Dan. 2:32, 36–38).
Nebuchadnezzar's reaction to its dishonor, however, makes it
clear that he fully identified with this image and considered its
dishonor his dishonor.

This chapter repeats the spiritual pattern seen in chapter 1 (see outline, page 14). It is outlined as follows:

1. The dilemma (vv. 1–7)
2. The decision (v. 12)
3. The test (vv. 13–25)
4. The reward (v. 30)
5. The results (vv. 26–29)

After Nebuchadnezzar's apostasy, the Jews were faced with another *dilemma*—again they could not obey both God's law and man's. If they bowed to Nebuchadnezzar's idol, they would break the first and second commandments; if they didn't bow they would break the law of Babylon (vv. 4–6). The *decision* Shadrach, Meshach, and Abednego made initially, though not specifically recorded (as in Dan. 1:8), was to obey God and trust Him to take care of the consequences of their obedience (see Dan. 3:12). (This whole trial is a very clear example of the principle of 2 Tim. 3:12!) The *test* occurred when they were accused and brought before Nebuchadnezzar for a public confession (another choice), then thrown into the seven-times-hotter furnace (vv. 13–25). The *reward* was their miraculous preservation (v. 25), sudden release (v. 26), public acclamation (vv. 26–27), and surprising promotion (v. 30). The *results* were that God was glorified in an official decree (v. 29), and, again, Nebuchadnezzar was converted, albeit temporarily, to at least an elementary faith in the God of Israel (vv. 26–29).

See "Converting belligerents into believers," chapter 2; also "The changing faith and favor of our enemies," chapter 3.

See 2 Timothy 3:12.

3:1–7 Enforced *universal* state religion—foreshadowing the tribulation. Nebuchadnezzar's actions here in erecting a golden image and enacting a legal order (decree) that it be worshiped on pain of death is no mere act of personal vanity. It is a direct foreshadowing of what Antichrist will do during the Great Tribulation. *The New Scofield Study Bible* notes:

Here is a case of enforced state religion, involving the

worship of a man-made image. This phenomenon, appearing at the beginning of the times of the Gentiles and continuing from time to time through history (e.g. Roman emperor worship, Japanese Shinto shrines, and Soviet veneration of Lenin), will reappear at the end of the age when, not only the dragon, but the beast and the image of the beast also will be worshiped under compulsion (Rev. 13:4–15; 14:9–11; 19:20; 20:4; cp. 2 Thess. 2:4). (pp 900–901)

One distinction must be made. Because he had divine permission to rule the world (many nations) at that time, Nebuchadnezzar's image-worship represents enforced *universal* state religion, whereas the forms of state religion Scofield described above, with the exception of Rome, were limited to single nations.

Following through with this typology, Meshach, Shadrach, and Abednego also typify the faithful Jewish Christian remnant of the Great Tribulation who will flee or suffer capital punishment rather than worship the image of the beast, which would both break the commandments and deny the Lordship of Christ. (See Rev. 14:12.)

See 2 Thessalonians 2:4; Revelation 13:14–15; 14:9–11; 19:20; 20:4.

Lesson: *In the Great Tribulation, Antichrist will demand—on pain of death—that all people worship his image.*

3:1 The changing faith and favor of our enemies. According to a notation in *The Modern Language Bible*, the Septuagint states that Nebuchadnezzar set up this image in the eighteenth year of his reign. So, as stated previously, this occurred approximately sixteen years after the events recorded in chapter 2. Sometime during this interim, therefore, Nebuchadnezzar apparently lost his faith in and fear of the God of Daniel and regained his characteristically heathen arrogance. If not, he would not have persecuted Shadrach, Meshach, and

586 BC

Abednego for their loyalty to God's law. And apparently he suffered another lapse of faith and resurgence of pride sometime
after the events of chapter 3; hence his need of severe divine
chastisement (Dan. 4). After that dreadful "rod," however,
Nebuchadnezzar was finally and fully convinced that Israel's
God was indeed God of all (gods), God over all (kings), God forever and ever. Hence, he penned his testimonial to this effect
(see Dan. 4:1–37). Apparently, this final conversion held for the
duration of his life.

We should look for this in our antagonists. At times they will
hate and defy us, and at other times, when God shows His hand
for us, they will repent and humble themselves and speak highly
of our faith. Then, as time passes without any signs of divine
intervention, they may turn again to despise and reproach us,
only to once more repent in the day they see God's hand at work.
Through it all we must remember that as long as we fear, trust,
and obey the Lord, we have *His* favor, regardless of outward
appearances, as did the faithful four both in times of trial and triumph. Therefore, we must not be moved by either the praises or
curses of those who know not our Lord. When they speak "fair
words" (Jer. 12:6), we must not flatter ourselves, and when they
ignore or belittle us, we must not lose confidence. Like the blow-
ing of the wind, our enemies change their opinions with the prevailing appearances. Like the unchanging Rock He is, our Lord is
steady and faithful to us always.

Shimei is a prime example of the fickleness of our enemies.
When David ruled with full divine favor, Shimei was silent. But
when Absalom successfully overthrew David, Shimei spewed his
venomous hatred and disdain for David (2 Sam. 16:5–14). Yet
later, when David was reinstated, Shimei repented and spoke
respectfully to David again (2 Sam. 19:16–23). Graciously,
David forgave Shimei when he confessed his sin; yet, wisely, he
recognized that Shimei's conversion was only skin deep and
wisely admonished Solomon to beware of him. (See 1 Kings
2:8–9.) Abimelech also behaved amicably toward Isaac when he
saw God's blessing continuing and increasing upon him. (See

Gen. 26:26–29.) Ahab "went softly" for three years after Elijah's terrible warning of doom (see 1 Kings 21:27–29) but later returned to his evil ways and hence was judged.

Lesson: *Our enemies' faith in God—and favor toward us—may come and go with the seasons of our lives.*

3:12 Isolation. Observe that Daniel is not included in the Chaldeans' accusation, nor is he mentioned at any point in this trial. Why not? Where is he at this crucial moment? The reader is simply not told.

One explanation may be that God permitted the rebellion of Daniel's three friends to come to the attention of the king before Daniel's (who, in light of his uncompromising decisions of chapters 1 and 6, surely took the same line of action). Since Nebuchadnezzar then acted in great fury and haste (Dan. 3:13, 22), only to see God deliver the three, he apparently was already humbled and reestablished in faith in (or fear of) the God of Israel before Daniel's rebellion came to his attention. Thus he did not persecute Daniel as he had his three friends.

Conversely, Daniel is tried alone in chapter 6, there being no mention of his three friends also defying the king's proclamation against prayer. One explanation is that they may have died by that time; Daniel himself was then over ninety years of age. Another is that on this occasion Daniel was challenged first, since we know he was the primary target of the evil men who conceived the plot (see Dan. 6:4). It was Daniel they lusted to destroy, not his three friends.

Whatever the whereabouts of Daniel in chapter 3 and his three friends in chapter 6, one thing is clear: God isolated His servants to test them more perfectly. While in chapters 1 and 2, the faithful four were tested together, here in chapter 3 and again in chapter 6, we see them tested alone. So we see that God sometimes isolates us, His servants, to test us. Why? Because the less human aid we have, the more we are forced to depend on God only; hence, the more our faith is increased and established.

When we find ourselves alone and severely tested, it is of some comfort to know that it is God who wants us so, in order that our faith may be more fully tried and increased by trial. Another reason God isolates us is that we may realize more fully His "very present" power to uphold, help, comfort, lead, and deliver us, even in the midst of great trouble (see Ps. 46:1) and human abandonment (see 1 Sam. 30:6).

Do you feel alone sometimes, humanly speaking, as if no other soul really understands, and so supports, you in your decisions and actions? It's no accident; God planned it this way. He wants you to make your decision to submit, obey, trust, give, or persevere all by yourself in Christ Jesus. Then the spiritual growth in you will be real and your own eternal possession. So accept your isolation and praise Him for it—and for the fact that He is with you always.

See Psalms 142:4; 102:7; Exodus 3:1–4; 4:24; Jeremiah 15:17; Daniel 10:7; John 16:32; 1 Samuel 30:6–8; Genesis 39:1; 32:24; Mark 1:12–13; 4:36; Luke 22:41–42; 2 Timothy 4:16–17; Acts 12:5–6; Revelation 1:9.

Lesson: *God sometimes isolates us to more profitably test us.*

3:8 Envy at the root? Notice that it was the "Chaldeans" (Dan. 3:8), the special class of wise men, who accused Meshach, Shadrach, and Abednego. Why? What was their motivation? Was it love and loyalty for King Nebuchadnezzar? Possibly, but this isn't likely. Was it anti-Jewish prejudice? Possibly, and this is likely, for the Jews were despised wherever they went during the dispersion (see v. 12, "certain Jews"). Or was there envy at the root of their decision to accuse the three? I believe this is very subtly implied.

Note that the three, along with Daniel, who was then chief of the wise men of Babylon (Dan. 2:48), were occupational rivals with the Chaldeans. All offered counsel to the king and hence were subject to comparison (see "The Chaldeans," chapter 2).

Remember, Nebuchadnezzar had already expressed his opinion that the wisdom of the faithful four was "ten times better" than all his other counselors (see Dan. 1:20), a finding that couldn't have set very well with the proud, renowned Chaldeans. Also, the faithful four (Daniel speaking for them all) had succeeded in revealing and interpreting Nebuchadnezzar's forgotten dream, when all the Chaldeans had failed (see Dan. 2:10–11, 27–29); that Daniel's three associates had shared credit for this revelation, perhaps due to their union with him in prayer (vv. 17–18, 23), is clear from his request that they too share in its reward (see v. 49). So there are solid grounds to support the likelihood that the Chaldeans were envious toward all of the faithful four. Apparently, they felt Daniel was too beloved by the king to be vulnerable to accusation—but not his three friends. Hence their accusation.

The Scripture also implies that envy was the motivation for the plot that Daniel's rivals contrived and executed against him (see "Preferment, promotion, persecution!" Dan. 6:3–4).

See "The Chaldeans," chapter 2.

See Daniel 6:3–4; Psalm 106:16; Genesis 37:3–4; Matthew 27:18.

Lesson: *Envy is sometimes the real, hidden reason people criticize or accuse others.*

3:10 "Fall down and worship"—Satan's age-old decree. King Nebuchadnezzar's order read that every subject of greater Babylonia must "fall down and worship" his image when signaled to do so by his orchestra. In this passage, the phrase "fall down and worship" is used in one form or another six times (vv. 5, 6, 7, 10, 11, 15). This wording is a subtle allusion to Jesus' temptation, in which the prince of pride himself personally called on our Lord Jesus to "fall down and worship me" (Matt. 4:9). Why this allusion?

It is because, as the spiritual head of the Gentile world, Satan was acting and speaking through King Nebuchadnezzar, who was then its political head. Remember, Satan always seeks embodiment in sinners that through them he may seek, albeit futilely, to carry out his infernal will—to usurp the praise (worship, glory), position, and power, and hence the very place and Person of God. (See Isa. 14:13–14.) Hence, he was tempting Meshach, Shadrach, and Abednego to bow to him just as he later tempted Jesus. He has since embodied many vain heads of state throughout the centuries and through them demanded, and at times received, similarly idolatrous veneration.

As a man of great pride (see Dan. 4:28–30; 5:20), King Nebuchadnezzar also symbolizes *all excessively proud people.* As he did through King Nebuchadnezzar, so Satan, as the *lord of pride,* acts and speaks through all vain people, trying to coerce others to "fall down and worship" him, not through overt Satanism (or Wicca), but rather through the arrogance of the servants of pride. Our temptation to bow down to Satan, then, will come to us through proud sinners (including carnal, apostate Christians). They demand that we kowtow to their "image" (vain self-conceit) or do as they wish when their will is clearly contrary to God's Word or leading in our life. If we refuse to yield to their will, in their "rage and fury" (Dan. 3:13) they will subject us to a "fiery furnace" of persecution (vv. 6, 21; see 1 Pet. 1:6–7; 4:12; 1 Cor. 3:12–13; Rev. 3:18); they will reject, denounce, deprive, slander, and oppose us, and energetically commit themselves to our downfall. But God will delight in us for not honoring the thing He most hates: pride. (See Prov. 6:16–17.) Hence He confers His blessing upon those who refuse to bow to Satan's spirit in proud people: "Blessed is that man who maketh the LORD his trust, and respecteth not the proud…" (Ps. 40:4). If, however, we slavishly honor the proud and obey the willful, we in effect worship their god, Satan, and so forfeit the blessing of the Lord.

Satan is also the *prince of this world,* that is, the invisible ruler of the present visible social order (see John 12:31; 14:30). So every time we "worship" (unduly reverence, overly praise) the things of this world, its present secular system, or unredeemed mankind's achievements or advancements in denial and independence of God, we do homage vicariously to this world's spiritual lord and ruler, Satan. *The Spirit-Filled Life Bible* notes, "Satan, as the god of this age (2 Cor. 4:4), forms many images by which he seeks to intimidate and seduce into bowing to the spirit of the world..." (p. 1236).

This does not imply that we should render deliberate indignities or mockery toward this present world system, which presently serves the Church, or ridicule mankind, which was originally made in God's image and still reflects that image, albeit imperfectly. Nor should we render indignities or mock even the most proud persons. That would be inconsistent with the love of God and the humility of the godly (see Ps. 1:1c). Rather, we should simply *not enter into* their praise. Mordecai did not mock, berate, or speak abusively toward Haman; he just refused to honor him (Esther 3:2–4; 5:9). To Haman, that alone was a cause of war (Esther 3:5–6; 5:9–14).

See Esther 3:2–4; 5:9; Psalm 40:4.

Lesson: *When we give undue reverence and praise to proud people, we honor Satan.*

Lesson: *When we give undue reverence and praise to this present unbelieving world system, or to unredeemed mankind, we honor Satan.*

3:1–7 Nebuchadnezzar's image—foreshadowing Christian and Jewish persecutions. The whole incident described in Daniel chapter 3 is a preview of things to come, both in Israel and the Church.

In Israel's history, Jews were subsequently faced with other calls to "worship" various notoriously evil leaders, such as Haman and the Caesars. In the Church's history, Christians faced Rome's decrees, first merely issued and later enforced, that its emperors be worshiped as divine; their refusal to worship was the chief cause of the long, bloody Roman persecution (A.D. 64–313). Much later, Christians also faced the Roman Church's own demands that its highest official, the Pope, be revered with the worship (reverence, faith) due only to God, blasphemously referring to him as the "Holy Father" and the "Head of the Church." And more recently, European Christians were called upon to support, if only tacitly, the cruel and vain despot, Hitler. Some, as the three Hebrew boys, refused to bow to Hitler's "image"; others even participated in plots to overthrow him (e.g. Dietrich Bonhoeffer); but far too many others, sadly, bowed weakly to Hitler's image, even taking a required oath of loyalty, not to Germany but to Hitler personally.

So here in Daniel chapter 3, God sets forth for all time His perfect will concerning His people and idolatrous figures, political or religious. The uncompromising obedience of the three Jews is exactly the line of obedience He wants us to take when faced with similar dilemmas either in national life or personal circumstances. When ungodly heads of state, or others given to vanity, demand idolatrous reverence, don't bow down!

The Book of Revelation declares plainly that one great, final test of this nature lies ahead for Israel and the nations in the Great Tribulation (see Rev. 13:14–15) and that many, surely remembering the exploits of Shadrach, Meshach, and Abednego, will pass it (see Rev. 15:1–2; 12:11b).

See Matthew 22:21.

Lesson: *Jews and Christians alike have been, and will yet be, forced to choose between honoring God's Word and bowing to the "image," physical or figurative, of vain leaders and sinners.*

3:1–7 Concerning authorities. Nebuchadnezzar was a king and hence an authority. While in this matter, which involved a royal decree distinctly contrary to God's will, the three Hebrews did not submit to Nebuchadnezzar, it should be remembered that at all other times and in all other matters they did. Hence, their refusal to comply with royal law was an uncharacteristic, not a characteristic, act; defying authorities was not their daily cup of tea. In seeking to emulate them as overcomers, we should be careful to follow the entire pattern they set before us. For that, we must learn to submit daily to all human authorities.

When faced with excessively proud, immoral, or evil authorities (e.g., the Herods and Caesars; and recently, for Americans, the Clintons), we must learn to divide the spirit from the office, refusing to respect wicked people yet submitting to their official authority in all normal matters out of respect for the Lord and His Word, which clearly and repeatedly calls Christians to obey, not defy, civil authorities and their laws. (See Rom. 13:1–7; 1 Pet. 2:13–15.) The only exceptions to this occur when: a) authorities demand action that is contrary to God's Word, dishonoring to Him, or harmful to his people (see Exod. 1:15–21); or b) when, as in Daniel 3, they demand idolatrous treatment.

The apostle Paul willingly submitted to the righteous authority of an unrighteous office-holder when he deferred to the justifiable objections of the obviously arrogant and unjust sitting high priest of Israel, Ananias (see Acts 23:1–5). Yet note that in no way did Paul kowtow to Ananias, or pretend or say he was a good man! Those who attempt to whitewash evil leaders, calling their evil deeds good and praising them profusely, in effect "bow down and worship" them and the god of their pride, Satan.

See Acts 23:1–5.

Lesson: *While refusing to "worship" the images of unjust or vain rulers, Christians must respect their offices and obey their laws, so far as they do not break God's Word, dishonor Him, or harm His people.*

3:1–12 When others don't bow down. Obviously, Nebuchadnezzar took great pride in his image. Hence, when the three Hebrews refused to regard the object of his pride, he was greatly offended and flew into a fit of rage. As one of the Bible's leading examples of a proud man, Nebuchadnezzar reveals much to us about our fallen nature. Hence, this incident speaks directly to us as Christians.

Nebuchadnezzar may be taken as a type of our proud, carnal nature, or "old man." As Christians, we still have this nature within us and must learn to recognize its manifestations and mortify pride whenever it arises in our hearts. Nebuchadnezzar's fit of rage here symbolizes our anger when people do not "bow down" (show respect or praise) to our "image," that is, our overly inflated self-esteem (see Rom. 12:3) due to our reputation, works, honors, achievements, knowledge, gifts, skills, office, or wealth. When they "regard not thee" (Dan. 3:12), by either ignoring or overtly disrespecting us, we often react with anger merely because they have not catered to our pride. Thus to some degree we reenact Nebuchadnezzar's folly, speaking or working against our offenders, or even persecuting them, without just cause.

This is one example of what Jesus meant by being angry with our brother "without a cause" (Matt. 5:22).

See 1 Samuel 18:8; Esther 3:2–6; 5:9–14; Matthew 5:22; Romans 12:3.

Lesson: *Sometimes we become angry with people merely because they do not honor us or praise the objects of our pride.*

3:12 The art of offense. "…these men, O king, have not regarded *thee*…" (Dan. 3:12, emphasis added). In making their accusation against the three Jews, the Chaldeans chose their words with evil skill. They wanted to sting the king, already swollen with pride, by making the Jews' actions seem more a personal affront than an act motivated by religious principle. They wanted Nebuchadnezzar to think the three had no respect for him as a person or king, which was not true. Meshach, Shadrach, and Abednego had already served Nebuchadnezzar for some time now (over sixteen years) with an appropriate submission and respect for his regal authority. Their problem was not with him but with his decree, which broke the law of their God.

Nevertheless, the Chaldeans, who were clever with their tongues, chose those words that would most certainly stir anger and offense in the king's heart. It was the art of offense at work. What do their actions teach us?

Primarily, they reveal we should beware when people speak of third parties (particularly those we have never met and so do not know) in such a way that implies they dislike us. Admittedly, what they say may be true (see Luke 13:31); or, as in this case, it may be the work of "he that soweth discord among brethren" (Prov. 6:19), trying to set us against someone who is not our foe and, as in Daniel 3, is also godly. Understanding and guarding against this serpentine strategy is part of our education in becoming "wise as serpents" (Matt. 10:16). We must deliberately not be quick to take offense at insinuation and innuendo. By doing this we obey Jesus' injunction to not judge by appearances but rather justly, by clearly verifiable facts. (See John 7:24.)

See Daniel 6:13; Esther 3:8; Proverbs 6:19.

Lesson: *When people describe the words or actions of third parties in words that pointedly offend us, we must defer our anger and judgment; our "messenger" may be trying to set us against an innocent, even a godly, person.*

3:13 The folly of fury...again! As seen earlier (Dan. 2:12), Nebuchadnezzar allowed his "rage and fury" to move him to act in foolish haste and evident self-opposition.

First, he spoiled his own public dedication service, or "Image Day," by stopping festivities so he could locate and execute the three Hebrew insurgents! Second, if he had killed the three, as he hoped and tried to do, he would have weakened his own administration by eliminating three of his most capable assistants and brought God's sure wrath upon himself for touching the Lord's anointed. (But, again, God graciously saved him from this.) Third, he lost an undisclosed number of his best soldiers, who were slain while carrying the three Jews to the edge of the fiery furnace (see vv. 20, 22).

See "The folly of fury," chapter 2.

See Daniel 3:19.

Lesson: *When angry, never make decisions or take action.*
Until you cool off, everything you say or do is likely
to be hasty, stupid, and self-opposing.

3:15a Another chance...to sin! Having heard from reliable sources that Meshach, Shadrach, and Abednego had defied his worship decree, Nebuchadnezzar already had grounds to summarily execute them. Yet he shows at least a speck of patience by calling them in to first confirm the report (vv. 13–14). Then he issues his ultimatum, which, though it is chilling, also offers them, from his perspective, a way out. So they are given a second chance to obey the offended lord of Babylon...and disobey and offend the Lord of heaven! (See Exod. 20:3–6.)

Since Satan is Nebuchadnezzar's inspirer in this incident, we see here one similarity between Satan and God: They both give people second chances. When His servants fail Him, God graciously and faithfully arranges another opportunity for them to obey, and thus succeed, in the exact area of obedience in which they have failed. (See Jonah 3:1–2; Gen. 42:15–20.) When God's servants fail to take up Satan's temptation, Satan too, in his diabolical "grace," gives us at least one more chance to sin (see Num. 22:15) and so "fall down and worship" him! Sadly, too many take up his offer (see Num. 22:21).

See Numbers 22:15; Judges 13:17; 16:16–17; Luke 4:5–8; Nehemiah 6:5.

Lesson: Satan always gives us a second chance to sin.

3:15c Challenging heaven!!?? It is one thing to challenge earthly opponents; from ancient times men have challenged one another to contests, duals, and wars. But to challenge heaven, by defying its omnipotent Master Spirit, is something else. When Nebuchadnezzar asked, "Who is that *God*, that shall deliver you out of my hands?" he was directly challenging God (emphasis added). He was saying, "I'm gonna do what I want with you, and what can your 'God' do about that?!" *The Modern*

Language Bible note calls this "a Pharaoh-like challenge" (see Exod. 5:2). Indeed, it was nothing less than the spirit of Antichrist speaking through Nebuchadnezzar. When incarnate and empowered, Antichrist will speak "great things" against God and heaven and those who dwell in heaven (translated saints; see Dan. 7:8, 20, 25; Rev. 13:5–6). Nebuchadnezzar's slur here also foreshadows the wildly mad challenge Antichrist will put forth when he gathers the armies of the earth to come to Armageddon...to do battle with Jesus (see Dan. 8:25; Rev. 17:14; 19:19). Have you heard such a challenge in your life?

This same Antichrist *spirit* operates today in our oppressors when they think, and sometimes dare to say, that they can do anything they want to us and God will do nothing about it. And, as in the case of the three Hebrews, sometimes it looks as if they are right for a season. But eventually it will be evident that they are as wrong as Nebuchadnezzar and Antichrist. As seen in this context, and in Christ's teaching (see Luke 18:7–8), God will answer every such challenge in His own time and way if we, His persecuted ones, will only believe and endure.

See Daniel 7:8, 20, 25; 8:25; Rev. 13:5–6; 17:14; 19:19.

Lesson: *Antichrist, the final "king of Babylon," will defy heaven; his spirit presently challenges the children of heaven daily.*

3:16–18 Obeying higher authority. Usually we think of the three Hebrew boys' act here as one of civil disobedience. When Nebuchadnezzar commanded them to worship his idol, they refused. Yet in reality, theirs was an act of obedience. They were obeying God's first and second commandments (Exod. 20:3–6).

Accordingly, Christians should always obey human authorities, except when such obedience would constitute disobedience to God's Word. Then they should obey higher authority by not yielding to the ungodly demands of lower authority. We see, then, that while God has ordained all human authority, human authority is not absolute. God's authority is always to be honored first.

In any conflict between human and divine authority, we should always obey the higher authority of God. (See Acts 4:19–20.)

This was why the early Christians refused to in any way worship their Roman emperors. See Christ's subtle commentary on this: "Yes, give Caesar taxes, for they are due him; but not worship, which is due only to God" (Matt. 22:21, paraphrased). It is also why Luther refused to submit to papal orders that he recant his teachings, which he derived directly from the Scriptures; he held that the Word of God was a higher authority than either the edicts of the pope or his councils. It is vital that we understand that to this day Luther's viewpoint is still right: The Word is the highest authority on earth, higher than the opinions of any church leader or council, higher than the laws or legal opinions of any national or international ruling body (see Ps. 138:2b).

See Daniel 6:10; Acts 5:29; 4:19; Esther 3:2–4; 5:9; 1 Peter 2:13–15; Romans 13:1.

Lesson: *In any conflict of authorities, we should always obey higher authority; the Word of God is the highest authority.*

3:16–18 Extreme loyalty. The three Hebrews here are the embodiment of extreme loyalty. They knew God could deliver them from Nebuchadnezzar's furnace and were willing to face its horrors, if necessary, to remain loyal to God. But even if God for some reason chose not to deliver them, they would not move from their position taken in obedience to His written Word. *The Living Bible* puts this best:

> Our God is able to deliver us...but if he doesn't, please understand, sir, that even then we will never under any circumstance serve your gods or worship the golden image you have erected.
>
> —DANIEL 3:17–18, TLB

Their faith was that they were confident of one thing: God's law was right, and departure from it would be at their eternal peril.

Hence, as long as they stood by that Word in their situational and personal conflicts, they too were right. So there they would stand, in Jesus' righteousness, come what may. This is clearly a large step beyond the faith that trusts and obeys because it believes God will—He must—give an immediate victory. It trusts God's character and stands with His Word, even if abject earthly defeat follows.

Again, the early Christians acted in accordance with God's Word and the gospel message, even when they had no hope of escaping Roman execution. In loyalty to His Father's will that He accomplish Redemption, Jesus gave Himself up to His betrayer and captors, knowing full well His Father would *not* deliver Him from the cross. Many Jewish Christians will accept martyrdom rather than the mark of the beast. Such utter loyalty is occasionally seen in the natural man. The soldier who accepts a suicide mission for the good of his fellow countrymen and nation has accepted that he probably will not return, yet he puts loyalty to his nation above his own life. In this age of extreme self-interest, such extreme loyalty is viewed as pure insanity. But before Christ's kingdom comes, extreme loyalty will again be seen in God's people.

See Job 13:15; Habakkuk 3:17–19; Esther 4:16; John 21:18; Acts 20:24; Revelation 20:4 (13:15).

Lesson: Christians with extreme loyalty to Jesus always choose to be loyal to God's Word, regardless of the consequences.

3:17 Confident of release—by deliverance or death. The three boys were unsure whether Jehovah would intervene to save them or let them die, but they were beautifully confident of one thing: He would release them from Nebuchadnezzar's tyranny. So they added the words, "And he will deliver us out of thine hand, O king" (Dan. 3:17). This points up that to the righteous, death, though it is unpleasant, is nevertheless a kind of release. Indeed, death releases us from:

- The carnal nature, the power of sin, and the control of Satan (Rom. 6:7; 6:16)

- The oppression of the wicked (Dan. 3:17)

- The agony of chronic illness or prolonged poverty (Luke 16:22)

- The vexation of living among sinners in this present world (2 Pet. 2:7–8)

- The weariness of our earthly labors (Rev. 14:13)

- The distress of carrying our crosses (Phil. 1:21, 29)

- The limitations of our mortal bodies (2 Cor. 5:1–8; 1 Cor. 15:51–53; 1 John 3:2).

These truths are very comforting when saints die. They have been released from this world into a much better one (see Phil. 1:21, 23; Ps. 16:11); they are in the Father's house, in Jesus' presence, at peace, without vexation, without tears, without burdens…in "paradise" (Luke 23:43).

So every Christian today may share the confidence of Daniel's three friends. We may be sure of one thing: We will be released from Satan (the ruler of this present world system and wicked oppressor here typified by King Nebuchadnezzar) either by the spectacular deliverance of the Rapture or by our physical expiration before that much-anticipated event. Either way, praise God, we may boldly tell the devil, "He will deliver us out of thine hand, O king of Babylon!"

See Romans 6:7; Luke 16:22; Revelation 14:13; 2 Peter 2:7–8; Philippians 1:21, 23; 2 Corinthians 5:1.

Lesson: *To the righteous, death is a release into a much better state of being.*

Lesson: *Christians may be confident that they will be released from all Satan's oppression one day, either by translation or death.*

3:24–30 God steals the show! Note the divinely caused reversal of events here. The day described in chapter 3 began as Nebuchadnezzar's finest, the day he was to unveil his treasured image and receive the accolades and homage of all his realm in full public view! "Image Day" was to be a grand and memorable spectacle that would permanently emboss Nebuchadnezzar's regal name and glory in Babylon's annals!

But "at that time" (v. 8), or while the great event was just getting underway, the Jews interrupted the proceedings by their uncouth rebellion. Then Nebuchadnezzar had to take the time and effort to locate, interrogate, and threaten them; and after their defiance he had to take more time to heat the royal furnace, bind the three, and toss them in to receive their just desserts.

But just when it seemed Nebuchadnezzar had successfully dispatched his interrupters, another Interrupter broke in: Jesus miraculously visited and preserved the three Jews (v. 25). Shocked, Nebuchadnezzar immediately called them out (v. 26). So captivated was he that he summoned all his "princes, governors, and captains, and king's counselors"—the same dignitaries he had invited to witness his high-profile dedication service—to see the wonder God had wrought (v. 27). After this, Nebuchadnezzar publicly praised the three as "servants of the Most High God" (v. 26) and explained to his wide-eyed compatriots how God had sent an angel to deliver his servants (v. 28), praising them further for their total commitment to their God (v. 28b). Then, surprisingly, in his final recorded acts of the day, he did two more things. First, he issued a decree forbidding any dishonoring of the Jews' God and, again, proclaiming Him to be greater than all gods (v. 29). Second, he promoted the now-vindicated rebels to higher office (v. 30). So his day ended.

What happened here? God interrupted Nebuchadnezzar's show of glory and totally eclipsed it with His own show of glory—an irrefutable public demonstration of His supreme power to deliver His own. And by day's end, the show, and the day, belonged to God.

Lesson: *Whenever the proud exalt themselves, invariably God eventually intervenes to upstage them by revealing His glory.*

3:24–30 God steals the show—foreshadowing the tribulation. A remarkable type of Antichrist, Hitler displayed his Nazi glory in massive, visually mesmerizing demonstrations at Nuremberg throughout the 1930s and when hosting the 1936 Olympics in Berlin, all the while boasting that his Reich would endure a thousand years. In fact, it was thoroughly dismantled in just over twelve years. Antichrist's kingdom and glory, though it will encompass the earth, will not last as long as Hitler's—about three and a half years, says the infallible Word (see Rev. 13:5–7).

As with Nebuchadnezzar, so with the beast. Nebuchadnezzar had just started to revel in his glory when God interrupted and stole the show, the day, and the glory. So the beast will erect his image in the Jewish temple in Jerusalem and institute universal enforced state religion (exactly as foreseen here in Dan. 3:1–7), only to have two spoilers—God's two witnesses (Rev. 11:3–6)—ruin his glory by the public denunciatory prophecies they will utter against him daily. Then, after only a brief show of ultimate vainglory, God will visit—again by sending Jesus to "Babylon" (Rev. 19:11–21); only this time He will utterly destroy the beast, his image, and his kingdom, and bind the ageless master spirit that inspired him, Satan (Rev. 20:1–3), then fill the whole earth with His glory. Thus, Antichrist's evil day will end and Christ's glorious day begin.

Lesson: Jesus' visitation—His return to earth at Armageddon—will interrupt Antichrist's day of glory and turn it into the glorious Day of the Lord!

3:19–30 Trial by fire—deadly but beneficial! Enraged at the three Jews' second refusal to bow and their polite but in-your-face rejection of his diabolical mercy, Nebuchadnezzar decided to torch them. (Nero had the same diabolical idea in A.D. 64.) So he ordered his furnace heated seven times more than its usual level. This was trial by fire—and it was awesome, even deadly!

But it was also very beneficial, even necessary to the full

spiritual maturation of the three. At least seven benefits resulted from this trial by fire:

1. Purification
2. Liberation
3. Knowledge
4. Glory (to God)
5. Salvation
6. Reward
7. Establishment

1. PURIFICATION: Seven is the number of perfection in Scripture. To perfectly purify someone or something, it was sprinkled, washed, or fired seven times (God's three purifiers: blood, water, fire). Nebuchadnezzar was purged of his pride by seven years of extreme discipline, and the world will yet be purged of sin by seven years of extreme judgments. (See Ps. 12:6; Dan. 4:16, 25, 32; 2 Kings 5:10, 14.)

Nebuchadnezzar's furnace was heated "seven times" (Dan. 3:19) more than usual. Hence, even though it is not directly cited, it is implied that the three Jews were purified in its fires (see Mal. 3:3–4).

2. LIBERATION: When they entered the furnace, the three Jews were "bound" (Dan. 3:21, 23–24), but in the furnace they were "loose" (v. 25). Hence, in the fire they were liberated from the ropes (hindrances, limitations) that previously bound them.

3. KNOWLEDGE: In the furnace, the three Jews received another special education; not an academic curriculum, as in the king's college (see Dan. 1:3–6), but an experiential one, in the school of the Spirit. There they learned intimacy with Jesus; they grew closer to Him in their great trouble than anywhere else (Dan. 3:25; see Ps. 46:1). Hence they came to know the Lord much better, specifically His comforting presence, which enabled them to be at peace (Dan. 3:24) when they should have been in a breathless panic, and His supernatural protection, which kept them from being burned (v. 25, "no hurt"), or even soiled by the stench of fire (v. 27). Furthermore, it was in the

furnace that they learned to walk with God (v. 25); at the beginning of their fiery trial they were unable to walk (v. 23).

4. GLORY TO GOD: The Jews' trial by fire brought glory to God. By word of mouth and by the king's decree, "the God of Shadrach, Meshach, and Abednego" was made known and highly honored before all the people of Babylon [the world] (vv. 28–29).

5. SALVATION: The three Jews' fiery trial became the stage for a supernatural revelation of Jesus by the power of the Spirit. Thus Nebuchadnezzar and his counselors and all other citizens of Babylon present saw Jesus for themselves. This, we know, led to Nebuchadnezzar's conversion, for he clearly expressed faith, albeit temporarily (see chapter 4), in the God of the Jews (Dan. 3:26, 28–29). Though not stated, it seems probable that other Babylonians too were converted by this remarkable and gracious manifestation of Jesus and His awesome power to save. (See John 11:45; 12:32; Ps. 40:1–4, especially 40:3b.)

6. REWARD: The three Jews were rewarded by being delivered, honored, and promoted to still higher offices in Babylon (Dan. 3:26, 30; see 1 Sam. 2:30; Mark 10:28–31; Luke 22:28–30).

7. ESTABLISHMENT: After clay is formed into a vessel, it is fired to make its form (shape or character) and function permanent. So the heavenly Potter, having formed the three Jews into the shape of uncompromising, courageous, loyal, trusting servants of His, put them into His kiln—Nebuchadnezzar's furnace—and fired them. Henceforth, their spiritual character and their capability of serving God acceptably were established and permanentized. Their subsequent promotion to even higher offices confirms that God had indeed established their character. The Lord only promotes those whom He has established through testing. (See 1 Pet. 5:10; Ps. 27:5–6; 40:1–2; 30:5–6.)

Also, other Jews were undoubtedly encouraged in their faith and so established in greater security in God in the midst of far-away Babylon. King Nebuchadnezzar's decree honored their God and so gave them a proper degree of acceptance (toleration) in

Babylon. Hence they were strengthened. (See "Winning for God and Christians," chapter 3.)

In their most immediate application, the three Hebrew boys represent uncompromising Christians who are tried by fire. These exceptional trials (Nebuchadnezzar's furnace was seven times hotter than normal, Dan. 3:19) are much more intense than normal daily trials. Hence, they are reserved for stronger Christians. Such intense ordeals benefit us precisely as Nebuchadnezzar's furnace did the three Jews.

They *purify* us by exposing latent faults—motivational and behavioral—we've never before seen in ourselves, and by forcing us to repent of secret sins we have stubbornly held to. The fires purify us to our very core, far deeper than the sprinkling of blood and water. They *liberate* us from every binding, chiefly fears (of people, failure, lack, trouble, etc.), including a whole host of carnal attitudes (pride, envy, prejudice, unkindness, etc.) that limit our ability to unite and work with other saints. By bringing us closer to Jesus than ever before, they greatly increase our experiential *knowledge* of God; when we emerge, we truly and deeply know the character (true personality) of our God. Hence we're confident of His unfailing faithfulness to provide, protect, deliver, guide, etc., and ready to do further exploits as occasion serves (see Dan. 11:32). When others hear how God has enabled us to endure our fiery trials without harm and has faithfully delivered us, He is *glorified* in their eyes. This in turn leads people, sometimes many, to believe on the Lord and be *saved* (see Ps. 40:1–3; John 11:45). Furthermore, God *rewards* us amply for our personal suffering and losses by delivering, honoring, and promoting us. Finally, at trial's end, our characters are fully formed, fired, and thus *established* (permanentized, or very likely to never change); hence God can, and will, entrust us with more of His work.

See Psalm 66:8–12; Malachi 3:2–4; 1 Peter 1:6–7; 4:12; 1 Corinthians 3:11–15; Revelation 3:18.

*Lesson: Though potentially deadly to our faith, trial by
     fire will bring us great spiritual benefit if we
     trust and obey God.*

3:19–30 Trial by fire—qualification implied. Though not
stated, it is implied that the three Hebrew boys had qualified for
this high-level testing. Observe they had passed two significant
tests approximately sixteen years earlier (chapters 1, 2), neither of which approached the severity of trial by fire; also, in
both of these earlier exams, Daniel was tested with them. By
passing these earlier, less severe trials, they unwittingly qualified for trial by fire, the highest form of human testing. Why?
Apparently God saw they had spiritual gold, silver, and precious
stones (figures of genuine faith, balanced truth, and unswerving
loyalty, the makings of God's choicest servants) in their souls.
God only tries by fire what is purified by fire. He doesn't waste
His time trying substances that can't stand the flame, such as
wood, hay, and stubble (figures of wrong beliefs, doctrines,
lifestyles). So only vessels of honor qualify for trial by fire.

Job was one such vessel. (See Job. 23:10b.) And he was
tested before his fiery trials recorded in the Book of Job. This is
proven by God's description of him as "a perfect and an upright
man,...who feared God, and |shunned| evil" (Job 1:1, 8) *before*
the awesome trial described in the balance of the book. Such
could only be said of someone previously tried and found
faithful—yet not in an extreme furnace like that that followed.

Also, Abraham was extensively tested (see Gen. 12–21)
before his great and final "trial by fire" on Mount Moriah.

Initially, only Christians who pass their preliminary trials
qualify for trial by fire; others do not. All Christians, however,
will at last meet some form of trial by fire, if not unto victory
and honor, then unto defeat, dishonor, and some degree of
spiritual disinheritance. (See 1 Cor. 3:13–15; 1 Pet. 1:6–7; 4:12,
17.) Lot is an example of this latter type who fail in trial by fire
(Gen. 19). Note that while the three boys were thrust into trial
by fire because of consistent uncompromising obedience to

God's Word, fire overtook Lot because he lived contentedly in full spiritual and moral compromise. Precisely this will occur again in the tribulation period; the fire will come on the whole world—surviving carnal Christians, Jews, and Gentiles—ready or not. (See Rev. 3:10.)

See Job 1:1, 8; 2:3.

Lesson: *Initially, only Christians who pass their prelimi-nary trials qualify for trial by fire; others do not. Ultimately, however, all Christians will experi-ence trial by fire, regardless of their readiness.*

3:25 Trial by fire—the goal. In trying us by fire, God has a clear goal in mind. It is capsulized in the words:

> ...loose, walking in the midst of the fire, and they have no hurt...

—DANIEL 3:25

Much to the chagrin of King Nebuchadnezzar, the three Hebrew boys were free, stable, upright, moving forward, without injury ("no hurt"), and closer to Jesus ("the form of the fourth") than ever before, despite the worst treatment he could dish up. It was at this point that he (lord of the furnace) called them out of their fiery trial (v. 26). So God does with us.

As Lord of our trials, God stands by our fiery furnaces, watching to see if and when we come to the spiritual state sym-bolized by the physical state of the three Hebrew boys at the moment of their release. When we reach that condition—consis-tently free from the control of any sin, consistently upright and stable, consistently moving forward in our duty or ministry, grow-ing ever closer to Jesus, with no open wounds in our spirits, and all *while still in a furnace of affliction*—God will approve us and call us forth to increased power and higher service: "Ye servants of the Most High God, come forth..." (v. 26; see Isa. 48:10).

If we are destined for very special service, God may keep us in the furnace even longer, that all His spiritual graces and overcoming strength may be perfected in us to the nth degree. A. W. Tozer said of Samuel Rutherford, "He had walked with God in the furnace so long that it had become as his natural habitat" (*The Root of the Righteous*, p. 136).

Has our uncompromising obedience to the Word brought us into a fiery furnace of trial? Have we, by grace, reached this goal? Are we on the way there?

See Isaiah 48:10.

Lesson: *In our fiery trials, God's goal is reached when we are free, upright, stable, steadily walking forward in duty, without offense in our spirits, and growing closer to Jesus daily.*

3:19–30 Trial by fire—foreshadowing Laodicea's final test. The three Hebrew boys' fiery trial is also a foreshadowing of the end times. The New Testament clearly and repeatedly declares God's intention to test Christians by fire (1 Pet. 1:6–7; 4:12; 1 Cor. 3:11–15). But Jesus goes further, making a tiny statement in Revelation 3:18 that intimates a huge fact about these End Times. His message to Laodicea speaks prophetically to this present materialistically dominated, morally compromised, spiritually deceived final period in church history. After rebuking this age for its spiritual lukewarmness, Jesus invites us all to "buy of me gold tried in the fire, that thou mayest be rich..." (Rev. 3:18). Plainly then, there will be fiery trials in this Laodicean period. If not, how could we buy faith tested in "the fire," as Jesus calls for? To have one's faith proven by fire, there must first be a fire in which it may be proven.

Therefore, by Jesus' own infallible Word we know God will arrange circumstances in this, the Church's final hour, in which uncompromising Christians (of the spiritual heritage of Daniel and company) will experience fiery opposition for their faith. By enduring this proving, they will be endowed with all the benefits of trial by fire, and they will not be released from their fiery trials until God's goal (see Dan. 3:25) has been accomplished in their souls. The Rapture will be their deliverance. (See Luke 21:36.) Hence, the experiences of the three Hebrew boys are not only examples for the Jewish Christians of the Great Tribulation, but also for overcoming Christians today in this terminal period of the Church Age.

See Psalm 66:8–12; Malachi 3:2–4; 1 Peter 1:6–7; 4:12; 1 Corinthians 3:11–15; Revelation 3:18.

Lesson: *Overcoming Christians will experience trial by fire in this final Laodicean period of church history.*

3:20 Opposed by Satan's strongest servants. When King Nebuchadnezzar chose to vent his wrath on the three Jews, he used "the most mighty men that were in his army" (Dan. 3:20). Thus he chose his strongest servants to bind them and put them through the experience of trial by fire. There is spiritual symbolism here.

King Nebuchadnezzar represents Satan, lord of the world (Babylon). His furnace represents the fiery situations that arise to try the faith, loyalty, and patience of uncompromisingly righteous Christians. And "the most mighty men that were in his army," who bound the three Jews and actually committed them into the fire, represent Satan's agents who persecute God's servants. As Nebuchadnezzar's mighty men but carried out his angry behests, so our prime enemies but carry out Satan's infernal hatred against us in all our persecutions and tribulations that we endure. Thus Satan, not the "mighty men" who oppose us, is our real enemy. (See I Peter 5:8–9; Eph. 6:12.) That Nebuchadnezzar chose his strongest ("the most mighty") servants is also illustrative.

When Satan wants to attack us for our uncompromising obedience to God, he usually does so through his strongest servants—people who are strongly held by him due to their sin. Remember, whoever yields to sin lets Satan into their disposition and thus becomes immediately subject to his influence. (See Rom. 6:16; 2 Tim. 2:26; John 12:6; 13:2.) The longer this satanic control exists, the more it strengthens, thus developing a "stronghold"; hence Satan more easily moves such persons to do his will. These evildoers, over whom Satan has a stronghold, are, spiritually speaking, Satan's strongest servants—or "the most mighty men" in his Babylonish, or diabolical, army of workers. Hence, they are his most effective means of waging spiritual warfare against saints.

For instance, King Saul, Shimei, and Nabal each were used by Satan to put David through fiery trials because they themselves were strongly bound by sin: King Saul through envy (1 Sam. 18:7–9); Shimei through cruel misjudgment of David (2 Sam. 16:7–8); and Nabal through covetousness (1 Sam. 25:11). If David had responded to them in an ungodly way, Satan would have successfully bound him (through them) due to his own sinful reactions. But David's submissive trust and obedience to God in his trials (David chose to forgive his offenders and not resist evil) made Satan's bindings disintegrate and fall off.

This helps us to remember:

1. Our real enemy is Satan, not the antagonists who "bind" us with confining, hindering troubles and cause us much pain.

2. Our antagonists are Satan's captives through sin. He is merely using them to oppose us. (See Eph. 6:12.)

This perspective makes it much easier for us to obey God: specifically, to give God thanks in the midst of our trials (1 Thess. 5:18); cease from anger and forsake wrath (Ps. 37:8); forgive as Christ taught (Mark 11:25–26), remitting the sins committed against us (John 20:23), and loosing the very people (Matt. 18:18) through whom Satan hopes to bind us by inducing sinful reactionary attitudes and actions. (God always honors such prayers, unless an evildoer has sinned the sin unto death; 1 John 5:16b.) This spiritual line of thinking and action both keeps us free and sets others free. And it makes us full-fledged, bona fide *overcomers in action!*

See 2 Timothy 2:24–26; Ephesians 6:12.

Lesson: When opposed by evildoers, we should remember: 1) Our real adversary is Satan; and 2) the people harassing us are strongly bound captives of Satan.

Lesson: Believing this, we should cease from anger, offer the sacrifice of praise, and forgive our enemies, remitting their sins against us and loosing them from Satan's control.

3:22 When slayers are slain. Despite the spiritual perspective advocated above, if our opposers have crossed the line of God's patience and sinned "unto death" (1 John 5:16b), they will end up as Nebuchadnezzar's mighty men—killed by their very effort to kill us. It is a heavy but true thought that, except for God's grace, there are lethal consequences to knowingly harming the body of Christ or any of its members. (See 1 Cor. 3:16–17; Ps. 105:14–15.)

For example, Haman put the Jews, especially Mordecai and Esther, through trial by fire and in the end was slain. King Saul put David through trial by fire and in the end was slain. Daniel's accusers put him through trial by fire (in the lions' den) and in the end were slain. King Herod (Agrippa I) put Peter and the Jerusalem Church through trial by fire and was thereafter slain. Yet upon some God showed mercy.

Paul was an exception to this otherwise harsh rule. He caused the persecution, affliction, imprisonment, and death of many Christians (see Acts 26:9–10; 8:3; 9:1), yet by grace obtained forgiveness because he had done so in ignorance (1 Tim. 1:12–15).

See Psalm 105:14–15; Isaiah 41:11; Daniel 6:24; Esther 7:10; Acts 12:1–19, 23; Matthew 18:6–7.

Lesson: Except for God's grace, there are deadly consequences to knowingly harming the Church or any Christian.

3:25 A "very present Help." Doubtless King Nebuchadnezzar saw Christ present—very present—with the three Jews he placed in his hastily fired crematorium. The "form of the fourth," whom he said was "like the Son of God" (Dan. 3:25, NKJV), was none other than Jesus. Noting this "Christophany (preincarnate appearance of the Messiah)," *The Spirit-Filled Life Bible* states, "This is a dramatic illustration of the presence and protection of the Lord with His people who suffer for their testimony."

Indeed it was an example for the ages of the grand truth expressed in Psalm 46:

> God is our refuge and strength, a very present help in trouble.
>
> —PSALM 46:1

While God is present with us at all times, He is a "very present" help in trouble. That is, He is at His best—an especially close and manifest helper—when our trials are at their worst. How kind and faithful He is, to manifest Himself most sweetly when we are most bitterly distressed. Thus, always, His grace is sufficient for the strain He permits. The very day we are pierced by a thorn in the flesh, that very day He draws near and anoints us with the Balm of Gilead. (See 2 Cor. 12:7–10.)

What a different perspective this gives us concerning very hard trials. When they come, our flesh shrinks: "Oh, no, Lord, not this!" Yet it is in these very "furnaces" that for the first time we experience Jesus' consummate consolations—His peaceful presence and inspiring, personalized Word—as never before. So, paradoxically, very difficult times become our best opportunities for very close fellowship with Jesus.

See Psalm 46:1; Luke 24:15; Genesis 28:10–16; 39:1–2, 20–21; 1 Kings 19:9; Acts 23:11; John 9:35–38; 20:19–20; 6:18–19; 2 Corinthians 12:9, 7–10.

Lesson: *Though always near us, God draws very near us when our trials become very distressful.*

3:26 Contentment extraordinaire! Note that King Nebuchadnezzar had to call the three Hebrew boys to get them to come out of his fiery furnace: "…Then [when called] Shadrach, Meshach, and Abednego came forth…" (Dan. 3:26b). Apparently, they had become comfortable there, even content, so much so that they were not seeking a means of escape. This is confirmed by the previous verse, in which Nebuchadnezzar sees the three merely "walking" around in the middle of his furnace, not frantically trying to climb their way out of his death pit (v. 25). This was contentment extraordinaire!

To be content while buoyed by the excitement of ever-increasing prosperity and success is normal for sinners, even for carnal Christians. To be content in quiet, mundane times is also somewhat normal for persons not presently agitated by active sin within. But to be content in adversity is evidence of divine grace. And, as we see here, to be content in the midst of extreme adversity—a vicious, murderous trial—is simply a wonder; it is evidence of extraordinary divine grace. What enabled the three to be content in such extremity?

Surely the manifest presence—the "very present" nearness (Ps. 46:1; see note above, Dan. 3:25)—of the Son of God was the key to their extraordinary contentment. Hence, we see that the presence of God, if cultivated by the believer's private communion and steadfast trusting obedience, is so strong, it [He] can keep us perfectly calm and content amid our worst trials, so much so that we don't even consider trying to escape; we just enjoy Jesus today and go on, trusting that God will make a way of escape when He pleases. We'll gladly receive His deliverance when He gives it, but we won't move a finger to seek or force deliverance on our own terms. The three were not the only ones to evidence such extraordinary tranquility amid tribulation.

The apostle Paul had to have this extraordinary grace to endure willingly all the fiery trials the "messenger of Satan" (2 Cor. 12:7) brought upon him. So did Peter, when he slept peacefully on the eve of his scheduled execution (Acts 12:6); and Jesus, when He napped contentedly in the midst of a powerful and frightening Galilean squall (Mark 4:38); and John, who evidenced extraordinary contentment by being "in the Spirit on the Lord's day" (Rev. 1:10) while exiled on the desolate, volcanic isle of Patmos. Surprisingly, the saintly Joseph seemed to lack this high level of contentment when he appealed urgently to the butler for release (Gen. 40:14–15); yet after "two full years" (Gen. 41:1) of additional waiting, he too became fully content with the Lord in his fiery trial. Then out he came, an inspiration to us all.

See "A very present Help," chapter 3.

See Philippians 4:11–12; 2 Corinthians 12:9; Psalm 16:11; Acts 12:6; 16:27–28; Mark 4:38; Revelation 1:9–10; Genesis 40:14–15; 41:1, 14.

Lesson: By the empowering grace of God's presence, it is possible for us to be so deeply content in the midst of very fiery trials that we don't even seek escape.

3:26 When adversaries become advocates. Here is a surprising fact: King Nebuchadnezzar both committed the three Jews to the fire and called them out of it! What a paradox! How could the same person both condemn and persecute God's people, then later release them, praise their faith, and promote them? As improbable as it seems, Nebuchadnezzar did just this. He was both their persecutor and their promoter, their adversary and their advocate. What is the explanation for this? Simply that Nebuchadnezzar was not the real persecutor of the three Jews but merely the "front man" for that invisible enemy, Satan.

While persecuting the three, Nebuchadnezzar was, practically speaking, *demonized*; hence demons, at Satan's behest, inspired the king to adamantly resist the worshipers of the one true God. But when Satan perceived that the worst he could do had no power to change (or stop) the three Jews' faith and obedience to God (see verse 25, "they have no hurt"), he withdrew from Nebuchadnezzar. After his departure, Nebuchadnezzar again became *humanized* and, returning to his former attitude toward the three, favored, praised, and promoted them. This is encouraging news to persecuted Christians.

We must follow the example of the three Hebrews by letting our "Nebuchadnezzars," or diabolically inspired detractors, see that we are continuing to walk with Jesus in the very fiery trials they have brought upon us, that we are perfectly unaffected by their worst treatment. Unless they have sinned the sin unto death (1 John 5:16b), when they see this and realize there is nothing further they can do against us, they may well one day give up the fight and, to our amazement, become our friends and supporters. Nebuchadnezzar's surprising reversal was not the only biblical case in point.

Abimelech persecuted Isaac only to later seek his favor (Gen. 26:26–33). Abner fought against David after King Saul's death, yet later defected and pledged his loyalty to David (2 Sam. 3:6–12). When the young Church persisted in its early fiery trials of persecution, a "great number" (Acts 6:7) of Jewish priests converted to Christianity. Saul of Tarsus persecuted Christians viciously for years, yet later, as the apostle Paul, he delivered Christians from the prince and power of darkness, incursions of error, and their relentless Jewish persecutors.

If Jesus were to ask you today, as He did Martha long ago, "Believest thou this?" what would your answer be? "Yea," or "nay, Lord"? Remember, to receive from Him you must believe in Him. (See Mark 11:24.)

See "Converting belligerents into believers," chapter 2.

See Proverbs 16:7; 28:23; Psalms 110:1; 47:3; Genesis 26:26–33; 2 Samuel 3:6–12; Isaiah 41:11; Acts 18:17 (with 1 Cor. 1:1); Revelation 3:8–9.

Lesson: *If we walk steadfastly with Jesus in the midst of our fiery trials, God may turn even our worst adversaries into advocates.*

3:27 Miraculous preservation. After calling forth the three Jews and inspecting them, King Nebuchadnezzar was impressed with the fact that their bodies were perfectly unharmed: "...these men, upon whose bodies *the fire had no power*..." (Dan. 3:27, emphasis added). Their hair wasn't singed, their clothes weren't burned, and they didn't even have the smell of fire upon them. They were miraculously preserved in his hideous, hissing crematorium.

God still does this for those who fear and obey Him with uncompromising loyalty and trust (like the three Jews). Their bodies are preserved from the harmful effects of their cruel and lethal trials. As we keep our minds peaceful with trust (Isa. 26:3–4), hopeful with promise (Ps. 43:5), and sharp with study (2 Tim. 2:15), as we keep our emotions under control (anger, Ps. 37:8; fear, Isa. 41:10) and our hearts joyful (Phil. 4:4), the supernatural grace of God preserves us from psychosomatic disorders despite our prolonged exposure to severe pressures that would otherwise ruin our health. Those who don't know the Lord, when exposed to the same pressures, utterly break down with stress-related disorders. (See Isa. 40:30.) As were Nebuchadnezzar's mighty men, they are slain by the flaming heat of their troubles (Dan. 3:22). And why have we not so fallen? Because, as our souls have prospered in the fire, so have our bodies also (see 3 John 2). And we are miraculously preserved, not only from apostasy and physical death, but also from stress-induced physical afflictions. Thus, in the end, we discover we have quite literally gone to hell and back with our health intact.

John Bunyan's health was miraculously preserved in his "fiery trial" of incarceration in Bedford jail. God kept him well and writing even while Bunyan was forced to live for twelve years in a filthy prison, one so purportedly vile that visitors sometimes became ill and died after breathing its infectious air. Yet it was in this, his hellish furnace, that Bunyan penned the manuscript for *The Pilgrim's Progress*, the most widely read book in the English language next to the Bible. For Bunyan, God kept the promise He made to the Israelites. (See Exod. 23:25.)

And will He not miraculously preserve our bodily health,

too, if we but trust and obey Him, and abide very close to His life-giving presence, whatever our fiery furnace?

See Daniel 6:22–23; Psalm 79:11b; 3 John 2; Exodus 23:25; Isaiah 26:3–4; 40:30–31; Proverbs 4:20–22.

Lesson: *If we fully trust and obey the Lord, His grace will miraculously keep our bodies from stress-induced disorders in even the most pressurized situations.*

3:29 From decree to decree. The three Jews' trial began with one Babylonian decree and ended with another. Their dilemma started when King Nebuchadnezzar issued a decree commanding all to worship his image (Dan. 3:4–6) and ended with his decree forbidding that anyone speak dishonorably of Jehovah (v. 29). Since Nebuchadnezzar's royal decrees were law, his second decree constituted a great legal victory for God and His people. It gave them a liberating sense of protection—legal protection—which they had not enjoyed previously in Babylon.

So it was in the Book of Esther. Mordecai and all the Jews were tried from the time Haman issued his decree in King Ahasuerus' (Xerxes') name ordering the genocide of the Jews (Esther 3:12–15) until Mordecai and Esther issued their decree, also in the king's name, enabling the Jews to avenge themselves of their unrepentant enemies (Esther 8:9–14).

So it was also in the Roman persecution of the Church. By imperial decree all Roman citizens were ordered to worship the reigning emperor. Beginning in A.D. 64, an increasingly bloody series of periodic persecutions ensued against Christians throughout the Roman Empire. This ended in A.D. 313 with the rise of Constantine, who issued another imperial decree giving full toleration to Christianity, and yet another in A.D. 324 giving Christianity full legal status. (Constantine's rise to power was at least partly God's intervention through human agency to relieve His oppressed people, similar to His intervention through King Cyrus to terminate the Jewish captivity; see Isa. 45:1–4.) In A.D. 392, Theodosius issued still another imperial decree making

Christianity the state religion of Rome—and forbidding pagan-
ism! (The first two legalization decrees were undoubtedly God's
hand and a great victory for Christians; the latter is questionable, as it also resulted from considerable compromises on the
part of the Church.)

So it will be again in the Great Tribulation. At the mid-point,
Antichrist will issue a law ordering all to worship his image (as
did King Nebuchadnezzar). Then will ensue the greatest trial
Israel and the world have ever known. It will end, however, when
Jesus returns at Armageddon, defeats Antichrist, and issues a
new "decree" ordering that all worship Him in Jerusalem for a
thousand years. (See Zech. 14:16–19.) Again, this will be a great
legal victory for God's people. Notably, all these legal reversals
were initiated not by the human shrewdness or political action
of God's people but by divine intervention.

Thus the ungodly laws of men begin periods of special trial
for God's people, and when God intervenes in power, the emer-
gence of new laws reverencing God and His Word mark the end
of these periods. Roe vs. Wade (1973) marked the beginning of
a terrible period of legalized mass murder in the United States.
When will come the law, or judicial interpretation, that reverses
it? Surely not until divine intervention—a mighty spiritual reformation marked by sorrow for sin and renewed faith in
Christ—sweeps the nation.

See Esther 3:7–15; 8:7–14 (divine intervention occurred
6:1–7:10); Revelation 13:14–18; 20:4 (divine intervention
occurs 19:11–21).

Lesson: *The fiery trials of saints often begin with ungodly
laws and—after some form of divine interven-
tion—end with godly laws.*

3:29 Winning for God and Christians. By overcoming their
trial by fire, the three Jews won honor and promotion, not only
for themselves but also for God and their fellow Hebrews. King
Nebuchadnezzar's decree, which was read in every village

throughout the kingdom, distinguished Jehovah as the greatest Deliverer of all "gods." (Though still confused by polytheism, at least Nebuchadnezzar understood and proclaimed Jehovah's supremacy!) No one was allowed to speak a word against Jehovah publicly. Thus God was greatly honored in the esteem of Babylon's religious community.

This encouraged every Jew. Not since they had fallen captive to the Babylonians had they felt so good about Jehovah or so secure in Babylon. Now being a Jew was honorable. There must have been much rejoicing in the synagogues of Babylon! Nebuchadnezzar's decree was tantamount to a toleration order. If Babylonians could not speak against the God of the Jews without risking death, they certainly had to be tolerant of His followers! So the Jews' faith, and hence their sense of security, were greatly strengthened. Consequently, they experienced religious liberation, a revival of sorts in the midst of their political captivity—all won by the exploits of three uncompromisingly faithful souls!

So it is with Christians today. By enduring and overcoming our trials by fire, we win not only honor and promotion for ourselves in Christ, but glory for God and liberty and strength for other Christians. (See "Fourfold honor," chapter 6.)

See "Trial by fire—deadly but beneficial," chapter 3.

See Philippians 1:12–14; Psalm 40:1–3; Acts 16:40; 27:33–36; Judges 7:23; 1 Samuel 14:22; 17:52.

Lesson: *By overcoming fiery trials, we win not only blessings for ourselves but honor for God and encouragement for all Christians.*

3:30 Promotion—after testing. God always rewards the faith that honors Him (1 Sam. 2:30). His reward to the three Jews was promotion to higher office; notice it was not given until they completed their trial. Before their trial they held high positions in Babylon (see Dan. 2:49a), but afterwards they held even higher offices, though their new titles are not disclosed

(Dan. 3:30). This was no accident. It was God's established way: Promotion always follows successful testing.

To receive such divine promotion, the three had to endure trial by fire. Before God promoted them, He thoroughly tested and humbled them, just as He did their forebears long ago. (See Deut. 8:16.) Too often believers forget this and take their viewpoint of promotion from this present world.

In this present system, we hope to emerge straight from academia, university degree in hand, and go right to the top of the sports, entertainment, business, political, financial, and industrial worlds. Our whole culture encourages such thinking. But rarely, if we were to rise so rapidly, would we have the humility, experiential knowledge, understanding, or compassion to experience such promotion without subsequently self-destructing. A long, honest look at the many professional athletes, entertainers, and preachers who have been undone by premature fame and fortune is all the proof we need that this is so. Once in Christ, believers tend to relive this world's prevailing fallacy by thinking that Jesus will take us to the top right away. But in the experiences of Daniel's three faithful friends—and those of Joseph, Moses, David, Mordecai, *et cetera ad infinitum*—we see God's way, and it is always promotion after trial, never before it.

Our reaction to the unpleasantness of testing, then, is crucial. If we won't have the testing, we won't have the promotion. It's as simple as that.

See "Trial by fire—deadly but beneficial," chapter 3.

See Proverbs 18:12; Matthew 23:12; Deuteronomy 8:16; James 1:12; 4:10; Psalm 113:7–8; Luke 14:7–11; Esther 8:1–2; Exodus 4:29–31; 2 Samuel 2:1–4a; Genesis 41:39–41; Luke 22:31–32; Acts 9:30; 11:25–26; Revelation 2:26–27; 20:4.

Lesson: *God promotes Christians after successful testing, never before it.*

CHAPTER FOUR

A COURAGEOUS AND HUMBLE MESSENGER

4:1–3 A WORLDLING'S WORD TO THE WORLD. Interestingly, Daniel wrote a very large portion of the book bearing his name (Dan. 2:4–7:8) in Aramaic. Since Aramaic was the language of Babylon, which ruled the world, it was the "world language" of the day. Hence, in this portion of Daniel's book God sends several vital messages specifically to the leaders and people of the Gentile world (see "Messages to the Gentiles," chapter 2). Nebuchadnezzar's salutation specifies that, indeed, he is speaking to the whole world: "Nebuchadnezzar...unto all people... that dwell in all the earth" (Dan. 4:1).

To corroborate and thus increase the impact of these messages, God chose to have one of them (Dan. 4) authored by one of the most prominent Gentile personalities of the ages, King Nebuchadnezzar, ruler of Babylon the Great, the first Gentile power to overrule Palestine during the captivity. Nebuchadnezzar was a worldling's worldling and a king's king (see Dan. 2:37a). God's reason for choosing Nebuchadnezzar is not stated, but perhaps He reasoned that if Gentile readers failed to heed

Israel's holy prophet, Daniel, maybe they would at least respect
the word of their most prominent leader!

So, in His passionate desire to convert the lost, God goes
the "second mile" in bearing witness to the unbelieving world.
Succinctly stated, this fourth chapter of the Book of Daniel is a
worldling's word to the world.

See "Messages to the Gentiles," chapter 2.

See Acts 5:34–40; 17:28.

*Lesson: When He pleases, God speaks to worldlings
through other worldlings who are prominent in
their eyes.*

4:1–3 An inspired Babylonian archive. *The Ryrie Study
Bible* notes, "This chapter is a public decree or state paper of
Nebuchadnezzar." As such, it would have been first proclaimed
throughout every nation, city, and village in King Nebuchadnezzar's vast empire (see Esther 3:14–15; 8:13–14), then
retained with his royal papers in a library or other literary
repository (see Ezra 6:1).

That a Babylonian monarch dictated this message makes it
Babylonian; that God gave the words and subsequently grafted
them into the Book of Daniel and the canon of Holy Scriptures
makes the decree inspired (and hence infallible). Hence, we find
in this chapter a very rare thing: an inspired Babylonian
archive.

4:4–33 The changing faith and favor of our enemies.
Implied here is that during the time between the events of
chapter three and those of this chapter King Nebuchadnezzar
experienced another change of heart, again reverting to unbelief and pride. He could not have thought, spoken, and acted as
he did here if the fear of Israel's God had been upon him as it
was on two earlier occasions (see Dan. 2:46–47; 3:26–29). *The
Spirit-Filled Life Bible* offers another perspective here, sug-
gesting that, while Nebuchadnezzar recognized God's greatness, superiority, and wisdom due to his previous experiences

with the faithful four, he wasn't about to fully acknowledge God's sovereignty over his personal life and vast kingdom. To believe that God is and that He is great is one degree of faith; to give Him all praise and surrender to His will in all matters is another. Clearly, Nebuchadnezzar was not yet subject to God, and his self-adulation was so great God could no longer overlook it. In either case, one thing is certain: Nebuchadnezzar needed, and received, severe divine chastisement.

See "The changing faith and favor of our enemies," chapter 3.

Lesson: *Our enemies' attitudes toward God and their favor toward us, His people, may change periodically. This may, or may not, indicate genuine permanent faith.*

4:5 He speaks through dreams. For the second time in Daniel's writings, we find God chose to speak to King Nebuchadnezzar through a dream (see Dan. 2:1) rather than a prophetic messenger. Later, we discover that God spoke twice to Daniel through dreams (see Dan. 7:1–14; 8:1–14). In fact, one or another form of the word *dream* occurs twenty-nine times in the Book of Daniel. God's usage of dreams is not limited to the Book of Daniel. Dreams were His preferred means of communication in the patriarchal period. (See Gen. 15:1; 28:10–15.) He also used them prominently in the four Gospels and in the Book of the Acts of the Apostles.

Today, clearly, the Bible is God's preferred means of communication with us. (See 2 Tim. 3:15–17.) Yet His extensive use of dreams in the Scriptures themselves tells us that we should not "pooh-pooh" all dreams as being too nebulous to be from God. Indeed, some dreams are nothing more than evidence of an overworked or troubled mind. (See Eccles. 5:3.) But the possibility always exists that a dream may be a real communication from heaven. It cannot be denied that the God of the Bible speaks through dreams, and, as seen in the examples given below, He speaks both to the redeemed and the unredeemed.

Therefore, it is wise to judge our dreams to see whether they proceed from the Lord. Dreams that come from God are:

1. Often *recurring* (Acts 10:16; Gen. 41:32; Job 33:14–15)
2. Always *timely*, dealing with current situations, problems, conditions
3. Often *corrective*, exposing sin or negligence (Dan. 4:4–27)
4. Given to *inspire hope*, revealing good things to come during or just before we enter times of distress, defeat, or grief (John 16:13; Gen. 28:10–15; Judg. 7:13–15; Acts 23:11)
5. *Instructive*, revealing or reminding us of vital spiritual truths (Acts 10:9–16)
6. *Ministerial*, revealing vital spiritual truths for God's people (Num. 12:6)
7. *Warnings* that alert us to the dangers of sin or prepare us for trouble ahead (Gen. 20:3–7; 31:24; 41:25, 28; Matt. 2:13; 27:19; Job 33:15–18)
8. Means of giving us *divine guidance* (Acts 16:9–10; Matt. 2:19–20)
9. Aligned with *biblical* principles (never contrary)
10. Accompanied by explanatory portions of *God's Word* (a dream and a word together; see Acts 10:15, 34–35; Deut. 10:17)

These references clearly show that the infallibility and pre-eminence of the Holy Scriptures cannot be used as an excuse to deny the legitimacy of dreams, for the Scriptures themselves bear witness repeatedly that God speaks to men through dreams (see Num. 12:6); it is contradictory, therefore, to use faith in Scripture to justify unbelief in dreams. Rather, we should avoid the dangerous extremes of this issue: denying all dreams or believing all dreams. Never should dreams be considered more important than the Word of God. (Some are slow to act in obedience to God's Word yet will act on a dream promptly without judging its merits.)

Summing up, the Bible is God's primary means of communicating with us; dreams are a secondary, yet legitimate, way He speaks.

See Daniel 2:1; 7:1–14; 8:1–14; Genesis 15:1; 28:10–15; 41:32; Job 33:14–15; Acts 10:16; 16:9–10; Numbers 12:6; Judges 7:13–15; Matthew 2:13, 19–20.

Lesson: *While God usually communicates with us through His Word, He sometimes speaks through dreams.*

4:7–8 The superiority of the Spirit…yet again! This reference reveals that Daniel again succeeded where Nebuchadnezzar's sages failed. Here is the Book of Daniel's third witness to the superiority of Spirit-born wisdom to that accessible by occultism and other psychic mediums. And in the "mouth" of two or three biblical witnesses, let every truth be established (2 Cor. 13:1). On this occasion, King Nebuchadnezzar twice declares his faith in the Spirit who indwells Daniel, calling Him the "spirit of the holy gods" (Dan. 4:9, 18). (It was because Nebuchadnezzar recognized the Spirit's superior wisdom years before that he placed Daniel over all his wise men: "O Belteshazzar, master of the magicians…" [4:9]; see 2:48.)

When we can have the wisdom of the Spirit of God through God's Word, biblical teachers, godly counselors, and answers to our prayer requests, why would we ever seek spiritual wisdom or moral guidance from any kind of worldly or occult source?

See "The superiority of the Spirit," chapters 1, 2, 5.
See Daniel 1:20; 2:24–30; 5:15–16.

Lesson: *The Spirit of God gives wisdom superior to any other kind, including all forms of occultism or secularism.*

4:8 He saves the best for the last. "But *at the last* Daniel came in…" (Dan. 4:8, emphasis added). Daniel was the last counselor called by King Nebuchadnezzar in this crisis, just as he was the last to be summoned in his earlier crisis (see Dan. 2:2–11, 16). Yet in both cases, Daniel's counsel was the best. Here we see a little known way of God.

God often saves the best for the last. He deliberately lets Satan go first, permitting his corps of imposters and deceivers to run their courses; then, at the last, He moves to bring forth truth, wisdom, or deliverance through His true servants. This pattern of divine action is capsulized in the memorable words of the governor of the marriage supper at Cana: "Thou hast kept the good [best] wine until now [the last]" (John 2:10b). Consider this long and illustrious line of last but best ones.

David was the last to face Goliath, yet he was Israel's best and only successful warrior. (See 1 Sam. 17:11–12, 32.) Though Lazarus' resurrection was the last of Christ's resurrections, it was His best (most glorious); there He conquered, not only death but also *burial.* (See John 11:1–44; 12:10–11, 17–18.) At Cana, Jesus' wine was reserved until the other supply was consumed, and though served last, His was the best. (See John 2:10.) Like Daniel's counsel, Joseph's was the last offered to his Gentile monarch, and it too was the best. (See Gen. 41:8–9, 15.) The Cushite was the last to report Absalom's death to David, but his message alone was true; hence, though grievous, it was the best word. (See 2 Sam. 18:28–32.) David was the last of Jesse's eight sons and the last called for Samuel's review, but because his heart was the best (most humble, trusting), he was chosen to be king. (See 1 Sam. 16:6–12.) On Mount Carmel, the false prophets called on Baal for help first; then at last Israel's best prophet, Elijah, called on God, who answered by fire. (See 1 Kings 18:25–39.)

When Israel's Messianic expectations ran high during the pharisaic revival, two false messiahs, Theudas and Judas of Galilee, appeared first on the scene (see Acts 5:36–37); then at last the joint ministries of John the Baptist and Jesus—God's best and only true Messiah—emerged. Paul was the last apostle called in the New Testament record, yet in quality of character and extent of ministry he proved to be the best (despite seeing himself as "least"; see 1 Cor. 15:8–9), out-performing even Peter and John. Though Christ's kingdom will be the last to appear on earth, it will in every way be the best: spiritually, morally, geographically, economically, culturally, and chronologically. (See Dan. 2:35, 44; 7:13–14, 27.) Israel's last revival, which will break out immediately after the Rapture of the Church and spread rapidly, re-evangelizing the entire world in three and a half years, will be the best (most effective and enduring) in its long history (see Rom. 11:26–29; Rev. 7:1–8) and will culminate in the translation of millions of Jews and Gentiles (see Rev. 7:9–17).

And last in this entry, and appropriately best, is what God will yet do in the true Church before the Rapture. The best is yet to be. God has saved the Church's best revival for its last. Jesus will come *to* His Church before He comes *for* His Church; He will reform and revive His people before He raptures them. The midnight cry will spark the lamp-trimming revival—a work of revival through repentance of sin and restoration of biblical ways among believers (see Matt. 25:1–13)—which will culminate in the Rapture of all overcoming Christians. During this period of unprecedented godliness and light, the glory of the Church's latter house will exceed that of its former, the first-century Church (see Hag. 2:7–9). Hence, Christ's last body of believers will be His best!

See John 2:10.

Lesson: *Often God's way is to save the best things for the last.*

4:8 Is He your Alpha or your Omega? In looking to Daniel, the Hebrew prophet, last, King Nebuchadnezzar looked to God Himself last, for Daniel was fully identified with God (see Dan. 2:47, "your God"). But we shouldn't expect anything else of him. King Nebuchadnezzar was a heathen, one who did not know the Lord. Though God had helped him on one occasion before (ch. 2), and demonstrated to him His unique ability to deliver His own (ch. 3), Nebuchadnezzar still had no intimate knowledge of God or His ways. So when trouble struck, instinctively he looked first to his own gods and to the help of flesh, in this case his council of occultists. Then, if they failed, he looked to God.

The same pattern of action should *not* be seen in our lives. Jesus is both the Alpha and the Omega, the First and the Last. And we who are coming to know Him more daily should always look first to Him by prayer the very moment trouble strikes (see Phil. 4:6–7), not to our own carnal reasoning or to the current wisdom, ways, and means of this world. When Christ came into this world, wise men sought Him. Wise men still seek Him... first.

Is He your Alpha or your Omega, the first or the last you look to when trouble strikes?

See Philippians 4:6–7; Numbers 14:5; 16:4; 2 Chronicles 20:1–4; Acts 4:24–30; 12:5; Isaiah 37:14.

Lesson: *We should look for God's help through prayer the first moment trouble strikes—not after we have exhausted other ways of obtaining help.*

4:13 "Watchers"—God's reporters. Three times in this chapter angels are spoken of as "watchers" or "holy ones" (Dan. 4:13, 17, 23). Their designation as "holy ones" (or holy angels) is found elsewhere in Scripture (see Matt. 25:31; Mark 8:38; Acts 10:22; Rev. 14:10), but only in the Book of Daniel are they called watchers. What does the term *watcher* imply?

Clearly, God's angels observe the words and deeds of humans, particularly the redeemed. And why? To give Him report of our manner of living under the sun. (See Gen. 18:20–21.) In this context, angels observed and heard King Nebuchadnezzar's arrogant pride and reported it to God. God then sent this vision/warning to the king and interpreted it through Daniel, who urged the king to repent (Dan. 4:27). But twelve months later, angels again observed Nebuchadnezzar's ongoing arrogance and reported it to God, who then ordered them to immediately pronounce and initiate his chastisement (vv. 31–33).

Angels observe us constantly for many reasons. They "encamp" around believers' persons, their family members, homes, and possessions, ready to alert them to dangers. (See Ps. 34:7; 91:11–12; Job 1:10.) They watch over sinners to determine when their sin is "full" and divine intervention is necessary. (See Gen. 18:20–21.) They eagerly watch the Spirit-empowered preaching of the gospel (1 Pet. 1:12), rejoice over every sinner that repents (Luke 15:10), and record the name of every spiritual newborn in the Lamb's Book of Life (Luke 10:20). As our spectators, they watch over saints in the arena of testing, to see if we will overcome and win eternal glory in Christ (Heb. 12:1). As God's historians, they watch over redeemed ones to record our deeds that, at the judgment, there may be a written record by which Jesus may reward us (2 Cor. 5:10; see Esther 6:2; 2:23). They watch over all who fear the Lord, to record special books of memorial for eternity (see Mal. 3:16); also, they record the works of the wicked for use at their judgment (see Rev. 20:12b).

This function as watchers is in addition to their duties as messengers (Luke 2:8–12), strengtheners (Dan. 10:18–19; Luke 22:43), spiritual warriors (Dan. 10:13, 20; 12:1; Rev. 12:7), visitors (Heb. 13:2), executioners (Gen. 19:13; Acts 12:23), and bodily guardians (Ps. 91:11–12).

As wonderful as angels and their ministries are, the New Testament pointedly warns us not to revere them unduly (Col. 2:18). It is also unwise (a distracting infatuation leading to idolatrous veneration and away from Christ) to seek to contact them. We are to worship and seek God only. (See Rev. 19:10.) Furthermore, as redeemed ones, we are called to spend eternity as a higher class of beings. Presently, the order is divine, angelic, human (see Heb. 2:5–9); eternally, the order will be divine, redeemed human, angelic. "Know ye not that we shall judge angels?" (1 Cor. 6:3). Hence, we should not worship a class of created beings that are destined to spend eternity beneath us in the theocratic order.

See Hebrews 1:14.

Lesson: Angels are God's "watchers," or reporters.

Lesson: Angels are our "watchers," or spectators.

Lesson: Angels are God's historians (writers of inspired history).

4:13 Familiar spirits—Satan's reporters. That righteous angels are holy watchers suggests that fallen angels are Satan's watchers and hence his reporters. The Bible term for these evil observers is "familiar spirits" (1 Sam. 28:9). Familiar spirits constantly observe human behavior and speech and so become familiar with all people. If people participate in an occultist (or psychic) session, these familiar spirits report their information to the familiar spirit(s) inhabiting the spiritualist (or psychic) medium. The medium then reports this information to his seeker and informs him that such knowledge has come from God by the operation of a divine gift. In most cases this deceives people. Because they know such information has been obtained supernaturally, they assume it has been gathered divinely, although in fact the information is the result of a diabolical work. Hence, demons too watch and report the words and deeds of people to their master, Satan, to further his evil work in their souls.

See 1 Samuel 28:7.

Lesson: Familiar spirits are fallen angels who report the words and deeds of men to their master, Satan. This is the explanation behind whatever facts are related accurately through occult or psychic readings.

4:15 Discipline and reuse, or destroy and discard? Though severe, God's message to Nebuchadnezzar (Dan. 4:4–27) was not without hope. There were two bright spots.

First, the stump was a subtle promise. The vision dictated that the stump of the great tree be left and banded with iron and bronze (v. 15). *The Ryrie Study Bible* says this band was for "preservation to prevent the stump's being dug up." But more importantly, it was a sign of restoration to come, for in his interpretation Daniel plainly reassured King Nebuchadnezzar that after he was disciplined he would be restored to his throne (see v. 26).

The second point of hope was Daniel's counsel. Upon finishing his interpretation, Daniel pleaded with Nebuchadnezzar to repent, specifically by seeking righteousness from, and doing righteousness before, God and by showing mercy to the needy. Had Nebuchadnezzar obeyed this counsel, it seems that his severe discipline could have been not only delayed, as Daniel hoped (v. 27), but altogether averted, as in the case of the king of Nineveh (Jon. 3).

These two things make it clear that God's plan was to severely discipline Nebuchadnezzar, then restore and reuse him in His purpose, primarily to write the great testimonial recorded in this chapter. If God had intended to kill Nebuchadnezzar, the tree would have been cut down and its stump removed.

The Lord will follow this same pattern in His upcoming dealings with the Church (see 1 Pet. 4:17), Israel (see Mal. 3:3–4) and the world. His judgment, though it may seem severe, will not cease until it has achieved its divine purpose; then God will reuse the entity He has judged (judgment is a divinely enforced return to divine order). He will use the Church to bear a mighty witness to His truth, grace, and power before the Rapture. He will use Israel to do the same during the first half of the tribulation. And He will use the world (the nations) in the same manner during the Day of Christ.

And this is His purpose in our lives individually. Though divine chastening at times is very grievous (see Heb. 12:1–17), God's purpose must always be remembered. He may cut down and cut away many things in our lives, our thinking, and our aspirations, but one thing, the "stump of its roots," the Root of David (Christ), always remains within us. If we will respond humbly and obey the Lord, He will freely restore and reuse us for His glory.

Lesson: *God's purpose in divine chastening is to discipline and reuse us, not to destroy and discard us.*

4:16 Do you want to be a beast? Of King Nebuchadnezzar's bizarre condition *The Ryrie Study Bible* notes:

> The king's illness was boanthropy (imagining himself to be an animal and acting accordingly), a condition that has been observed in modern times. Probably the king was kept in one of the royal parks during his insanity.

God's punishment of King Nebuchadnezzar—rendering him bestial (see Dan. 5:21)—was no coincidence. Failing to respond to God's repeated miraculous witnesses through the faithful four (chapters 1–3), Nebuchadnezzar had become truly as a beast to God. He had no knowledge of or communion with God, nor would he respond to His voice. He was a man content to live solely for the satisfaction of his fleshly appetites and pleasures and visible worldly ends. (See "How do you see the system?" chapter 2.) In this dream, God was warning Nebuchadnezzar:

> If you insist on thinking and living with no more awareness of me than a beast, OK, have it your way. I'll make you think, eat, live, and even *look* the way a beast does.

God does something similar to this when disciplining rebellious Christians. If we stubbornly insist on living for the lusts of our flesh (as do beasts), God may one day "decree" a similar captivity for us. That is, He may give us over to sin and demonic influence so much that for a season we live a very carnal, base, and unspiritual existence. It is the same principle as His judgment against the Israelites when they lusted for flesh in the wilderness; to judge them, He simply gave them what they wanted...until they were sick of it. (See Ps. 106:13–15.) Sadly, there are many of God's children out in Babylon's fields today, roaming about and thinking, eating, living, and even looking more like bestial sinners than saints!

See Romans 6:16; 2 Timothy 2:26; John 8:34.

Lesson: Beware! If you persistently live (or desire to live) carnally, God may give you over to sin for a season!

4:17 The larger purpose of the vision: "The heavens do rule." King Nebuchadnezzar's vision here was more than a personal message from God. It was one of God's messages to the entire Gentile world. Note the Spirit asserts it was given "to the intent [for the purpose] that [all] the living may know" (Dan. 4:17). Hence, in the larger sense, God was speaking not merely to King Nebuchadnezzar but to all who live on the face of the earth (all Jews and Gentiles, including and especially heads of state).

Exactly what was it God wanted us to know? It was "that the Most High ruleth in the kingdom of men" (v. 17). In other words, "the heavens do rule" (v. 26). That is, God controls all human actions in this satanically ruled world. Men rule, but God *overrules*—always. Heads of states (good and evil) and other governmental authorities rule only by God's permission. By stating that He sometimes appoints "the basest of men" (base in God's sight—proud, arrogant, self-willed, unscrupulous—yet often attractive to and enthusiastically approved by men), God discloses that His permission of a ruler's authority is *not* His personal approval of that ruler's character.

See "Messages to the Gentiles," chapter 2.

Lesson: "The heavens do rule"; that is, God overrules human rulers and kingdoms—always.

Lesson: God's permission of a ruler's authority is not His approval of his character.

4:17,25,32 The larger principle of the vision: God is the giver of all things. The greater principle underlying God's vision to King Nebuchadnezzar was this: No one can "receive" any good thing—victory, authority, wealth, assets, blessing, favor (popularity), growth, spouse, children, truths, messages for the Church or the world, gifts (natural or spiritual abilities), knowledge, wisdom, opportunities (open doors), deliverance, healing, etc.—unless it is "given" by God from above. It was this John the Baptist tried to teach the Pharisees: "A man can receive nothing, except it be given him from heaven" (John 3:27). Divine permission precedes human acquisition—always. Before we may acquire something, God must "give" it (grant permission for us to acquire it). And if He does not grant it, we will not acquire it, no matter how diligently we work, pray, strive, or connive. Note that God repeatedly informs Nebuchadnezzar that He has *given* him his kingdom (He "giveth it," Dan. 4:17, 25, 32). It was this that, in so many words, the king later humbly acknowledged (see vv. 34–35). Just here a question arises: Why, then, did Satan claim the authority to "give" the kingdoms of this world to any he would?

Here is the explanation: Satan gives worldly authority but not unless God first gives him heavenly permission to do so. Until Christ returns to earth, God has in a sense leased the world (existing social order) to the "prince of this world," Satan (John 12:31; 14:30; 2 Cor. 4:4). While Satan is its immediate ruler and thus divinely authorized to "give" its rulership to whomsoever he will (see Luke 4:6; Rev. 13:2; 13:5, 7), God remains its eternal owner (Ps. 24:1) and overseer. Nothing happens, good or ill, without His permission.

See John 3:27; 19:11; Job 1:12; Psalms 66:12; 68:10–11; Daniel 1:17; 4:17; 5:18–19; 7:25; Exodus 12:36; Deuteronomy 8:18; 10:4; James 1:5–7, 17; Ephesians 6:19; Revelation 3:8; Colossians 4:8; 1 Corinthians 3:5; 12:7–10; Genesis 41:15–16;

24:27; Joshua 1:2; 8:18; Ruth 4:12–13; 1 Samuel 1:11; 30:23; Acts 7:9–10; 9:34; Luke 1:74–75.

Lesson: *We cannot receive anything—good or ill—unless it is given us by God.*

4:17 Base rulers: a divine judgment. Regardless of the moral quality of leadership, God gives it (see preceding note). When He gives good leadership (Harry Truman, Dwight D. Eisenhower), He is blessing His people for their collective righteousness and approval in His sight. The queen of Sheba recognized that Solomon's kingship was God's blessing upon Israel (1 Kings 10:9). When He gives poor leadership—the "basest of men" (Dan. 4:17)—He is judging His people for their ongoing sinfulness in His sight. There are other possibilities, too.

If He gives a good but naïve leader in lukewarm times (Jimmy Carter), or an openly evil or self-serving one (Bill Clinton, Lyndon Johnson), He is permitting the continuing downward spiral of sin and judgment because His people, however religious, are not yet repentant; they still stubbornly persist in clinging to their idols. If due to the prayers of His righteous remnant (see 2 Chron. 7:14) God gives a good leader in an evil time (King Hezekiah, Abraham Lincoln), the purpose is that either through the new leader or merely in his term God may visit the land in reformation and revival.

Leaders, particularly elected ones, both reflect and predict the moral state of the people. A.W. Tozer wrote:

> The history of Israel and Judah points up a truth taught clearly enough by all history, viz., that the masses are or soon will be what their leaders are. The kings set the moral pace for the people...
>
> Whatever sort of man the king turned out to be, the people were soon following his leadership. They followed David in the worship of Jehovah, Solomon in the building of the Temple, Jeroboam in the making of a calf and Hezekiah in the restoration of the temple worship...

> A good man may change the moral complexion of a
> whole nation; or a corrupt and worldly clergy may lead
> a nation into bondage...
>
> —THE BEST OF TOZER, P. 74

As Tozer observes, these principles of divinely given leadership apply in churches just as much as in nations. What kind of a Christian leader do we support and follow? And more importantly, what kind of Christian leaders are *we* becoming— base or blessed?

See Ecclesiastes 10:16–17; 2 Chronicles 2:11; 7:14; 1 Kings 10:9; Isaiah 45:1–4; Proverbs 29:4.

Lesson: God judges sinful nations—whether His own or Gentile—by permitting evil or inadequate leaders to come to power.

Lesson: God blesses nations—whether His own or Gentile—by bringing good leaders to power.

4:19 Courage—the story of Daniel's life—in miniature. After hearing the king's dream, Daniel instantly understood the basic theme of God's message...and it wasn't good news!

First, the sheer horror of the dream was stunning: King Nebuchadnezzar, Daniel's personal employer and the head of the most powerful and stabilizing nation on earth, would soon lose his mind, be deposed by his counselors, experience a mysterious bestial physiological transformation, and spend seven years in humiliating, utter insanity!

Second, Daniel realized that, considering Nebuchadnezzar's typically volatile reaction to unpleasant news (see Dan. 2:12–13; 3:13–15, 19–20), his interpretation of this message would not be well received. In fact, he might be next in line to prove God's keeping power in a fiery furnace. (See Daniel 3.) Fears, perhaps such as these, troubled his mind for "one hour" ("a while," *The Amplified Bible*). *The Modern Language Bible* states, "Then Daniel...was stunned and stood aghast for a time, his thoughts appalling him..." (Dan. 4:19). (See also *The Living*

Bible.) But despite the nervous counsel of his fears, Daniel pulled himself together and courageously delivered his message of judgment to the most powerful man in the world (vv. 19c–26). Not only this, but he also added a loving word of personal exhortation (v. 27).

To Daniel's surprise, and contrary to the king's previously established pattern of bad reactions, Nebuchadnezzar did not fly into a rage. Apparently he said nothing, good or ill. Why? Probably because he too was stunned. But also, and most significantly, because God restrained him. And why did God restrain him? Because Daniel obeyed God, telling every detail of a very disturbing message without hiding or distorting any portion to avoid an adverse reaction.

This brief "one hour" in which Daniel grappled with fear, rose above it, and prophesied a most unwanted message at great personal risk is the story of Daniel's whole life in miniature. Courageous loyalty to God's Word and obedience to His voice regardless of possible adverse consequences—that was Daniel, his heart, his way, his life.

See 1 Samuel 3:15–18.

4:16,25,32 Perfect discipline—"Until you know..." Repeatedly this chapter states that Nebuchadnezzar was disciplined "seven times" (vv. 16, 25, 32). Seven is the biblical number of perfection. For any process of cleansing or refining to be done perfectly, or thoroughly, it was repeated seven times. (See Lev. 8:11, 33; 14:7; 2 Kings 5:10; Ps. 12:6.) Hence, figuratively speaking, "seven times" means *until completely or perfectly finished.* Fittingly, then, in two of these references (Dan. 4:25, 32) God further specified that the king's discipline continue "till thou know," or until he fully understood the great lesson, "the heavens do rule" (v. 26). Here the limit on Nebuchadnezzar's discipline is set in two ways: time and condition. It would end when: 1) seven years had passed, and 2) Nebuchadnezzar's attitude was thoroughly transformed from pride to humility.

The New Scofield Study Bible notes simply, yet profoundly,

"This discipline was effective," then invites us to contrast the vastly different attitudes the king manifests in Daniel 4:30 and Daniel 4:37. Indeed, God's instructive punishment was perfect: It continued until the king was a profoundly and permanently changed man.

Whenever we force Him to, God disciplines us perfectly, too. He corrects us either by sending seven times of trial or by keeping us in a trial "until we know..."—that is, until we're convinced of, and fully accept, God's will. Simply put, perfect discipline lasts *however long it takes for us to learn the lesson God is teaching us*. When Nebuchadnezzar emerged from perfect discipline, God never again had to speak to him about his pride. When God releases us, we never again need divine discipline in the areas of our life and conduct that necessitated the discipline.

Lesson: God disciplines us perfectly—until He completely finishes His purposes and we learn all our lessons and fully accept His will.

4:25 "Until you know..."—foreshadowing the tribulation. As God chastened King Nebuchadnezzar, the first head of the Gentile world system of rule, so He will chasten the entire Gentile world itself during the tribulation. For "seven times" He will pour out His plagues of wrath on this Christ-rejecting, Antichrist-worshiping world "until it knows," and fully accepts, that "the heavens do rule." And when God is finished, His discipline will be effective: The nations will serve Him with the same voluntary humility Nebuchadnezzar evinced after his "plagues" (v. 37).

Lesson: In the tribulation, God will chasten the nations "until they know," and fully accept, that He shall rule them.

4:25 "Until you know..."—He *can* be very severe. This message to King Nebuchadnezzar—that God would take his mind from him if necessary to humble him—also reveals something about God we need to know. *God will use whatever means He must use, however severe, to at last impose His full and complete will in His own world.* He intended for King Nebuchadnezzar to rule humbly in recognition of His (God's) sovereignty, and He gave him ample warning (vv. 4–26), counsel (v. 27), and time (vv. 28–29) to repent and comply. When he did not, God suddenly and unexpectedly moved with shocking severity. So He will do again during the Great Tribulation. (Have you considered the *severity* of the trumpet and bowl judgments lately? See Rev. 8–9, 11, 16.)

And so He will do in our lives if we force Him. God intends that every Christian walk in humble recognition of His sovereignty over his life. Are we responding to His faithful warnings, loving counsel, and gracious "space to repent"? Or will we, as King Nebuchadnezzar did, force Him to use means He would rather not have to use? That we believers are God's own adopted sons and daughters does not exempt us from this possibility: Ananias and Sapphira were also His children. (See Acts 5:1–11.) The Israelites too were His people, but He judged them severely twice during their long history (as in the Babylonian captivity and Roman dispersion in A.D. 70).

Though little regarded, this is a truth we need to hear in this day when the love of God is generally mistaken for endless permissiveness even though judgment is about to begin "at the house of God" (1 Pet. 4:17). Indeed Jesus is our wondrously gracious Good Shepherd, but if He must strike, or even wound, His persistently straying sheep with His rod, He will do so—to save it from the jaws of the wolf and ultimate judgment.

See Daniel 9:11–12; Romans 11:22; Leviticus 10:1–5; Acts 5:1–11; Luke 19:41–44; 1 Corinthians 11:31–32.

Lesson: *If we stubbornly refuse to let Him rule our lives,*
God may deal with us very severely.

4:27 The liberation of obedience. Daniel's words describe the bonds of sin upon King Nebuchadnezzar and advise him how to be free of them. What was Daniel's counsel? Do righteousness and show mercy; in other words, obey God's will to the extent you know it. This is how Daniel told Nebuchadnezzar to "break off [the bonds and chains of] thy sins." In *The Amplified Bible* Daniel said, "Liberate yourself from your iniquities by showing mercy" (Dan. 4:27).

This is the simplest remedy imaginable. What is it that brings one under the dominating power of sin? Sinning! Disobeying the known will of God. So what will release us from sin's power? Obedience! Willing compliance with God's will, particularly in the area of mercy—being kind and speaking and acting kindly to all, especially those through whom the Lord is testing our love (such as enemies, offenders or hard-hearted ones).

The importance of these simple principles cannot be overstated. Rebellion to God binds us; submission and obedience to Him—especially mercifulness—liberate us (John 8:31–32). Moreover, they deliver us from divine judgment. *The Modern Language Bible* notes, "Nebuchadnezzar needed to be told that 'righteousness delivers from death' [Prov. 10:2]; and that a primary virtue of a ruler is justice."

When distressed by the bonds of their sins, many faltering Christians look to the wrong sources for deliverance. Rather than always hope for deliverance by the laying on of hands and the fervent prayers of righteous leaders, should we not also begin consistently surrendering to and obeying God's Word and His guidance in our lives? Even if we were miraculously liberated by God's grace, how could we remain free without the liberation of obedience?

See Romans 6:16; John 8:31–34; Isaiah 58:6–11; Job 42:10; Psalm 18:25; Proverbs 11:17.

Lesson: *Disobedience to God's will binds us with the bonds of sin; submissive obedience to His will releases us from those bonds.*

4:27 A prophet with compassion. Daniel's counsel to King Nebuchadnezzar reveals a compassionate heart, one that did not desire to see anyone suffer and would take whatever action possible to prevent anyone from coming to harm. Note how he seems to plead with the aloof Babylonian king:

> O King Nebuchadnezzar, listen to me—stop sinning; do what you know is right; be merciful to the poor. Perhaps even yet God will spare you.
>
> —DANIEL 4:27, TLB

Thus Daniel spoke the truth in love, appealing for a response that would cause his hearer to be fully and permanently reconciled with God. What a contrast to the prophet Jonah, who so obviously wanted to see his audience (the Ninevites) suffer. Unlike Daniel, Jonah spoke the truth without love.

As Christians, we are all light-bearers, or messengers of divine truth, to people. But is our heart in our message? Do we really want our hearers to get right with God? Are we compassionate (Daniel, Joseph, Jeremiah) or callous (Jonah) prophets?

4:27–28 Licking your ministerial wounds? Though Daniel was called of God, heavily anointed by His Spirit, well proven in ministry, humble in manner and compassionate in heart, his gracious words of counsel (v. 27) were still rejected by King Nebuchadnezzar. Consequently, at the end of a twelve-month grace period, "all this came upon the king..." (v. 28). Here's a lesson for everyone who speaks for God: If even *Daniel's* words were sometimes rejected, ours will be, too, at times.

Too often we become offended when our messages are rejected, and we step back, sulk, and lick our ministerial wounds. But we need not be offended. The rejection of a message has nothing to do with its inspiration or right-ness. In this case, Daniel's message was absolutely heavenly—inspired and infallible—but rejected nonetheless.

Let every rejected minister take heed. Don't fret at your

messages' rejection. Rejection is not necessarily a sign that a message is either of sub-standard content or delivery, or is spiritually off the mark. It may mean just the opposite: You said *exactly* what God wanted you to say...and exactly what your hearers didn't want to hear. (See Ezek. 2:6–7; 3:10–11.) Just be sure you stay close to the heavenly Speaker and continue recording and speaking everything you hear (Matt. 10:27). Let one standard guide you always—not what the churches want you to say but "what the Spirit saith unto the churches" (Rev. 2:7, 11, 17, 29; 3:6, 13, 22). Then whatever the reaction—apathy or acclaim—you will know you're a faithful messenger of Christ.

See 1 Samuel 8:6–7; Ezekiel 2:6–7; 3:10–11.

Lesson: *Even the messages of God's most extraordinary spokespersons are sometimes utterly rejected.*

4:29 A grace period. Twelve months passed between the delivery of God's Word to King Nebuchadnezzar and its execution. This silent period was no accident, nor was it evidence of divine forgetfulness. Rather, it was a divinely ordained grace period for the king—a fixed time given by God during which His subject could consider responding to His call to repentance. But when grace expired, chastening fell hard upon the king exactly as God had foretold it (Dan. 4:28–36). Throughout Scripture we see God giving grace periods to people after they have sinned and been clearly warned of judgment.

Once the pre-flood world became utterly corrupt, God appointed an additional 120 years of grace, during which He raised up Noah, who preached righteousness, foretold the coming flood, and set an example of hope by building the ark (Gen. 6:3). The three days Joseph's brothers spent in Egypt's prison were intended for them to consider their ways and repent of their envy and evil deeds toward their brother (Gen. 42:17), and it was effective (vv. 21–22). The plagues of Egypt gave Pharaoh not only abundant proof of God's superior power but repeated opportunities to repent. (See Exod. 7:25.) The "forty days" Jonah referred to in his preaching was God's grace period to Nineveh, during which the Ninevites wisely chose to repent (Jon. 3:4). The many years during which numerous prophets steadily warned Judah of impending judgment was God's grace period, which, sadly, ended in Babylonian captivity (2 Chron. 36:15). The forty years that followed Jesus' crucifixion afforded the Jews a time to reflect upon their rejection of Him and the subsequent powerful rise of His Church. But when this time ended, they had not repented, and God executed His judgment in the form of a devastating Roman invasion. (See Luke 19:41–44; 23:27–31.) Jesus warned the church at Thyatira that its grace period, which He described as a "space to repent" (Rev. 2:21), was about to expire (v. 22).

To this day God gives grace periods. These times may be used or abused. If we repent, we use them wisely, and God delights that His goodness (forbearance) has indeed led us to lasting repentance (Rom. 2:4). But if we continue sinning, He bears with us, but only until His appointed space to repent expires (Luke 13:6–9). Then He visits in swift, inescapable judgment. The entire Church Age is a grace period, during which God is deferring His worldwide judgments in hopes that multitudes will be saved (2 Pet. 3:9). Even this final period of the Church Age, this Laodicean era, is a grace period. Soon God will begin His End-Time, worldwide process of judgment by judging the sin and lukewarmness of His people (1 Pet. 4:17).

This compassionate and temporary deferring of judgment is often misunderstood by the unrepentant as:

1. A sign of divine approval (see Ps. 50:21)
2. Evidence of divine indifference (see Eccles. 8:11; Zeph. 1:12; Ps. 10:11)

Hence, they abuse God's grace by continuing in sin despite His forbearance (Heb. 10:26–29). In such cases, God's grace period becomes the sinner's deception period. (See 2 Thess. 2:10–11; Esther 6:6.)

See Revelation 2:21–22; 2 Peter 3:9; Luke 13:6–9.

Lesson: After warning sinners, God usually allows them a grace period before executing judgment.

Lesson: Often God's grace periods become sinners' deception periods.

4:30 The defeat of pride. King Nebuchadnezzar's chief flaw is here exposed: He was a man of excessive pride (Dan. 4:30; 5:20). In this reference, pride manifests as the attitude that takes all credit for achievement or success. Nebuchadnezzar flatters himself by indulging in the false premise that solely by his personal strength he has built Babylon to its current greatness, and, therefore, all honor should go to him. It was this pride that caused him to suddenly fall, as Satan did. (See Luke 10:18.)

The opposite of Nebuchadnezzar's pride is the attitude that refuses to take all credit to itself and insists on sharing the credit with God and other people. Sharing honor, sharing credit, acknowledging others' gifts, contributions, efforts, sacrifices—this is the best way to defeat the pride that takes all honor unto itself. It also develops in us the humility of Christ.

Daniel showed this humility by asking King Nebuchadnezzar to promote his fellow faithful Jews (see Dan. 2:49) and by carefully crediting God for his interpretive ability (see vv. 28–30). Paul too was careful to acknowledge those who helped him (Phil. 4:3; 2 Tim. 1:16–18). Nabal, however, seemed to forget everything his own men, and David's, did for him (see 1 Sam. 25:11). His words reveal he was desperately sick with the same deadly "I-my-me-mine" syndrome that had infected Nebuchadnezzar's heart.

See 1 Samuel 30:26–31; Philippians 4:3; 2 Timothy 1:16–18; Luke 22:28–30; Esther 8:1.

Lesson: Acknowledging those who help us achieve or succeed helps defeat the pride within us.

4:31 Pride deposes. "The kingdom is departed from thee"

(Dan. 4:31). With these divinely spoken (apparently audibly, as in Exod. 3:4) words, God deposed King Nebuchadnezzar due to his ongoing pride (see Dan. 5:20). Elsewhere throughout Scripture we learn that God raises or promotes only the humble (see Matt. 23:12). Hence, God's Word reveals there is a direct connection between our attitude and God's actions in promoting or demoting us. Our current attitude determines the direction in which God is currently taking us, up in honor or down in humiliation. Simply put, pride demotes and humility promotes.

See Proverbs 15:33; Matthew 23:12; Daniel 5:20, 30; 2 Chronicles 26:16, 21.

Lesson: *Pride demotes; humility promotes.*

4:31 A sudden intervention. After a long silence, God visited King Nebuchadnezzar with great suddenness. While Nebuchadnezzar strode about calmly and quietly in his palace, all the anxiety he may have felt when Daniel interpreted his dream twelve months earlier was gone. Long gone. He hadn't a worry in the world; his kingdom was prospering and running as efficiently as a well-oiled machine; personally, he was happy and at ease. So confident was he that he spoke aloud the proud thoughts of his overinflated heart (Dan. 4:30). And suddenly, out of nowhere, God spoke back, pronouncing judgment, and executing within the hour His sentence of insanity upon the king (vv. 31–33). Thus the long story begun a year earlier was over in a matter of minutes. Nebuchadnezzar spoke; then God spoke; then God acted. The startling speed with which God intervened was an uncannily accurate foreshadowing of God's future sudden judgment of Nebuchadnezzar's grandson, Belshazzar. (See Dan. 5:30.) It also reveals how God comes to His people sometimes with great suddenness.

God appeared to Moses suddenly in the burning bush (Exod. 3:1–12), and through Moses' ministry He appeared suddenly to the elders of Israel (Exod. 4:29–31). Through

Hezekiah's zealous reforms, God suddenly purged the temple and restored divine order in worship (2 Chron. 29:35b–36). John the Baptist (and God who sent him) suddenly appeared on the religious scene in Israel (Luke 3:2–4). The Holy Spirit fell on the 120 suddenly, and the church was born (Acts 2:2). The Lord appeared to Saul of Tarsus suddenly on the Damascus Road to end his persecution of the Church (Acts 22:6). Later, He delivered Paul and Silas from the Philippian jail with a sudden earthquake (Acts 16:25–26). God will visit, purge, and raise up (by teaching, training and testing) His Church suddenly by a "midnight cry" and lamp-trimming revival (Matt. 25:6–7; Mal. 3:1–4; Rom. 9:28). Sometime afterwards, Jesus will suddenly appear and catch away His people (1 Thess. 4:17; 1 Cor. 15:51–52). After the Rapture, revival will suddenly break out in Israel, led by the 144,000 Jews (Rom. 11:26; Rev. 7:1–8; Zech. 8:20–23).

God's apparent slowness to act in our behalf during the trial of our faith may deceive us by lulling us into an attitude of non-expectation. If so, the shocking suddenness of His actions will always bring us back to the full consciousness of this important fact of faith: God's withholding of His intervention does not diminish His ability to act suddenly. He may act openly at any moment and will always act at precisely the time He appoints.

See "A swift response," chapter 5; also "A surprisingly swift judgment," chapter 5.

See Proverbs 27:1; 29:1; Acts 2:2; 5:1–11; 12:23; 16:25–26; 22:6; Ezekiel 12:25; 24:15–18; 1 Thessalonians 4:17 (1 Cor. 15:51–52; Mark 13:36); 5:3; Numbers 12:4; Leviticus 10:1–5; 2 Chronicles 29:35b–36 (Rom. 9:28); Luke 12:20; 24:15, 31; Daniel 5:5, 30; 2 Kings 7:1.

Lesson: *God sometimes intervenes in our lives very suddenly.*

Lesson: *God's withholding of His intervention does not diminish His ability to act suddenly. He may act openly at any moment and will always act at precisely the time He appoints.*

4:33–37 Losing the best thing you have. As punishment for his excessive pride, King Nebuchadnezzar lost the best thing he had. No, that wasn't his throne, palace, harem, fame, or royal fortune. It was his *mind*, his sanity. During his seven years of awful captivity, he was out of his mind. King Nebuchadnezzar suffered a *psychosis*, "a mental disorder characterized by symptoms, such as delusions or hallucinations, that indicate *impaired contact with reality*" (*Webster's Encyclopedic Unabridged Dictionary of the English Language*, emphasis added). Specifically, his mental disorder was boanthropy (see "Do you want to be a beast?" chapter 4; also Dan. 5:21). Physical health is an extremely important blessing, but mental health—a sound, clear-thinking, emotionally stable mind grounded firmly in reality—is even more valuable (see Prov. 18:14). Are you thankful for mental health? Many have lost theirs due to the intense and inescapable pressures of life in a vicious, sinful world. Others have lost their mental health because, as Nebuchadnezzar, they were excessively proud.

That this chapter so plainly teaches that God took Nebuchadnezzar's sanity as punishment for his pride draws a subtle connection between excessive pride and loss of reason. God who gives us our capacity for clear thinking (see 2 Tim. 1:7) may confound us for our sins (see Jer. 1:17b). If stronger measures are necessary to humble us, He may permit us to be stricken by the scourge of emotional instability or, in drastic cases, mental illness. We do well to remember that a surprisingly high number of Americans are under psychological or psychiatric care, most due to the excessive stresses of our time to be sure, but others perhaps as the just reward of excessive pride and rebellion to God.

See 2 Timothy 1:7; Jeremiah 1:17; Proverbs 18:14.

Lesson: *Those who harbor thoughts of vanity may bring upon themselves a noticeable loss of sound reasoning (mental confusion or inefficiency). If persisted in, this may lead to emotional disorders or mental illnesses.*

Lesson: God gives us sound minds, and He can take them away.

4:34 A personal captivity period. "And at the end of the days..." Note that King Nebuchadnezzar was not released from his insanity until the God-ordained time of punishment was served, in this case seven years (see Dan. 4:16, 23, 25, 32, 36). This reveals that God sentenced him to suffer a personal captivity period and affixed an unchangeable time limit on that period, just as He was doing simultaneously with the nation of Israel, which was serving a seventy-year captivity. (See Jer. 25:8–11; 29:10.) Why? Because Nebuchadnezzar had refused to obey God's Word after a reasonable period of instruction, warning, and forbearance.

God does the same thing today to rebellious Christians. If they refuse to hear their "law" (Bible) and their "prophets" (such as pastors, teachers, counselors, mentors and prophets) and stubbornly refuse to respond when God graciously gives them "space to repent," along with many other unmerited kindnesses, God may thrust them into a personal captivity period. During such a time, they will suffer satanic control (still subject to greater divine control) and be unable to fully recover themselves from the grip of sin and sorrow until their God-appointed time limit is reached. Until that release, all God's purposes and blessings in their lives are put on hold. Not until His rod has finished its dreadful but effective work will they be free to walk in spiritual normalcy (trust, obedience, peace, joy) again. (See 2 Tim. 2:25–26.)

Spiritual Israel (the Jewish people worldwide) is under such a time-judgment right now due to their crime of rejecting Christ. According to God's Word, they will not escape the bonds of unbelief, sin and sorrow as a people until the time of the Rapture of the Church. Then God will remove the veil on their hearts, they will see who Jesus is, and they (a large percentage of Jews worldwide) will believe in and walk with Him in uncompromising faith and obedience. (See Rom. 11:25–26.)

See Daniel 4:16, 23, 25, 32, 36; Jeremiah 25:8–11; 29:10; 2 Timothy 2:25–26; Romans 11:25–26.

Lesson: God sometimes places persistently rebellious Christians in timed periods of spiritual captivity.

4:35 A second great revelation—"None can stay His hand." Besides the great fact, "the heavens do rule," King Nebuchadnezzar learned that no one can stop God's work: "He doeth according to his will...among the inhabitants of the earth, and *none can stay his hand*" (Dan. 4:35, emphasis added).

To understand the expression "none can stay His hand," we must remember that man is made in the image (form) of God. Though God (the Father) is "a Spirit" (John 4:24) and has no material body, He does have a form and speaks freely of His "face," "hand," "back," "feet," and "eyes" throughout Scripture. Since men work with their hands, the natural assumption is that God does the same. Hence, to try to "stay His hand" is to attempt to stop God's work. God is omnipotent. Hence, the works of His hand are unstoppable.

Do we have the faith King Nebuchadnezzar had? That is, do we restfully believe that God's work can't be stopped? Are we confident that, if we are abiding close to Him and doing His work as called, His power is with us and we will ultimately prevail over everyone and everything that opposes us? Provided, of course, we don't get discouraged or weary in well doing and give up the good fight!

See Isaiah 43:13; Psalms 21:11; 66:3b; 110:1; John 12:19; Nehemiah 6:15–16; Exodus 1:12.

Lesson: Because God is omnipotent, His work cannot be stopped.

4:34,36 Chastened, restored, *increased, honored!* At the end of Nebuchadnezzar's captivity period, God restored his reasoning and sound mind (Dan. 4:34, 36). At this point, the king was fully and finally purged of his sin. Daniel chapter 4—the king's written testimonial (see vv. 1–3, 4–36)—chronicles and proves this fact. Further proof appears in its final statement, in which the now-repentant king gives full honor and praise to God only (v. 37). Thus the reader sees that Nebuchadnezzar has received, not rejected, God's chastening. For this reason, God restored his sanity ("understanding"), throne, counselors, palace, sovereignty, honor, judicial sharpness or acumen ("reason"), and cheerfulness ("brightness") (see vv. 34, 36). Surprisingly, God didn't stop with this. He then increased Nebuchadnezzar by adding "excellent majesty" to the humbled monarch, beyond that which he previously held. *The Modern Language Bible* calls this "exceptional greatness"; *The Amplified Bible* states "still more greatness." The point here is that God *added* a new blessing to the king's life he did not have before. That God added greatness to the king means He also honored him.

So God does today with every soul who receives His chastening (Heb. 12:7). Our reaction to recognized divine chastening is crucial. If we rebel further, God chastens us further; if we continue rebelling, we risk terminal judgment. (See 1 Cor. 11:30.) But if we "break" under God's rod and repent, He deals with us as He did with King Nebuchadnezzar. When our punishment or captivity period ends, He restores all that we previously had and even adds new blessings and honors to us. Why? These are tokens of His appreciation of our submission to His correction and of the fact that we now honor Him (and Him alone) for all our blessings, accomplishments, gifts, and successes, as Nebuchadnezzar did in this testimonial (Dan. 4:1–37). Other scriptures confirm this.

One of the psalmists testified that God blesses the man who is taught by (or who receives) His chastening (Ps. 94:12–13). After King David fully surrendered to the divine Shepherd, he came to see His means of correction—"thy rod and thy staff" (Ps. 23:4)—as comforting blessings; then God set a table full of blessings before him, gave him a fresh anointing of the oil of the

Spirit, and assured David that God's goodness and mercy would be with him the rest of his earthly life and throughout eternity (vv. 5–6). After Job repented of his proud, self-justifying attitude (Job 42:6), God restored and increased him (vv. 10–17), and honored him before his enemies (vv. 7–9). After God stroked Jacob with a bitter rod of correction at Shechem (Gen. 34:1–30), Jacob repented and returned to Bethel (Gen. 35:1–15). God then increased and honored him in his later years in Egypt (Gen. 47:1–10, 27–28). After David received God's correction through Abigail (1 Sam. 25:35), God honored David by pleading his cause against Nabal and increased him by giving him a new, beautiful, and spiritual wife—Abigail! (See 1 Sam. 25:39–42.) After Esther received God's correction through Mordecai (see Esther 4:13–14), God increased her value and esteem before the king and before all the Jews, and honored her by inscribing her name on a book of the Bible.

See Job 42:7–9, 10–17; Hebrews 12:7; Psalms 23:4–6; 94:12–13; Proverbs 22:4; 1 Samuel 25:36–39, 42; Esther 4:13–14.

Lesson: God restores (recompenses), increases, and honors Christians who receive His chastening.

4:37 Converting kings. The Book of Daniel reveals that the faith exploits of the faithful four played a key role in the conversion of two great Gentile kings, each of whom was currently the most powerful man in the world.

In chapter 3, King Nebuchadnezzar was initially converted to faith in Jehovah by the example of Shadrach's, Meshach's, and Abednego's victorious and uncompromising faith and the divine intervention it brought on (see 3:26, 28–29). Chapter 4 adds that, after suffering severe discipline because of his subsequent refusal to surrender to Jehovah's sovereignty, Nebuchadnezzar fully surrendered to and highly praised the Lord (v. 37). In chapter 6, King Darius the Mede was converted to faith in Israel's God by Daniel's uncompromising loyalty and faith and the amazing deliverance it invoked. (See Dan. 6:25–27.) Thus Daniel's book discloses how Nebuchadnezzar and Darius met the Lord.

While as *souls* Nebuchadnezzar and Darius were no more important to God than any other soul, as *kings* they were more useful to His purpose and plan in the earth. Because they occupied the supreme position of governmental authority, they were able to procure great favor for the Jews and hence God's Word, His ways of living, and His worship. In other cases, while the victories and gifts of God's children did not convert Gentile rulers, they won their full trust and loyalty and motivated them to do all they could for God's people and will. For instance, God used the exploits of Esther and Mordecai to put favor in the heart of the Persian ruler Ahasuerus (or Xerxes), who then gave the two a free hand in issuing royal decrees favorable to the Jewish people. (See Esther 8:1–14; 10:3.) Joseph's divine gifts of interpretation, prophecy, and counsel convinced Pharaoh that God was with him, after which Pharaoh used the full might of Egypt's throne to implement God's plan of salvation throughout the nation and the world. The equivalent today would be for the spiritual victories of uncompromisingly righteous Christians to come to the attention of the president of the United States and for him thereafter to use the full power and influence of his office to in every way favor the gospel, people, and purpose of God throughout the nation and the world.

But remember what brought about the regal conversions and favors disclosed in the Book of Daniel: not shrewd politics, media image-building, or seeking and following popular lines, but uncompromising obedience to God's Word in an ungodly society and unyielding endurance in fiery trials. Many of us would love to be used of God to convert a king, but few are willing to pay the price the faithful four paid.

See Daniel 6:25–28; Esther 8:1–14; 10:3; Acts 13:12; Genesis 41:37–40, 46–49, 55.

Lesson: *The faith exploits, victories, and gifts of God's overcomers sometimes convert heads of state, who then use their authority to promote God's interests and will in their nations.*

CHAPTER FIVE

READY AT A MOMENT'S NOTICE

5:1–4 SACRILEGE...AGAIN! Chapter 5 opens with a description of King Belshazzar's wild and wanton royal extravaganza. Not long after his famous dinner party got underway, Belshazzar (son and co-regent of Nabonidus) brought forth the golden and silver cups and bowls that his grandfather Nebuchadnezzar had taken from the Jewish temple. He and his thousand guests then drank from them solely for their pleasure. It was an open act of sacrilege (unauthorized seizure and/or disrespectful use of things held sacred), for these vessels were holy unto the Lord— to be used only by God's priests, according to God's law, in God's house, and for God's worship. (See "Sacrilege," chapter 1.)

Though separated from Nebuchadnezzar's sacking of the now-razed temple by many years and miles, Belshazzar's unauthorized and disrespectful use of God's temple instruments nevertheless constituted yet another attack upon, and robbery of, God's holy temple. In a sense, Belshazzar was putting the ugly finishing touches upon the horrifying crime Nebuchadnezzar had begun years earlier. Then, to add insult to injury, the Babylonian aristocrats had the audacity to praise their own gods while drinking from Jehovah's holy bowls (Dan. 5:3–4). This in-your-face idolatry stirred God's fierce jealousy (see Exod. 20:3–5)—hence, His immediate response by message (Dan. 5:5) and by startlingly sudden and lethal punishment (v. 30).

God's strong and wrathful response underscores the fact that sacrilege was, and still is, most offensive to heaven (see 1 Cor. 3:16–17). It also helps us understand why Nehemiah was so angry when the temple was misused and neglected in his day (see Neh. 13:4–14), as was Christ when the temple courts were misused and its heavenly Owner's will dishonored (see John 2:13–17; Mark 11:15–18).

The Spirit-Filled Life Bible note here capsulizes the real issue in this passage:

> God's response to Belshazzar's irreverent use of God's holy vessels is a warning that whatever God has sanctified is not to be profaned...Regarding holy things as common is always dangerous. Those guilty will be "weighed in the balances, and found wanting" (Dan. 5:27).

We should consider, then, the spiritual application of this message to our "temple" and other holy things. Today the temple of God may mean several things:

1. The body of believers in Christ worldwide (see 1 Cor. 3:16–17; 3:9; 1 Pet. 4:17)
2. Any local church body
3. Any gathering of Christians for Bible study, prayer, worship
4. Any ministry (believers united and organized for ministry)
5. Every Christian's individual body (see 1 Cor. 6:19–20; John 2:19–21; also "tabernacle," 2 Cor. 5:1–2, 4)

Other holy things (dedicated exclusively to God and His use) are: the Bible; chosen ministers; Christian ordinances (baptism and the Lord's Supper); church funds and properties;

gifts and operations of the Spirit; spiritual movements, missions, and other works initiated and favored by God. To misuse, attack, willfully interfere with, speak against, or treat contemptuously any of these or other holy things is to be guilty of sacrilege. One form of sacrilege particularly noted in Scripture is partaking of the Lord's Supper "unworthily" (1 Cor. 11:29)—in an unworthy manner of conduct (see vv. 20–22) or unworthy spiritual condition (see v. 31).

Where do we stand in relation to holy things? Are we sacrilegious or sanctified? Do we provoke or please the Lord? God help us be very respectful of everyone and everything that is holy!

See 1 Corinthians 3:16–17; Nehemiah 13:4–9; John 2:13–17; 2:19–21; Psalm 105:15; 2 Kings 2:23–24; 1 Samuel 26:9–11.

Lesson: *God is angry when His Church, our physical bodies, or any other holy things, are misused, dishonored, or defiled.*

5:1–4 No time to party. History informs us that on the night of Belshazzar's feast Babylon was besieged; the Persian armies were encamped outside the city walls, ready to take the city according to God's Word. (See Isa. 21:1–10.) That Belshazzar chose to hold a drinking party at such a time is most revealing. It proves him to be one of three things: 1) exceptionally intellectually inept, 2) extremely overconfident, or 3) completely disconsolate. Either he was very stupid, very presumptuous, or very discouraged by the siege. To everything there is a season and a time to every purpose (see Eccles. 3:1), but obviously, with such a momentous conflict imminent, any average Joe would recognize it was no time to party—but not Belshazzar. A bold and wise leader he was not.

Wise leaders realize that, while there is indeed a time to relax in wholesome casual or social activities, there are other times when such activities must be avoided like the plague. The seriousness of the hour, the imminency of danger, the relent-lessness of our enemy, and the need for alert on-the-spot lead-ership demand all the leader can give—and then some. Have we the wisdom to know when *not* to leave our posts?

See Nehemiah 5:19; Exodus 17:12; contrast with 2 Samuel 11:1.

Lesson: A wise leader realizes there are times when he must not leave his duties.

5:2 The folly of drink. Scripture carefully notes that Belshazzar's command to bring out the vessels of God's temple was given "while he tasted the wine" (Dan. 5:2). Apparently this was not his original intention but rather one that came to him spontaneously, either from within his own mind or at a guest's suggestion, *after* he began drinking his royal wine. Hence, in addition to its revelations on "the folly of fury" (see chapter 2), the Book of Daniel here discloses to the reader the folly of drink.

Alcoholic beverages impair our reasoning faculties and inspire irresponsibility and folly—always. Belshazzar here does something under the influence of alcohol he may not otherwise have done, either out of respect or fear of the Jewish deity. But God's response makes it clear: Inebriated or not, he was responsible for his own actions.

So it is with us. When we drink any alcoholic beverage, our reason is immediately impaired. Consequently we make deci-sions, speak words, and take actions that we would not normally do. While the Bible does not forbid consumption of alcoholic beverages, it clearly warns readers of its many dangers and of our inescapable responsibility for our own actions—sober or drunk.

See Proverbs 31:4–5; 23:29–35; 21:17; 1 Samuel 25:25, 36; Isaiah 5:11–12; 5:22–23; Genesis 9:20–21; 19:30–36.

Lesson: Alcoholic beverages impair our reasoning facul-ties and inspire irresponsibility and folly— always.

5:1–31 The "handwriting on the wall." God interrupted Belshazzar's blasphemous party by causing the fingers of a man's hand to appear near the lampstand (to ensure their detection by all) and to write a message of doom to the Babylonian monarch on the palace wall. This judgment was then executed on the same night. Babylon fell to the Medo-Persians, and Belshazzar was dethroned, slain, and replaced by another king (Dan. 5:30–31).

Here is the origin of the universal cliché "the handwriting is on the wall," meaning everyone can see that the cause is lost and the end is at hand.

5:5 A swift response. Note that within an hour (literally sixty minutes) of the time Belshazzar began to dishonor the temple vessels, God intervened: "In the same hour came forth fingers of a man's hand" (Dan. 5:5). That's quick. That's very quick. The swiftness of God's actions here reflects the strength of His feelings. He was not angry—He was *furious* at Belshazzar.

Conversely, when God is very delighted, He also acts with great suddenness. (See Acts 16:25–26; Dan. 3:24–25.)

See "A sudden intervention," chapter 4; and "A surprisingly swift judgment," chapter 5.

See Numbers 12:4; 14:10; 16:42, 44–45; Acts 12:23; 16:25–26; Daniel 3:24–25.

Lesson: When strongly aroused by anger or delight, God sometimes responds swiftly.

5:7–8,15 The superiority of the Spirit—a fourth witness. For the fourth time in this book we see Daniel obtaining and ministering wisdom to the king when all other sources of wisdom—natural and supernatural—failed. (See Dan. 1:20; 2:27–28; 4:7–8.) In this case, no one present could understand the Aramaic words (apparently encoded) God wrote on the palace wall, later deciphered as "number, weigh, divide." (Note it is stated *four* times that Daniel was to "read this writing, *and* show…its interpretation," clearly signifying that the individual words themselves were also not understood; see Dan. 5:7, 15–17, emphasis added.) Nor could anyone understand the *message* God hoped to convey—no one except Daniel, a man filled with and dependent upon the Spirit of God (see vv. 11, 14).

Thus, the Book of Daniel strongly establishes the fact that God's wisdom, born of His Spirit, is always superior to the wisdom of man (represented by the Chaldeans) and that of occult practitioners (represented by the astrologers and soothsayers).

See "The superiority of the Spirit" entries, chapters 1, 2, 4.

Lesson: The wisdom the Holy Spirit gives overcoming Christians is greater than that possessed by secular wise men or occultists.

5:6 Changing countenances. "Then the king's countenance was changed..." (Dan. 5:6; see also 5:9, *The Living Bible*). The Book of Daniel notes, perhaps more clearly than any other, changes in people's countenances. Our countenances (facial expressions) are direct reflections of our thoughts and emotions. Just as our words do (see Matt. 15:18), our countenances also betray our true disposition and overall state of being. As we think in our hearts, so our countenances appear (except, of course, when we consciously alter our facial expressions to hide our true feelings).

Scripture describes many kinds of countenances: angry countenances (Dan. 3:19; Esther 7:7); troubled countenances (Dan. 5:9–10); fearful countenances (Dan. 5:5–6); perplexed countenances (Dan 4:19); intelligent countenances (Dan. 4:36, "brightness"); insane countenances (Dan. 4:16; 1 Sam. 21:13–14); fierce countenances (Dan. 8:23; cold, demonic, like Hitler); proud countenances (Prov. 6:17; 21:4; Ps. 101:5); envious countenances (1 Sam. 18:9); vexed countenances (1 Sam. 1:12, 18); happy countenances (Prov. 15:13); sad countenances (Gen. 40:6–7); grieved countenances (Job 2:13b; Neh. 1:4; 2:1–3); hurt countenances (Luke 22:61); confused countenances (Dan. 9:7–8); healthy countenances (Dan. 1:15; 1 Sam. 16:12; Ps. 42:11); disapproving countenances (Gen. 31:2, 5); approving

countenances (Ps. 4:6; Num. 6:25–26); determined, bold countenances (Isa. 50:7; Luke 9:51); illuminated countenances
(Exod. 34:29–35); glorified countenances (Matt. 17:2).

In light of this, overcoming Christians (especially pastors,
counselors, and other leaders) should learn to read peoples'
faces. A change in countenance is indicative of a change in
one's inner thoughts. When sin enters, our facial expressions
change: Cold, hard looks betray cold, hard hearts. When bro-
kenness and humility return, our countenances soften. Joseph
obviously learned to read the countenances of the prisoners to
whom he ministered (Gen. 40:6–7).

On the other hand, Jesus advised us to consciously alter our
facial expressions so we would not betray our religious sacrifices
(Matt. 6:16–18). In times of conflict, we may need to do this for
a different purpose: to not betray our true intentions or actions
to the enemies of the Lord, an indiscretion that could result in
faithful Christians suffering harm or loss. (See Exod. 1:18–19; 2
Sam. 17:19–20.) This is part of our education in becoming "wise
as serpents, and harmless as doves" (Matt. 10:16). To live among
ravenous wolves, we sheep have to be very discreet.

Lesson: *Our countenances (facial expressions) reflect
our true thoughts and emotions. We should learn
to read others' countenances and, when necessary, disguise our own.*

5:12 Ready at a moment's notice. "Now let Daniel be
called..." (Dan. 5:12). In the heat of the crisis, King Belshazzar's
mother remembered Daniel and recommended him to the king.
Obviously, then, the king must have forgotten Daniel.

Proof that Daniel was personally unknown to King
Belshazzar is seen in these facts: 1) He didn't call for him initially, as he did his other royal consultants (v. 7). 2) His mother,
the queen, had to describe Daniel's gift, depth of wisdom, and
office to him (v. 11). 3) The queen described Daniel as a man
from another era long ago, specifically the period of
Nebuchadnezzar's rule (v. 11). 4) Belshazzar did not recognize

Daniel by sight and had to ask him to confirm his identity (v. 13).

Why did Belshazzar not remember Daniel? Three reasons seem probable: 1) Daniel had not served in the Babylonian cabinet in approximately twenty years. 2) Belshazzar was a very poor student of history, unaware of his famous grandfather's most famous and gifted adviser. 3) He was simply too inebriated to think clearly.

Whatever the reason for the king's idle mind, it is evident that, though technically unemployed for twenty years, Daniel had not been idle. That he steps in at this moment of national crisis and delivers a spiritually precise message straight from the heart of God is most enlightening. It proves that, like Joseph, Daniel was a man who lived in constant touch with God; if he were not, he either would have received no understanding or would have had to get himself in shape, spiritually speaking, by confessing sin and drawing near to God by prayer, worship, and Bible meditation. But he didn't have to *get* ready because he *was* ready. Whether on the stage or on the shelf, Daniel was always fit and ready for the Master's use. Whether God's people were walking in revival or apostasy, he stayed tuned to heaven. Not only when his ministry was "in season," but when it wasn't in demand, he still lived and walked closely with the Lord. Hence, he was one of God's minutemen—ready for divine service at a moment's notice. We should emulate him in this regard because we never know when the Lord will call us to a task. Committed athletes keep themselves in top form during their off-seasons; committed scholars stay full of reading; committed musicians practice day and night. How much more should overcoming Christians keep their souls strong, upright, and close to the heart of God at all times?

Others of God's minutemen and minutewomen were Simeon, Anna, Micaiah, Joseph, the apostle John, the apostle Paul, and the apostle Peter.

See 2 Timothy 4:2; Genesis 40:3–4, 12–13; 41:12–16; Luke 2:25–35, 36–38; 2 Chronicles 18:12–13; Revelation 1:9–10; Acts 11:25–26; 10:19–20; 13:2–3.

Lesson: We should walk so closely with the Lord at all times—including seasons of ministerial inactivity—that we are ready for His use at a moment's notice.

5:16,29 Working all things together for good. To induce Daniel to read the handwriting on the wall, King Belshazzar offered him, among other things, authority over one-third of the kingdom of Babylon. Belshazzar was the eldest son of Nabonidus, who had married Nebuchadnezzar's daughter and was the official ruler of Babylon. Belshazzar became the acting ruler because Nabonidus had been out of the country for the past ten years (living in Tema of Arabia.) Thus, by virtue of his successful interpretation, Daniel became the third ruler over Babylon and so temporarily held sway over one-third of that vast empire in the final hours before it fell to the Medo-Persian armies (Dan. 5:29). That Daniel became "king for a night" was not accidental but providential. It was God working all things together for His servant's, and His people's, good. (See Rom. 8:28.)

Foreseeing the imminent fall of Chaldea, God brought Daniel back to the court of Babylon at just the right moment. Remember, it was God who sent the handwriting that caused Belshazzar to call Daniel and offer him in desperation the highest office in the land. In that high position, Daniel's faithful character, soaring intellect, and unique gifts were readily made known to the incoming king, Darius, who undoubtedly heard of the dramatic events that unfolded during Belshazzar's final hours in office. The uninterrupted sequence of the verses describing this remarkable transition of power—Belshazzar's death (Dan. 5:30), Darius's accession (v. 31), Daniel's appointment (Dan. 6:1–2)—imply that it was Daniel's shining in Belshazzar's darkest hour that recommended him as an invaluable administrator to the new king Darius, who, with such vast additional responsibilities suddenly thrust upon him (reorganizing a large fallen nation), must have been delighted to have such a man in his administration. Hence, the Holy Spirit records Darius's pleasure at making Daniel his top government official: "It *pleased* Darius to set over the kingdom...three presidents, of whom Daniel was first..." (6:1–2, emphasis added).

So God coordinated all things together to exalt His choice servant that, from his new position of authority, he could execute His will to the blessing of His people.

See Romans 8:28; Esther 10:1–3; Genesis 45:7–8; 50:20.

Lesson: *If we obey and follow Him uncompromisingly (as Daniel), God works all things together for our good and the good of His people.*

5:10–12 High recommendations. Observe the high recommendation of Daniel that the queen mother gave her son, King Belshazzar (Dan. 5:10–12). Daniel was Spirit-filled, a man with God-like wisdom, someone with an excellent attitude (personal "spirit"), filled with knowledge (vital information), an interpreter of dreams, a discerner of riddles and obscurely written statements, and a former member of King Nebuchadnezzar's cabinet. (Note that "father" [Chaldean *ab*] as repeatedly used in this chapter [vv. 2, 11, 13, 18] carries a duel meaning of "ancestor" or "predecessor to the throne.") Her confidence in Daniel's God-given wisdom and skill was absolute. Call him, she said calmly, and you'll get your answer (v. 12b).

Other servants of God—Joseph, David, Mordecai, Timothy—who walked with Him in submissive trust and obedience, and who served His will diligently and faithfully in humble places, received similarly high recommendations. These were more than personal compliments; they were praisings of the Holy Spirit's work in forming their characters over many years of spiritual training.

The Lord will do the same today for us if we diligently fear and obey Him. He will have people in key positions notice His gifts and work of grace in us and use their high recommendations to bring us into our predestined places of service. (See Prov. 18:16.)

See Proverbs 18:16; 22:29; Genesis 41:12–16; 1 Samuel 16:11, 18; Esther 8:1; Philippians 2:19–23; Matthew 25:21.

Lesson: God inspires key people to recommend highly those who serve Him diligently, faithfully, and with holiness in humble places.

5:12,16 The gift of "unknotting knots." *The Amplified Bible* translates the phrase "dissolving of doubts" (Dan. 5:12, 16) as "solve knotty problems"; so does *The Living Bible* (v. 12); *The Modern Language Bible* renders it "unravel knots" (v. 12); and *The Spirit-Filled Life Bible* margin says the literal meaning is "untying knots" (v. 12).

Walter Beuttler, late missionary and Bible teacher with the Assemblies of God, illustrated this matter of "untying knots" by telling of his young daughter's failed attempt to tie her shoelaces. Seeing her struggling with the task at hand, Beuttler offered his help. "No, Daddy," she replied confidently, "I'll knot it myself." And, as Beuttler tells it, "She did just that!" The result was a knotty mess. He went on to draw a parallel to the knotty messes we Christians often make of our lives by refusing our heavenly Father's graciously proffered help—through His Word, His Spirit, His ministers, and our loving, spiritually minded friends—and by going on stubbornly in selfish and sinful living.

The problem with bad, tightly bound knots is that one hardly knows where to begin to try to unravel the whole mess. Similarly, there are people whose lives are so entangled, troubled, confused, wounded, misguided, and self-opposing due to years of sinful and selfish living that Christian counselors hardly know where to begin. In fact, they don't; really, they *can't*. But the Holy Spirit (who is omniscient) knows, and He can show the willing, prayerful worker a divinely prescribed path that will lead to the deliverance of even the most hopelessly knotted lives. It requires a special gift of wisdom as well as an extraordinarily patient and loving heart to extricate such souls from their "knots." Daniel had these abilities in him by the work of the Spirit of God.

So may we today, if we will: 1) abide very close to Jesus; 2) let patience have her "perfect work" (James 1:4) in us as we deal with troubled lives; and 3) pray with persistent faith for wisdom and divine deliverance. May God thus develop within us the gift of "unknotting knots." Many Daniels are needed for this task in this day when changing values and sins against the family have left millions wounded and psychologically and spiritually bound up in knots so tight and unyielding that no mere human wisdom and compassion can bring them through to the promised land of deliverance.

Lesson: *We need Christians with the Spirit's special wisdom and patient compassion who, through their prayers, labors, and counsel, may liberate hopelessly bound lives.*

5:20 Pride—an inflator. By inspiration Daniel states that King Nebuchadnezzar's pride lifted him up: "But when his heart was lifted up...in pride" (Dan. 5:20). That is, he became inflated with a disproportionate sense of self-importance and henceforth thought he was more important than he was. So we see that pride is a dangerous inflator. It pumps into our heads all kinds of overly self-important thoughts that make us no longer think soberly about ourselves, highly enough of God, or highly enough of others.

See 1 Corinthians 8:1b; Romans 12:3.

Lesson: *Pride fills our minds with overly self-important thoughts, leaving us puffed up with too much self-esteem, too little esteem for others, and little or no fear of God.*

5:20 Pride—a spiritual hardening agent. Daniel's description of Nebuchadnezzar's sin further states that pride hardened Nebuchadnezzar's mind (literally *spirit*, or heart). So we see that pride not only overinflates one's self-esteem; it is also one of many sins that harden our minds (or hearts). Consequently, we become indifferent about our relationship to God and callous in our attitude toward people (see Matt. 24:12). Echoing this truth, which is further expounded in Psalm 95, Hebrews 3:15 commands Christians, "Today...harden not your hearts..."

Conversely, as pride hardens us, humility softens us. Jesus, therefore, bids us come to Him and learn of His humility, His meek and lowly attitude toward His heavenly Father's will (see Matt. 11:28–29).

See Psalm 95:8; Hebrews 3:15; Matthew 11:28–29.

Lesson: Pride hardens our minds and hearts.

5:20 Pride—a demoter. Daniel further points out that, as seen previously, pride was the reason God deposed Nebuchadnezzar from his throne (see "Pride deposes," chapter 4). Just as surely as humble, uncompromising obedience to God's Word promoted the three Jews to higher office (Dan. 3:30), pride demoted Nebuchadnezzar. Pride was also the reason King Belshazzar was now to be deposed. Said Daniel to the young and haughty monarch: "And thou, his son [grandson], O Belshazzar, hast not humbled thine heart, though thou knewest all this, but has lifted up thyself against the Lord of heaven" (Dan. 5:22–23; see Dan. 3:30). Other kings deposed for their pride were Uzziah, Saul, and Herod. Each of these divine demotions was but a reenactment of the original fall of Lucifer (Isa. 14:12–15).

What is the Spirit saying here to the Church? Simply that whenever we walk in pride, we lose—suddenly or gradually— whatever power, position, or authority we had gained. Always, our power is diminished; always, our authority is stripped away; always, we go lower in the chain of command.

See Daniel 5:22–23, 30; Proverbs 16:18; 18:12; Luke 10:17–19; 1 Samuel 15:17; Acts 12:22–23; 2 Chronicles 26:16, 21; Isaiah 14:12–15; Matthew 23:12.

Lesson: Just as surely as He promotes those who humbly obey Him, so God demotes all who walk in pride.

5:20–21 Pride—a transformer. These verses describe King Nebuchadnezzar's complete transformation—mentally and physically—into an animal-like state.

Spiritually, he was utterly carnal, without any awareness of, or desire to know, a higher being. Psychologically, he thought of himself as an animal. Emotionally, he had only those instincts and feelings possessed by beasts. And physically, a distinct change occurred in his bodily conditions, functions, and limitations. Normally, a person cannot eat grass, especially a large quantity of grass, without becoming sick; yet Nebuchadnezzar ate grass for seven years. Normally, an unclothed human being cannot be exposed to rainfall, dew, and varying temperatures for twenty-four hours a day without becoming sick; yet somehow Nebuchadnezzar's body survived this for seven years. Clearly, his bodily functions were altered as was his mind. Hence, Nebuchadnezzar was completely—monstrously—transformed as a result of his pride. (See "Do you want to be a beast?" chapter 4.)

Spiritualizing this, once pride gains complete control, it transforms us progressively into an ugly, beast-like personality. Just compare the personality of someone during their humble years with that of their years of pride and vanity. How pride transforms simple, caring, truthful people into callous liars, ruthless plotters, and malicious oppressors—from beautiful people to ugly beasts! In its numerous biographical portraits of God-changed souls—Jacob, Zacchaeus, Saul of Tarsus, Mary Magdalene—the Bible teaches us the transformative power of righteousness. Through Nebuchadnezzar, the Bible shows us a counterbalancing truth: the transformative power of sin!

King Saul was transformed by pride (envy is a form of pride; see 1 Sam. 18:6–9; 15:17) from being David's loving mentor (1 Sam. 16:19–22) to being his cruel persecutor (1 Sam. 18:29); from God's anointed prophet-king (1 Sam. 10:5–7) to His desolate, demonic enemy (1 Sam. 28:16); from Israel's prime deliverer (2 Sam. 1:19–24) to its chief troubler (1 Sam. 22:11–21). Wise Christians fear nothing but sin.

See 1 Samuel 10:5–7; 15:17; 16:19–22; 18:29; 22:11–21; 28:16; 2 Samuel 1:19–24.

Lesson: When pride gains control within us, it begins transforming us into an ugly, beast-like personality.

5:22–23 Responsible to obey the truths we know. Daniel charges King Belshazzar with the crime of not obeying the revealed will of God: "And thou…hast not humbled thine heart [obeyed God's will], *though thou knewest all this*" (Dan. 5:22, emphasis added).

As believers, we are responsible to know God's will. Hence, our most basic responsibility is to learn His Word, which reveals His will. We are all under orders to "study [God's Word] to show thyself approved unto God" (see 2 Tim. 2:15; 1 Tim. 4:13–15; John 8:31–32). Then, as we see with Belshazzar, we are also responsible to obey God's will, including everything we have learned, as we have opportunity. The light—the knowledge of God's will—may shine into our hearts in various ways:

1. ACADEMICALLY, in Bible reading, study, teaching
2. EXPERIENTIALLY, by reflection on God's dealings in our lives, especially His chastisements
3. OBSERVATIONALLY, by our reflection on His dealings with others, based upon their testimonies or chronicles

Specifically, Daniel (and God) rebuked Belshazzar for not walking in the light of his grandfather's (King Nebuchadnezzar's) divine chastening, which illuminated Jehovah's hatred of pride and His determination to punish those who walk in it. (See Dan. 4:1–37.) The whole story had been rehearsed in Belshazzar's hearing, as it had throughout all Chaldea, many times over the years. Belshazzar may be taken as an example of unsaved persons (Babylonians) who have heard portions of God's Word secondhand (related by believing parents, friends, spouses, or ministers) or testimonies of God's past or present chastisements of Christians. Though they do not know the Lord personally and are largely ignorant of His Word, they are still responsible to obey the biblical principles and lessons to which they have been exposed. King Manasseh (a Jew by birth) affords us with an example of a carnal Christian (a reborn one who disobeys). Though he didn't seek or know the Lord closely, the Lord still disciplined Manasseh for rebelling against the truth he knew, specifically the way of faith and obedience he had seen so clearly and continually in the life of his righteous father, King Hezekiah (2 Chron. 33:1–11).

Belshazzar's rebuke and subsequent judgment reminds us all that we are responsible to live according to all the truth we know. All divine truth—Bible verse, experience, testimony—is spiritual "light," and we must walk in the light we have. (See 1 John 1:7.) To do this makes us "doers of the Word"; to fail renders us "hearers only" (James 1:25)...and spiritually kin to King Belshazzar.

See 2 Chronicles 33:1–13; James 1:25; 1 John 1:7; John 13:17; Matthew 7:26–27; Luke 6:46, 49.

Lesson: *God holds us responsible to obey all the truths we have learned, academically, experientially, and observationally.*

5:17–24 Defiant unbelief or unbelievable defiance? While Daniel's inspired rebuke reveals Belshazzar's fatal error—walking in pride when he knew better—it does not reveal his real, inner thoughts, that is, the attitude that prompted his arrogant act of sacrilege. Two things seem possible.

Defiantly, Belshazzar may have refused to believe the story of Nebuchadnezzar's divine chastening. He may have held that the king's insanity was unrelated to either his enormous ego or a direct act by the God of the Jews. Or he may have believed the story but was so audacious, so evilly bold, so without care for the consequences of his brazen self-will, that he defiled the vessels of God's temple knowing it would evoke divine retribution, a kind of "in your face and I don't care what you think or do about it" act. Belshazzar was either a committed disbeliever or the consummate rebel.

See Matthew 28:11–15; Luke 18:2,4.

5:25–29 On the shelf? Stay ready! Finally, after being out of high office for more than twenty years, Daniel again found himself appointed to serve two more Gentile monarchs—not only Belshazzar on this fateful evening (Dan. 5:25–29) but also the incoming king, Darius, in his new administration (Dan. 6:1–3). That at this time he was ready to serve—in the Spirit (Dan. 5:14) and still accurate in his prophecies and interpretations (vv. 17–30)—proves that Daniel had not been put on the shelf because God was displeased with him. Rather, he served a lengthy "season in the dust" only because God didn't need his gifts and skills during those years. Now God needed Daniel's services again, so off the shelf he came! God's actions here are comparable to what we do with our own household property every day.

Sometimes we place instruments on a shelf because they are not usable; something is defective or broken or otherwise out of order. We shelve other items only because we don't need them at the moment. So God does with His instruments, His vessels. Not all "shelved" vessels (ministers, disciples) of God are vessels unto dishonor, set aside by the Master because they are unfit for His use. Some, as Daniel in this context, are there merely because God doesn't need them at the moment. When He needs their services, He simply reaches for them and puts them to use, just as He did with Moses, Joseph, Saul of Tarsus, and the apostle John. He does the same with His secular instruments whom He uses to further His plan among the nations.

For ten years Winston Churchill was deliberately ostracized from the highest levels of English government, but when World War II broke out, within days he was appointed Lord of the Admiralty and, only months afterward, prime minister. Long forged in extraordinary adversities, Churchill proved an extraordinary "instrument for his (God's) work" (Isa. 54:16) in perhaps the world's greatest crisis to date.

That Daniel, like Churchill and these others, was suddenly recalled by God to serve at a moment's notice points up the truth that vessels unto honor keep themselves "fit for the master's use" (2 Tim. 2:21). Like year-round athletes, they stay in good shape spiritually, "in season, out of season" (2 Tim. 4:2), by diligently watching and praying (Luke 21:34–36). And, as Joseph did in prison, they keep their ministry gifts sharp by exercising them regularly in obscurity. We should, then, make it our aim to always stay spiritually fit—close to Jesus, sanctified, and well practiced in our gifts and ministries in the day of small things. We never know when the Master may call us from our Tarsus (as Saul, Acts 11:25–26), Midian (as Moses, Exod. 3:1–12), Babylon (as Daniel, Dan. 5:13–29), or Patmos (as John, Rev. 1:9–10)!

See "Working all things together for good," chapter 5; also "At a moment's notice," chapter 5.

See 2 Timothy 2:21; 4:2; Exodus 3:1–12; Genesis 17:1; 41:14; Acts 11:25–26; Revelation 1:9–10.

Lesson: When God puts us on the shelf for a season, we should keep ourselves spiritually fit and ready for His use.

5:25–28 Words or messages? While the letters of the three Aramaic words that appeared on the wall were understood by everyone at Belshazzar's party, the words they formed and the message they conveyed were not. Only Daniel, who is described as a *Spirit-filled man* (Dan. 5:14), deciphered the words (apparently encoded) and grasped the message God was conveying. By the Spirit's help, he gave unity and meaning to the inscrutable words and their indiscernible message. And why did the Spirit so richly endow Daniel with such penetrating wisdom and spiritual illumination? Because of Daniel's uncompromising loyalty to God and His Word (see Dan. 1:8, 17). *The Amplified Bible* notes:

> Any wise man present probably could recognize the four inscribed words, but only the uncompromising

man of God—who knew God by daily fellowship and communion with Him, who was so dedicated to Him that God could speak to him and through him—only such a man could tell what the words really meant. Blessed—happy, fortunate, prosperous and enviable—are those who dare to be a Daniel! (p. 1003)

It is the same today. When the Bible is read or studied, the unredeemed see but words, while Spirit-filled souls (Spirit-baptized *and* uncompromisingly obedient to God), especially ministers (teachers, pastors, prophetic scholars), hear messages from God for themselves and others. And why? Because the Holy Spirit puts it all together for them, giving the sense, the essence, and the application of the principles of God's words, welding them into clear, timely directives from heaven. Thus, as Daniel did, they decipher God's words and interpret His messages to us.

When we read our Bibles, do we discern messages from God, or do we see mere words? The answer lies in our response to these questions: Have we received the Holy Spirit? And are we obeying Him without compromise?

See John 6:63; 2 Corinthians 3:6; Acts 8:30–31; John 16:13–15; 14:26; Revelation 2:7.

Lesson: *When we are Spirit-filled (Spirit-baptized and uncompromisingly obedient to God), the Spirit helps us see messages from God in the otherwise meaningless words of the Bible.*

5:25–28 The message of the last day. As a man of Babylon (a biblical symbol for the world), Belshazzar represents all worldly men. So the message God sent to him applies to all the inhabitants of this present world.

The message was comprised of three words: *Mene* (repeated for emphasis), *tekel*, *upharsin*. Translated, these three words mean "numbered," "weighed," and "divided" (or "divisions." When this word is used in its singular form *peres* [v. 28] it means "divided"; some translators feel *upharsin* [v. 25] means "and divided").

To pin down the meaning of God's message, let's ask: What was God saying to King Belshazzar at this time? And also, what did He do to him? Here's a free translation:

> I have numbered the days of your administration in Babylon, and they've reached their end. Today is your last day. I have weighed your character (decisions, acts, and attitudes) in the balances of My judgment, and it's time to give My decision (judgment): Your evil deeds far outweigh your good; hence, you are worthy of punishment. Furthermore, I have divided your kingdom (or house, consisting of possessions and authority) and given it to someone else. After today, your office (authority) and your palace (possessions) will be his.

So on this worldly man's last day, God *numbered* him, *weighed* his character, and *divided* his house and gave it to others. This is a message to all of us about our last day:

1. *Mene*—Our days in Babylon (the world) are *numbered* by God; one day will be our last (Exod. 23:26; Ps. 90:12; 71:15; Prov. 27:1).

2. *Tekel*—God is judging our characters every day, *weighing* our righteous and unrighteous decisions, deeds, and attitudes, and He will one day render a decision (judgment) in our case (Heb. 9:27; Rom. 14:12; 2 Cor. 5:10).

3. *Upharsin*—Our personal kingdom (authority, place, and possessions) will then be *divided* and given to others. No matter now fervently we love them and how firmly we hold to them, all our worldly authority, places, and possessions will be taken from us and given to our earthly successors. Thus the point is made that our worldly authority, places, and possessions are temporary, not permanent (1 Tim. 6:7).

See Exodus 23:26; Psalms 90:12; 49:10; Proverbs 27:1;

Hebrews 9:27; Romans 14:12; 2 Corinthians 5:10; 1 Timothy 6:7.

Lesson: God has numbered our days in this world; our last day is coming.

Lesson: At our last day, God will judge us, rewarding or punishing us for the sum of our decisions, deeds, and attitudes.

Lesson: At our last day, God will take all our worldly authority, places, and possessions and give them to others.

5:17–29 Daniel—a faithful prophet. Observe the unrelieved heaviness of the word Daniel delivered here. That he without hesitation delivered such a stern message of judgment to a powerful heathen monarch reveals that Daniel was unswervingly faithful to God. Whatever God spoke to his heart, that he spoke to the people. (See 2 Chron. 18:13.) There was no attempt to toughen soft messages or to soften hard ones. Such faithfulness in delivery demands a courage born of deep faith in God. One must trust that God will take care of the adverse reactions and retaliations that arise when unpleasant truth is spoken in His name (James 5:10–11; 2 Chron. 18:26; Isa. 30:10–11; Jer. 1:19; 36:21–26).

Anyone can deliver a favorable word from God, but it takes faith and courage to speak His messages of criticism, warning, or judgment.

See Genesis 40:16–19; Matthew 24:2; 2 Chronicles 18:16–22; 2 Samuel 18:31–32; Acts 20:27.

Lesson: Faithful ministers speak both favorable and unfavorable messages with equal faithfulness.

5:29 A surprising reward. Despite the unpleasantness of Daniel's interpretation (Dan. 5:17–28) and his potentially offensive indifference toward his monarch's generosity (v. 17), King

Belshazzar still rewarded Daniel (see v. 29). Daniel's reward consisted of:

1. MATERIAL BLESSINGS: Scarlet (literally "purple") clothing, likely taken from the royal wardrobe (see Esther 6:8–9).

2. MATERIAL WEALTH: A "chain of gold"; probably royal jewelry and very expensive.

3. PUBLIC HONOR: A "proclamation concerning him, that he should be the third ruler in the kingdom." A public announcement was issued describing Daniel's outstanding interpretation and consequent promotion.

4. HIGHER OFFICE: Daniel assumed—albeit briefly—the highest position he ever held—the lofty position of tri-regent of Babylon.

How incredible that a prophet should be favored with such a regal reward for informing his sovereign that his doom was imminent! What explains this? Why was Daniel rewarded?

The reason is: "The laborer is worthy of his hire" (Luke 10:7). Belshazzar's compensations were in reality *God's* rewards. God was rewarding Daniel for walking faithfully with him during the previous twenty-plus years of obscurity and also for not withholding His unpleasant word from the king on this occasion. Daniel's loyalty to God in the dark and his boldness to speak for Him in the light honored and pleased God; hence, though Daniel didn't covet honors or rewards, God delighted to give him both. (See 1 Sam. 2:30.) God's worthy laborer had done his work and was due his pay, so God paid him. How could a faithful God do anything less for His faithful servant? (See Hebrews 6:10.)

See Luke 10:7; Hebrews 6:10; 11:6b; 2 Chronicles 15:7; 1 Corinthians 15:58; 9:9; Psalm 84:11; 1 Samuel 2:30; Galatians 6:7.

Lesson: *God always rewards ministers who remain unswervingly loyal to Him.*

5:30–31 A surprisingly swift judgment. Just as God's response to Belshazzar's sacrilege was swift, so was His performance of the judgment He pronounced through Daniel. "In that night"—literally within a few hours—the word God had spoken was fulfilled.

See "A sudden intervention," chapter 4; also "A swift response," chapter 5.

See Ezekiel 12:21–25; 24:15–18; Acts 5:1–11; 2 Chronicles 26:16–20; Isaiah 37:33–36.

Lesson: While God typically delays the performance of His judgments, He sometimes fulfills them with stunning swiftness.

CHAPTER SIX

PREFERRED, PROMOTED, PERSECUTED—STILL UNCOMPROMISING!

6:1–3 DARIUS: A WISE ADMINISTRATOR. Obviously Darius the Mede[1] believed in delegating authority. Upon assuming the throne of Babylon, he immediately appointed 120 princes ("satraps," or government officials) or provincial governors (Dan. 6:1–3), whose task was twofold: 1) govern, and 2) collect tribute.

The general governance of the people was according to the royal decrees, which were both directives and laws. This passage, however, seems to speak more directly to the governors' latter duty of collecting the king's tax. Also a believer in establishing clear lines of accountability, Darius placed over his provincial governors three presidents, of whom Daniel sat first (v. 2). These presidents superintended the governors' daily work and, most importantly, ensured that all taxes collected were delivered in full to the seat of government in Babylon (and not into the pockets of the governors, as was later done by many Jewish publicans; see Luke 3:12–13). This clearly understood chain of authority ensured that Darius would not suffer "damage," or loss of revenue, due to dishonest satraps.

Thus, Darius established, at least in part, delegation of authority, a clear chain of command, and a system of checks and balances in Babylon. Consequently, he was not overworked, his administrators were not left in confusion, none of them had a disproportionate amount of authority, and they all were accountable for their official actions. Quite unlike his predecessor, Darius the Mede was a wise administrator.

See Matthew 17:25–26; Nehemiah 5:4; Ezra 6:8; Luke 2:1–3.

Lesson: Wise administrators delegate authority, establish clear lines of command and require their subordinates to be accountable.

6:3 A good attitude! And faithful! King Darius preferred Daniel because he had "an excellent spirit" (Dan. 6:3; see Dan. 5:12). Context implies that this means Daniel had a great attitude toward his work. (While Daniel's initial appointment as a president [Dan. 6:2] was based on his previous reputation, Darius's desire to make Daniel his prime minister [v. 3] arose purely from Daniel's outstanding performance in his new post.) It also states Daniel was "faithful"—utterly trustworthy and thoroughly dutiful (v. 4). His impeccable integrity and outstanding industry made Daniel the perfect choice for the top "Internal Revenue Service" post in Babylon—hence the king's vision of higher service for Daniel.

Spiritually, the pattern here was this: For faithfully executing his duties with a good attitude, God's servant was given favor with his superior, who immediately looked to promote him.

See Proverbs 22:29; Daniel 5:12; Genesis 39:1–4; 39:21–22; 1 Kings 11:28; 1 Samuel 16:18–19; 17:14–15; 18:5, 14–15, 30; Psalm 40:8; Colossians 3:23; Ecclesiastes 9:10.

Lesson: If we do our duties faithfully with good attitudes, the Lord will give us favor with men, and promotions to higher service.

6:3–5 Preferred, promoted, persecuted! In these verses we read three chronological occurrences in Daniel's life. Daniel was:

1. *Preferred* above his peers (Dan. 6:3a)
2. *Promoted* above them (Dan. 6:3b)
3. *Persecuted* by them (Dan. 6:4–5, 6–23)

While envy is not explicitly stated to be the cause of Daniel's persecution (as it was in Joseph's case; see Gen. 37:11; Acts 7:9), it is implied by the order of the facts presented. For example, Daniel 6:3 tells us how Daniel was preferred by Darius and selected for promotion, and the following verse begins, "*Then* the presidents and princes sought to find occasion against Daniel..." (v. 4, emphasis added). So it was "then"—when Daniel's preferment and promotion were fresh on the minds of his fellow administrators—that they turned against him. Since no other explanation for their sudden antipathy is given, that implied by the context is the one the Holy Spirit gives us: They were envious. Envy is angry discontentment and ill will at another's possession of something one keenly desires oneself. Hence, however wrongly, they felt Daniel had been given the job they deserved!

So we see that envy, stirred by one's preferment and promotion above his peers, led to persecution. *The Living Bible* agrees that "jealousy" was the cause of Daniel's persecution (v. 4). Other factors may have exacerbated the hatred from Daniel's peers. A note in *The Modern Language Bible* implies that anti-Jewish prejudice was also a factor: "They were doubtless prejudiced against an alien holding high position in the government" (p. 880). The full truth be known, both were probably true in Daniel's case. He was hated, not only because he was a Jew but because he was an extraordinarily faithful and favored Jew!

Daniel's persecution took two forms: 1) a dirt hunt, which proved unsuccessful (v. 4), and 2) an entrapment, which succeeded initially (vv. 5–23) but later backfired (v. 24).

Daniel's experience is something every aspiring overcomer

should mull. We are all eager to win God's approval and rewards, but are we also aware that there is a backlash of persecution that inevitably attends such blessings? When God's favor blesses or promotes us in life, we should not be surprised if our worldly peers or carnal fellow Christians, moved by envy, arise and give us a hard time. (See Dan. 3:8.)

See "Envy at the root," chapter 3.

See Genesis 37:11; Acts 7:9; Daniel 3:8.

Lesson: *When worldly peers and carnal Christians recognize God's blessing upon us, envy may sometimes drive them to persecute us without cause.*

6:4 Be prepared: Your enemies will seek cause! As agents of the accuser of the brethren, Daniel's enemies sought a cause—any cause—to accuse him. So driven were they that when they couldn't find one, they contrived one by creating a dilemma in which he could not be loyal both to divine law and Persian law.

Their actions are a subtle warning to us: If we too are uncompromisingly righteous, our enemies will do the same to us. With great passion, they will one day seek a cause—any cause—against us. What will save us in that hour? How can we prepare for our enemies' treachery? Again, Daniel is our example.

One thing saved Daniel from his enemies' desire to malign him: *He was faithful!* Scripture states, "He was faithful [honest, loyal, thorough in the execution of all duties], neither was there any error or fault found in him" (Dan. 6:4). This alone made him irreproachable. We too must be faithful so we may be beyond reproach in the hour our detractors seek feverishly to reproach us. (See 1 Cor. 4:2.) We should make it our ambition to be so faithful that, like Daniel, our enemies may only attack us on the grounds of our faith!

One difference between Daniel's times and ours stands out. His Persian critics apparently searched for "current dirt" (Dan. 6:4). Our generation digs and sniffs for dirt all the way back to our cradles! The business of reputation assassination has reached its ugly climax in our time. No previous generation has ruined people with the zeal and efficiency of the modern slander machine known as "the press." This is all the more reason to heed this lesson from Daniel. Faithfulness will prepare us for whatever onslaught our enemies bring.

See 1 Peter 2:14–15; 4:12–16; Acts 24:13–21; 2 Timothy 2:2; Nehemiah 7:2; Genesis 39:6, 22–23; 1 Samuel 22:14.

Lesson: *We should strive to be irreproachably faithful so that when our enemies seek a cause of reproach they will find none—other than our faith!*

6:6–7 Be prepared: Your enemies will lie! Daniel's enemies lied to Darius by telling him that "all" (Dan. 6:7) his government leaders had "consulted together" (v. 7) and proposed the new thirty-day ban on prayer to any entity other than himself: "We presidents, governors, counselors and deputies have unanimously decided that you should make a law..." (v. 7, *The Living Bible*). The truth was that the king's most trusted official, Daniel, had no part in the decision. It was an expertly crafted lie: a collection of partial truths that, due to the omission of a carefully selected fact, created a false impression of a person, act, or event.

If Daniel's enemies didn't mind lying about him, neither will ours mind misrepresenting us. We mustn't be naïve. The awareness of an approaching attack saves us from the sudden shock of its unexpected onset. Every uncompromisingly righteous Christian from the beginning of this age—from Jesus of Nazareth to the apostle Paul to Martin Luther to John Wesley—has felt the stinging scourge of sinners' tongues. Are we prepared to be misrepresented for Jesus' sake?

See Luke 6:22; John 15:20–21; Psalm 31:13, 18; Acts 24:4–9, 11–13; 2 Timothy 3:12.

Lesson: *We may expect to be willfully misrepresented by our enemies at one time or another in our walk.*

6:3 Be prepared: The preemptor will visit you. As stated earlier, Daniel's storm of persecution arose just when King Darius was about to appoint him to a newly created office atop his administration (Dan. 6:3), and the natural (human) reason for this attack was envy. But there is another view we should consider.

From the supernatural perspective, Satan, the real inspirer of Daniel's enemies, was attempting to preempt Daniel's promotion to higher office, perhaps fearing that Daniel's increased authority might enable him to do even more for the cause of God and the welfare of His people, the Jews. (See Esther 10:3.) But thanks to divine intervention, the preemptor's attack failed. Scripture notes that after the storm of trouble passed Daniel "prospered" (Dan. 6:28). This seems to indicate that he was then promoted to the position the king had envisioned for him before the opposition arose (v. 3).

As the preemptor, Satan still attempts to stop whatever God is doing—to deliver or bless Christians, or promote the cause of Christ—just before it happens. Just before the heavenly vision is fulfilled, the enemy attacks with hellish fury. However, if we persist in steadfast prayer, service, and faith, as Daniel did (see vv. 10, 16b, 23b), God will faithfully intervene to thwart the preemptor's thrust and establish us in the vision He has given. Are we prepared to recognize and overcome the preemptor when he visits us?

See "A pattern of preemptive persecution," chapter 8.
See Exodus 1:16–22; Matthew 2:16–18.

Lesson: Satan always tries to preempt the blessing or promotion of God's uncompromising servants. We must be prepared to overcome his schemes by steadfast prayer, service, and faith.

6:7 Be prepared: Your prayer life will come under attack. The deadly plot hatched against Daniel had both natural and supernatural objectives. Naturally, Daniel's enemies used his devotion to prayer merely as a convenient way to entrap and punish him. They could not have cared less whether he prayed; they just wanted to get him into the den of lions—and out of their lives! But supernaturally, Satan had another reason for inspiring them to draft a decree that explicitly forbade prayer to God.

Their decree could have addressed many areas of Daniel's consecrated walk: his diet (Dan. 1:8), interpretations (v. 17), study (Dan. 9:2), or worship (Dan. 3:18). Why did they target prayer? Because Satan—the real mastermind behind their plan—wanted desperately to stop Daniel from praying! The record reveals Daniel's prayer life was extraordinarily regular (Dan. 6:10) and effective. Many Jews were praying during the Babylonian captivity, but when Daniel prayed, mighty things happened: deliverances, messages, visions, interpretations, prophecies, and angelic visitations. (See Dan. 2:17–23; 4:19; 9:3, 20–23; 10:12–14.) The result was distressing disruption in the kingdom of darkness and life and hope for the children of light. Therefore, the plan to put Daniel in the lion's den was not only an attack on Daniel's faith and his very life but also an attempt to stop his prolific prayer life. Why? Prayer is the main and most enduring work of any redeemed person.

For this reason, every Christian who prays regularly and effectively (in obedience, faith, and steadfastness) may expect to encounter spiritual attacks occasionally for the purpose of spoiling the effectiveness or reducing the regularity of their petitions. This is why Ephesians 6:10–18 describes praying Christians under attack from evil spirits. Are we prepared for our prayer life to come under attack? Are we willing to persevere in prayer, as Daniel did (Dan. 6:10), until God delivers us from the turbulence?

See Ephesians 6:10–18; 1 Thessalonians 5:17; Luke 11:9–10; 18:1.

Lesson: *Satan attacks praying Christians to reduce the regularity and effectiveness of their petitions.*

6:7 Power through flattery. Though they lived in ancient times, Daniel's enemies knew how to win friends and influence people: flatter them. Hence, their request was carefully designed to flatter King Darius. Their suggested law put him on the highest pedestal—with the gods! To eastern monarchs, who frequently claimed divine status, this was a very self-gratifying thought. Unquestionably, this flattering notion helped Daniel's enemies gain influence over the most influential man in the world...to further their own ends! Watch for flattery.

Flattery appeals to and, when accepted, activates pride. When pride is stirred, we become subject to the lord of pride, Satan. He then can weaken, deceive, mislead, or otherwise move us from righteousness and the will of God, exactly as Darius—a good man—was moved in this context. (The activation of pride, as that of any sin, gives the enemy a spiritual "foothold" [Eph. 4:26–27] or "advantage" [2 Cor. 2:9–11], which he immediately uses to work against us, other Christians, or the cause of Christ.) Unquestionably, flattery is the work of the serpent.

Are we becoming "wise as serpents" (Matt. 10:16)? If so, we will watch for flattery and beware lest we let it move us. At the same time we will understand that compliments are always in order and sometimes help wise men further their righteous agenda. (See Acts 26:3.) The difference between the two is:

- A *compliment* is a sincere and true word of commendation rendered to bless or encourage, whether or not favor results (see John 3:2).

- A *flattering* statement is an insincere and baseless (or exaggerated) commendation, used solely to hide malice and to further a selfish or evil purpose (see Matt. 22:15–16).

Because flattering is a form of lying, it is a sin for Christians to flatter one another or others. Because compliments are a form of giving, we should freely give them. And if a compliment may be truthfully rendered to those whose assistance we seek, we may with clear conscience render it. Only good can result. It will always bless the one to whom it is due. (Doesn't it bless *you* when someone commends your worthy attitude, effort, or work?) And, if God wills, it will garner favor for the work of Christ. So we will be as subtle as a serpent but as harmless as a dove.

See Proverbs 26:24–26, 28; 29:5; Matthew 10:16; 22:15–16; Acts 12:20–22; 24:2–3.

Lesson: *Flattery captivates, enabling flatterers to influence the unsuspecting to help them do evil.*

Lesson: *True compliments always bless people and may encourage them to discern and assist the work of the Lord.*

6:8–9 Legalized illegality. Daniel's enemies didn't contrive this law for the people's good, or for any cause of justice, or to help the Persian state or royal family. Their legal maneuverings were solely to do something utterly wrong: ruin a good man. Hence, while their means were legal, their end was illegal—in God's eyes if not man's. Theirs was no just or necessary use of the legislature (6:6–8) or courts (6:12–15) of Persia, but rather an abuse of its system of law, an attempt to harness its irresistible power to achieve an immoral—really criminal—end. Their actions are best described as "legalized illegality"—an illegal end achieved by legal means.

Jesus plainly warned us that some of us would face hearings before hostile and unjust authorities (Mark 13:9–11). Stephen faced just such a hearing before the Sanhedrin—the ruling Jewish legal body in first-century Israel—and was both falsely charged and summarily and illegally executed (Acts 6:11–14). The Jews frequently attempted to use legal venues to nail the apostle Paul to a cross of injustice. In Jerusalem, they met hastily after Paul was falsely arrested, hoping to justify legally his execution then and there (Acts 23:1–10). In Corinth, they brought him before Gallio, claiming he was advocating an illegal religion (Acts 18:12–17). Earlier, in Philippi, enraged Jewish occultists claimed he was causing trouble throughout the city by teaching Christians to disobey Roman authority (Acts 16:20–21). So not surprisingly, Paul described his hearing before Caesar (which resulted from the Jews' earlier unjustified legal charges in Jerusalem) as a kind of den of lions (2 Tim. 4:16–17). Generally, poor or crude evildoers kill their enemies with fists, knives, or guns; refined, well-educated, well-heeled murderers, individually and collectively, use the courts to eliminate their enemies. Hence James writes, "Do not rich men oppress you, and draw you before the judgment seats?" (James 2:6). He later charges these prominent enemies of Christ, "Ye have condemned [by legal judgments] and killed [ruined] the just; and he doth not resist you" (James 5:6). Of this latter reference, *The Ryrie Study Bible* states, "This probably refers to the practice of the rich taking the poor ('the righteous') to court to take away what little they might have, thus 'murdering' them" (p. 1862).

The same is done today when people bring criminal charges or file suit without cause, attempting to use the power of the courts to ruin people whom they merely dislike or cannot control. Defaming allegations, public ridicule, the emotionally grueling burden of prolonged litigation, the issuance of unjust legal judgments, the imposing of unbearable financial awards—these are the "dens of lions" innocent Christians sometimes find themselves thrust into in this day.

See Mark 13:9–11; Acts 6:11–14; 16:20–21; 18:12–13; 23:1–10; James 2:6; 5:6; 1 Kings 21:5–14; 2 Timothy 4:16–17.

Lesson: *Sometimes legal authority (legislative, judicial) is used to achieve illegal (unjust, even criminal) ends against Christians and Christian organizations.*

6:4–9,10–11 Walking into a trap. Well informed of Daniel's beliefs and personal habits, his enemies met in secret to draft a plan to entrap him. Knowing he prayed three times daily, that seemed the area in which they could most easily ensnare him. So they devised the idea of the royal decree forbidding prayer, hoping that Daniel—whose uncompromising faithfulness they well knew (see Dan. 1:8–16; 3:16–18, 28)—would not obey it. True to character, he did just that: "Now when Daniel knew that the writing was signed, he went into his house...and prayed and gave thanks before his God, as he did |previously|" (Dan. 6:10; see v. 11). Thus he saw their trap and calmly walked straight into it.

One of the Proverbs speaks of the folly of setting a trap that one's prey can see (Prov. 1:17); conversely, it implies that walking straight into a trap one can see is folly as well. Oddly, both follies seemed to have occurred here. Daniel's enemies must have known that Daniel, a man of renowned wisdom and repeatedly confirmed supernatural discernment, would have suspected something amiss, yet they set their trap anyway. At the same time, Daniel understood clearly the consequences of his actions, yet he walked straight into the trap set before him. Why? Because in his mind his choice was fall for the trap or fail God by neglecting prayer and so compromising his wondrous daily fellowship with God, the source of all his strength, insight, and ministry (prophetic utterance). So Daniel did something a bird would never dream of doing: He walked straight into a fowler's snare.

Daniel wasn't the only believer who did this. Thousands, perhaps millions, of Christians did the same thing during the long and bitter Roman persecution (A.D. 64–324). Rather than worship Caesar as divine, they boldly confessed Jesus as their only God, knowing well the terrible consequences of their profession. So they walked straight into entrapment and suffered loss of property, liberty, and sometimes life. Ironically, thousands were killed by wild animals, including lions, in Rome's "den of lions"—the Coliseum. Bible scholars agree that Daniel and his three loyal Jewish friends are types of the faithful remnant of Jewish Christians who will endure the fiery trial of the tribulation period. But are they not also divine illustrations of uncompromising

Christians from the Roman persecution all the way through to the final trials of this age?

The Bible affords us with many examples of uncompromisingly loyal saints who, as Daniel did, walked straight into traps rather than fail God: the three Jews (Dan. 3:16–18, 28); the apostle Paul (Acts 20:22–24); Jesus of Nazareth (Matt. 20:17–19); and the apostle Peter (John 21:18–19; 2 Pet. 1:14).

Lesson: Overcoming Christians will knowingly suffer rather than give up their fellowship with God or disobey His Word.

6:10 Unchangeable Christians! Just as God's character, Word, and ways are immutable (see Mal. 3:6), so are His uncompromising servants. They do not change their ways with the times. Observe Daniel in the worst of times.

When Daniel realized that his established way of steadfast daily prayer could put him in jeopardy with the Persian authorities, he didn't change his way but "prayed, and gave thanks… [just] as he did |previously|" (Dan. 6:10). Had it been able to speak, self-preservation surely would have urged Daniel, "*Change,* man, and avoid trouble!" Worldly wisdom would have added, "Everyone else is doing it; why not you?" And perhaps they did so speak in Daniel's mind. But he didn't yield. Further evidence of Daniel's unchanging character is seen in that he is just as uncompromisingly righteous in his nineties (chapter 6) as he was in his teenage years (chapter 1). Obviously, his full sanctification was finished early and held firm throughout his life. Thus he typifies unchangeable Christians.

While God is sanctifying us, all of His teaching and chastening have one goal: to change us from our old selves into Christ's image. But once that transformation process has changed us into Christ's character image (as it had Daniel; see 1 Thess. 5:23), it is God's will that we become unchangeable, like Him. So we see two seemingly contradictory seasons in our spiritual life: During our formative Christian training, constant change is our way of life; yet when we become established in the mind, standards, words, and ways of Christ, God wants us thereafter to be unchangeable. No matter what is popular in our generation, regardless of the worldly disadvantages of faithfulness, He wants us to stay as we are "in Him"—to continue in the same simple biblical beliefs, moral values, and spiritual ways of living He has so faithfully and patiently taught us. Thus the unchangeable God seeks unchangeable Christians.

Uncommitted Christians sell out their beliefs, morality, and devotional habits when the times turn evil and loyalty to God seems futile or self-opposing. But unchangeable Christians quietly put their trust in God and stay the course. It is the highest compliment to the Holy Spirit's work in our lives when others say of us, "He (or she) is always the same." The same is true of Daniel—and God!

See Acts 20:24; Romans 8:29; Malachi 3:6; Hebrews 13:8.

Lesson: Like God's character and His Word, uncompromising Christians are unchanging.

6:10 Exemplary devotion. *Webster's Encyclopedic Unabridged Dictionary of the English Language* defines *devotion* as "earnest attachment to a cause, person, etc.; profound dedication, consecration." Evidence given throughout the Book of Daniel reveals that Daniel's devotion to God was exemplary. It was marked by:

- REGULARITY. Daniel served God through devotional acts "continually" (Dan. 6:16, 20)—three times every day (vv. 10, 13) and in every season of his life, whether prosperous or adverse.

- THANKFULNESS. Daniel took time to worshipfully thank God (for His wondrous Person and manifold blessings) (v. 10).

- HUMILITY. In prayer, Daniel supplicated, or humbly begged, God for help (v. 11); he also humbly confessed his and his people's sins (Dan. 9:4–8).

- PETITIONS. In prayer, Daniel made specific requests of God (Dan. 6:13; 2:17–18, 23; 12:8).

- DISCIPLINE. Daniel practiced prayer with fasting (Dan. 9:3; 10:2–3).

- MEDITATION. Daniel often pondered God's Word thoughtfully and prayerfully (Dan. 9:2; 10:1, 14, 21).

- PERSISTENCE. Daniel pursued the spiritual goals he set with great determination (Dan. 9:3; 10:12); even amid great adversity, he continued praying (Dan. 6:10).

- BOLDNESS. Though not a religious exhibitionist, Daniel was unashamed of his devotion; he didn't mind that others knew he prayed to God (vv. 10–11).

Jesus has called every Christian to walk in the way of devotion (Mark 3:13–15; Matt. 6:2–4, 6, 16–18, 33; 11:28–30). Daniel sets a wonderful example for us to follow.

See Psalm 55:17; Matthew 6:2–4, 6–8, 16–18, 33; 11:28–30.

Lesson: Ideal devotion to God is marked by regularity, thankfulness, humility, petitions, discipline, meditation, persistence, and boldness.

6:10 Higher than the laws of the land. All Daniel had to do to comply with the king's decree was simply *not pray*. The law did not mandate that all Persians and foreign nationals pray to the king (an idolatrous act for any Jew). Rather, it stated that *if* prayer were rendered during the next thirty days, it had to be directed to him. Hence, it was a forbiddance of prayer to any other deities or persons during this period only. As far as God's law was concerned, Daniel could have kept this ordinance; only his fellowship with God, not his loyalty to God's Word, would have suffered. His uninterrupted persistence in prayer (Dan. 6:10) demonstrates his unwillingness to surrender his devotional life—personal fellowship with God—for the sake of compliance with Persian law. Hence Daniel put his fellowship with God above the law of the land. By today's standards, many Christians would have condemned him as a disrespectful radical.

Many pastors and believers today speak of our nation's Constitution and laws with the highest reverence. And indeed Scripture itself authorizes the rule of man's law until Christ comes. But while the Bible reveals the ordinances of man are unquestionably authoritative and explicitly commands Christians to obey them (Rom. 13:1–7; 1 Pet. 2:13–15), it also teaches that there are things that are higher than our nation's laws. Specifically, they are God's law, as seen in the three Jews' courageous decision to defy Nebuchadnezzar's idol worship (chapter 3), and our fellowship with (devotion to) God, as seen in Daniel's refusal to stop praying to God merely because the laws of the land forbade him from doing so (chapter 6).

In short, when man's laws forbid the Christian to exercise his devotion to Christ or command him to act in some way clearly contrary to the Scripture, the Christian is obligated not to obey but to *disobey* man's laws. Such is not an act of disrespect for the rule of law but rather a living testament of respect for something he holds, and rightly so, in even *higher* regard: the rule of God. The laws of heaven are higher than the laws of the land. Accordingly *The Ryrie Study Bible* notes, "Daniel's example is one of legitimate disobedience to the government" (p. 1319). Again, Rome's early persecution of the church centered around this very issue. The Christians refused to worship the Caesars as divine because God's Word forbade such idolatry; hence, they demonstrated their faith that God's Word took priority over Caesar's whenever the two conflicted.

See Exodus 1:15–21; Esther 3:2; Acts 4:19; 5:29.

Lesson: *The rule of God is higher than the rule of law. When they conflict, God's laws and our devotional fellowship with God take priority over man's laws.*

6:10 Uncompromising *devotion*. By refusing to surrender his fellowship with God for even one day, Daniel displayed uncompromising devotion to God. Obviously Daniel considered his private time with God precious and nonnegotiable. So besides being uncompromisingly obedient to God's Word (chapter 1), Daniel was also uncompromisingly devoted to God. He was an extraordinary God-chaser.

Do we follow his example? Are we taking time for Jesus daily, no matter what our schedule or activity level? Or are we letting other things, interests, or people get in between us and our private time with Him? We should be flexible when necessary, to be sure, but never should we forget to take time for personal fellowship with our Lord. Daniel would rather have died than give Him up.

See Psalms 105:4; 65:4; 27:4, 8; 2 Chronicles 26:5; Mark 3:14.

Lesson: We should not compromise our daily devotional time with Jesus.

6:13 The art of offense. In an attempt to heighten the king's indignation, Daniel's accusers crafted a two-part lie against him. First, they claimed he held no respect for King Darius: "That Daniel...regardeth not *thee*..." (Dan. 6:13, emphasis added). Second, they accused him of having no respect for the rule of law: "...nor *the decree* that thou hast signed..." (v. 13, emphasis added). Daniel had both respect for the king and for his laws, yet, as shown above, Daniel held his devotion to God in even higher regard. Nevertheless, his enemies sought to misrepresent him in hopes Darius would believe Daniel was lawless and, most importantly, without any respect for him personally. Once implanted, that lie would have insulted the king and prompted him to speedily enforce the dire penalty of his decree. Thus with diabolical skill Daniel's enemies practiced the evil art of offense.

While this evil art worked on King Nebuchadnezzar (Dan. 3:12), it did not on Darius, who already knew and deeply respected Daniel (Dan. 6:1–3, 14). His prolonged effort to deliver Daniel and his steadfast support even while executing his sentence proves he had no doubt of his innocence.

Are we on the alert for the art of offense? When people relate the words or actions of others in such a way that we are offended, we should not rush to judgment. The speaker may be deliberately trying to offend us so as to turn us against another without cause. A prayerful, patient, objective inquiry will always reveal the truth of the matter.

See "The art of offense," chapter 3.

Lesson: When people describe the words or actions of others in such a way that pointedly offends us, we must be slow to anger and judgment. Our messenger may be trying to set us against an innocent person.

6:14 A royal friend indeed. It is said, and rightly, "A friend in need is a friend indeed." Daniel's excellent character won him the approval of King Darius, who then became his friend in need. Note the facts that reveal just how much the king admired Daniel.

- By grace, Darius *selected* Daniel to live and work closely with him (v. 2).

- He *approved* of Daniel's work and conceived a vision of higher service (v. 3).

- He blamed himself for making the decree that incriminated Daniel (v. 14) and *labored in thought* all day to devise a way to not punish Daniel (v. 14b).

- He spoke *words of encouragement* to Daniel as he entered his trial (v. 16).

- He wouldn't indulge and *couldn't rest* while Daniel suffered (v. 18).

- He *rose early and ran* to the lions' den to discover Daniel's condition (v. 19).

- "Exceedingly glad," he *rejoiced* that Daniel overcame his trial (v. 23).

- He promptly *avenged* Daniel of his cruel enemies (v. 24).

- He issued a royal decree *honoring* Daniel's God and Daniel's faith (vv. 25–27).

- He *prospered* Daniel by fulfilling his vision (v. 28, probably by making him prime minister, as planned earlier; v. 3b).

Exactly what characteristics impressed King Darius and won his friendship for Daniel? Five are brought out in this chapter:

1. An excellent attitude (v. 3)
2. Faithfulness in work (v. 4)
3. Uncompromising devotion in prayer (v. 10)
4. Complete trust in God (vv. 10, 23b)
5. Continual service to God (vv. 16, 20)

Thus by his exemplary *attitude, faithfulness, devotion, trust,* and *service* Daniel won the approval and committed friendship of an earthly king. Overcomers do the same today.

As we walk as Daniel walked and continue in the study and obedience of God's Word, doing whatever it commands and following wherever the Spirit leads, we win the approval and friendship of Christ, our heavenly King. (See Rev. 19:16.) He then becomes our royal Friend indeed (John 15:14–15) and favors us in our times of need in the very ways Darius favored Daniel in this chapter.

See John 15:14–15; 8:31–32; Romans 8:14; Revelation 19:16.

Lesson: If we walk in Daniel's attitude, faithfulness, devotion, trust and service, and do whatever the Word commands and the Spirit leads, Jesus will be our royal Friend indeed.

6:14 Other friends, too. Darius was, of course, an unbeliever. As a non-Jew, he did not know the Lord. Yet he became totally committed to the uncompromisingly righteous man of God, Daniel. So while as a king he symbolizes Christ, as a man he symbolizes the unbeliever.

Accordingly, if we walk as Daniel walked, we will occasionally win admiration and friendly favors in time of need from unbelievers (Acts 27:3, 43; 28:16) and sometimes even our former enemies (Prov. 16:7; Dan. 3:26–30).

See Proverbs 16:7; 17:17; 18:24; 27:6, 10, 17; Job 6:14; 19:21; John 15:15; Acts 27:3, 43; 28:16.

Lesson: *If we walk in Daniel's attitude, faithfulness, devotion, trust, and service, even unbelievers will occasionally admire, befriend, and help us in time of need.*

6:8,12,15 If *Persian law* was immutable and irrevocable... This context repeatedly states that Persian law could not be changed or revoked. Once written, a decree was permanently effective, unless another law was written subsequently superceding it (see Dan. 6:8, 12, 15; Esther 1:19; 8:8). Thus the immutability and permanence of human law is strongly emphasized in this chapter.

If men's laws, once enacted and written, are unchangeable and permanent, how much more are God's laws—the decrees of His holy Word? If Persian law *had* to be carried out, how much more *must* God's Word—His promises, threats, and prophecies—be fulfilled? Once written, God's Word cannot be changed to suit individuals, generations, or cultural innovations; nor can it ultimately fail to come to pass, for it is in effect permanently. Hence, it must always eventually come to pass exactly as written. (See Mark 14:49b.)

See Matthew 24:35; Isaiah 40:8; Mark 14:49b; John 12:48; 13:18; 19:23–24, 31–37; Revelation 22:18–19; 2 Peter 3:3–7.

Lesson: *The words of the Bible cannot be changed or revoked; they will all be fulfilled one day exactly as they are written.*

6:15–16 *Not* above the law. "Then the king commanded..." (Dan. 6:16). While some American presidents have obviously felt themselves above the law (recently Nixon, Clinton), there was at least one Persian head of state who did not. When Darius's evil administrators gathered and heavy handedly reminded him that the law now required him to do something most unpleasant, he did it (vv. 16–17). Thus he acted, not for fear of them but out of respect for the rule of law. Where are the leaders today—especially heads of state—who realize humbly that they are not above the law?

Lesson: Leaders are not above the law.

6:17 The king's purpose will not be changed. After committing Daniel to the den of lions, King Darius sighed heavily and pressed the imprint of his royal signet ring into the wax seal that was poured either upon or around the stone door of the den of lions. Why did he do this? "That the purpose might not be changed concerning Daniel" (Dan. 6:17). Officially, his actions signified the immutability of the punishment that was established by his decree. Daniel had offended a Persian law, and he had to be punished as specified in that law. Nothing and no one, not even the king himself, could alter that solemn purpose—the will of the state.

Figuratively, however, this "purpose" speaks of something else: the sovereign and immutable purpose of God. While it was Daniel's enemies who conspired to put him in the den of lions, it was God who permitted their evil plan to succeed. Hence, whatever their cruel designs, God had His own reasons for letting Daniel be thrust into such a severe trial. They were:

- TO TEST AND THUS ESTABLISH His servant's loyalty, faith, and endurance

- TO DEMONSTRATE HIS UNLIMITED POWER to deliver His own (vv. 22, 27)

- TO EXPOSE AND PUNISH God's enemies (vv. 13, 24)

- TO REVEAL GOD'S JUST JUDGMENTS (v. 24)

- TO REVEAL GOD'S SURE REWARDS: preservation (vv. 22–23), deliverance (v. 23), honor (vv. 26–27), and prosperity (v. 28)

- To GLORIFY God (by another public decree; vv. 25–27; see Dan. 2:46–47; 3:29; 4:1–37)

- To ENCOURAGE all future believers to remain uncompromisingly obedient to God

These reasons comprise God's "purpose," which the text reveals was not to be changed concerning Daniel. Nor has it been changed concerning us.

In these morally lukewarm final days of the church age (see Rev. 3:14–22), when many Christians consider adversity a thing of the past and prosperity the only way of life, we may imagine that God has changed His mind about sending strong testing to His people. If so, let us think again...and listen carefully to what the Spirit is saying to us in Daniel 6. The king of heaven has set His seal to this fact: As Daniel was, this generation of Christians will be strongly tested, and *His purpose will not be changed!* All that remains is for us to humbly accept this and patiently and loyally endure our dens of lions as they come our way. If we will do so, every benefit seen in Daniel's trial will be revisited in our own.

See "Trial by fire" chapter 3.

See 1 Peter 1:6–7; 4:12; James 1:2–4, 12; Matthew 7:24–27; 13:21; 1 Corinthians 3:13; Revelation 3:18; Psalms 7:9; 11:5; Proverbs 17:3.

Lesson: God has purposed to test His people, and His purpose will not be changed.

6:16–23 Faithfulness delivers the faithful. Twice in this passage (Dan. 6:16, 20) the point is made that Daniel's continual service to God won him deliverance from otherwise certain death. The lesson here is simply that *God delivers faithful servers.* If we are faithful (consistent in our devotion and in the performance of our God-given duties and ministries; see v. 10) in serving God, God will be consistent in releasing us from our afflictions and deadly traps.

See Psalms 34:19; 91:3; 1 Corinthians 10:13; 2 Timothy 4:17–18; Acts 23:12–16; 27:23–24.

Lesson: If we serve God faithfully, He will faithfully deliver us from all tests, afflictions, plots, and traps.

6:22 Angels for the innocent. Daniel told Darius that God had sent an angel to save him by supernaturally closing the lions' mouths, then added that this was because God considered him innocent of any wrongdoing (Dan. 6:22).

Do we want angelic intervention, when necessary, to save us in dangerous trials? Then let us follow Daniel's example and be innocent of wrongdoing in God's sight. Undoubtedly Daniel was condemned by both his accusers and the public, but not by God.

See "Caution: Angels at work," chapter 9.

See Psalm 34:7; Acts 5:19–20; 12:11; Proverbs 10:2; 11:4, 6a.

Lesson: To enjoy angelic protection, we must be innocent of sin and wrongdoing.

6:23 Faith protects; unbelief exposes. This verse declares that "no manner of hurt" was found upon Daniel "because he believed in his God" (Dan. 6:23). Clearly, then, his firm belief in God's ability to protect him from harm in this otherwise deadly situation was the prime reason he escaped unharmed. It seems clear that if he had doubted, he may have been harmed; if he had openly disbelieved, he may have been killed. It is the word of Christ: "According to your faith be it unto you" (Matt. 9:29).

We should take heed. If we believe God, He will protect us from all evil, permitting only those troubles, afflictions, and wounds He sovereignly selects to test our faith and conform our characters to the image of Christ. But if we do not believe in His protecting power, other things God never intended to touch us may enter and harm us. In Daniel's experience we see that it pays to: 1) be innocent of sin (see note above), and 2) believe in divine protection.

We must remember that faith is both a *fruit* and a *choice*.

As a fruit of the Spirit (Gal. 5:22), faith thrives only when there is no ongoing sin present to quench the flow of the Spirit in our lives. As we abide in the Vine and in His Word, His Spirit, which is our life-sap, flows freely into and through us on a daily basis, and the fruit of faith manifests naturally and easily. But I defy you to deeply trust God while at the same time allowing any sin to remain active within your life. You cannot do it, because practicing sin always quenches faith by cutting off the vital flow of life from the Vine, who is holy. (Forgiven sins—faults confessed and forsaken—do not hinder our confidence in God.) But if we walk in the light of the truth we have, the measure of faith we have received from God (Rom. 12:3) thrives by the power of the Spirit, as long as we stay in God's Word (Rom. 10:17) and make the simple choice to believe. Like unbelief, faith is a choice: "Preserve me, O God; for in thee do I put [choose to place] my trust" (Ps. 16:1). The difference is that faith is a choice to trust God's character and promise in the face of contradictory evidence, whereas unbelief is a choice to believe the negative evidence.

See 2 Chronicles 20:20; Daniel 3:25; Galatians 5:22.

Lesson: *Faith in God, which is a fruit and a choice, protects us in the very same dangerous situations in which others who do not have faith experience harm.*

6:24 A cruel harvest. King Darius threw Daniel's accusers—along with their wives and children—into the lions' den where they were devoured. Some commentators note here that this punishment, which was very cruel and unusual by today's standards, was typically Persian. While true, its divine oversight makes it something more—not merely a Persian but a divine judgment. *God* chose this punishment as appropriate for those who tried to destroy His prime servant.

"How could a loving God be so cruel?" we ask. He wasn't. The severity of this punishment was determined by the men who suffered it. When they chose such a barbaric fate for Daniel, an innocent and harmless child of God, they unwittingly chose it for themselves. Why? Because God's principle of sowing and reaping (Gal. 6:7) was activated the moment they executed their plot against Daniel. Once they sowed it (Dan. 6:10–15), nothing could halt the inevitable process. Hence, the crop they reaped was as bitter as the seed-acts they maliciously and methodically sowed.

It behooves us to think twice before we accuse the innocent or actively work toward their undoing, because in due season the very acts we sow against them will come back upon us (see Gen. 42:21–22), and neither prayer nor grace will stop the harvest.

See Galatians 6:7; Proverbs 11:8; 11:6b; Psalm 64:2–4, 7–8.

Lesson: Evildoers will reap the very cruelties they have sown toward the innocent.

6:24 Avenged "speedily." Note that on this occasion God didn't wait around to deal with Daniel's sworn and unrepentant enemies. He immediately prompted Darius to issue their execution order, and they were slain the minute they entered the lions' den.

See Proverbs 10:25a; Psalm 73:18–19; Esther 7:5–10; Luke 18:8.

6:25–27 Fourfold honor. Because Daniel had honored God by his uncompromising devotion and unflagging faith, God honored Daniel through Darius's royal decree. This was the principle of 1 Samuel 2:30 in action: "Them who honor me I will honor."

Note that Darius's decree called on all people to fear Daniel's God, declaring Him to be alive and real (Dan. 6:26, in contrast to other purported deities); unchanging and utterly faithful to His servants ("steadfast forever," v. 26; compare vv. 16, 20); sovereign forever (v. 26); and a master of miraculous rescues (v. 27). Furthermore, he declared God's kingdom to be perpetual (v. 26b). By so honoring Daniel's God, Darius also honored Daniel, God's notable servant; the Jews, the people of Daniel's God; and Judaism, Daniel's religion. Hence, Daniel's uncompromising devotion and brave endurance reaped fourfold honor:

1. For God
2. For God's servant
3. For God's people
4. For Judaism (true religion)

The same occurs every time a Christian overcomer is honored. He or she wins honor for himself, God, all Christians, and Christianity (current true religion).

See "Winning for God and Christians," chapter 3.

See 1 Samuel 2:30; Daniel 3:29; 5:29.

Lesson: When overcoming Christians are honored, so is their God, their people, and their religion.

6:28 Promotion and prosperity—God's way. Daniel is said to have "prospered" during Darius's reign (Dan. 6:28), though only for a brief time (in his nineties, his life was nearly over). We may reasonably assume that after emerging from the den of lions Daniel was promoted to the position the king had envisioned for him (prime minister, v. 3) before the great crisis erupted. Considering Darius's former preference for Daniel (v. 3) and now his rapturous joy at his deliverance (v. 23), it is unthinkable that he would *not* have gone ahead with his former plans. Such a promotion would have inevitably meant more material prosperity for Daniel, blessings such as increased wages and benefits and other perks. Thus this chapter, which describes the man of God's passage through breathtaking adversity, ends appropriately on a note of triumph and divine prosperity. Hallelujah! The preemptor failed and the uncompromising prophet triumphed and came into a season of godly prosperity!

Note well, however, *how* Daniel came to promotion and prosperity: not by moral compromise, ingratiation, and blind conformity, but by showing uncompromising devotion and brave obedience to God in a most difficult trial. (See chapter 2.) Do we have ears to hear what the Spirit is saying here? If we imagine God will give us only promotions and prosperity without our first giving Him uncompromising devotion and brave obedience in our trials, we are naïve and biblically uninformed. Yes, God desires to promote and prosper His people, but in His way, not ours. Daniel shows us God's way to power and prosperity.

See "Power and prosperity—by courage or compromise?" chapter 2.

See 3 John 2; 1 Peter 5:10; Deuteronomy 8:15–16.

Lesson: *God prospers and promotes Christians who give Him uncompromising devotion and brave obedience in their trials of faith.*

---

[1]During this period of history, Cyrus, King of Persia, was the prime monarch of the greater Medo-Persian Empire. Darius the Mede (not to be mistaken for the Persian King Darius I Hystaspis), introduced in Daniel 5:31 and described throughout the following sixth chapter, was his Median appointee as co-regent and ruled over all the territories formerly comprising the "realm of the Chaldeans" (Dan. 9:1), including Babylonia, Assyria, Syria, and Palestine. As Daniel does, this commentary treats Darius the Mede as a full-fledged Persian monarch, despite his obvious deference to Cyrus. To support this I note: 1) Darius the Mede is described as a co-regent, implying full regal power (Dan. 6:28); 2) His decrees are stated to have full Persian legal authority, the "laws of the Medes *and Persians*" being referred to three times (Dan. 6:8, 12, 15, emphasis added); 3) His decree praising Daniel's God was sent, not only to Babylonian provinces but to "all people, nations, and languages that dwell in *all the earth*" (Dan. 6:25, emphasis added). Hence, I refer to him as a Persian head of state and his laws as Persian.

THE MESSAGES
OF A
MASTER PROPHET

A mong the writings of Israel's prophets, the Book of Daniel stands tall. Though comparatively few, Daniel's words are incomparably powerful—and timely. Yet, as seen in Part One, Daniel's character stands even taller than his messages. Uncompromising in righteousness, unsullied in holiness, unceasing in devotion, unsurpassed in insight, unwavering in service, and divinely beloved, he was in every way a master prophet.

In Part Two, we examine the latter six chapters of Daniel's writings. There he has endowed us with some of the richest prophetic legacies ever given. These priceless foretellings have inspired and kept on course countless Jews and Christians down through the centuries. Truly, they are *the messages of a master prophet*.

CHAPTER SEVEN

A VERY SURE PROPHECY OF WORLD HISTORY

7:2–7 DANIEL'S GREAT VISION: A PRECISE DESCRIPTION OF GENTILE KINGDOMS. In Daniel's vision of the four beasts rising from the sea of humanity, the Spirit gives us a very precise description of the order and distinguishing characteristics of the four successive Gentile world governments that will arise before Jesus comes: Babylon, Medo-Persia, Greece, and Rome.

Babylon

"The first was like a lion..." (Dan. 7:4). The lion is king of beasts and hence the most regal and honorable of animals. The lion Daniel saw had "eagle's wings," fittingly, since the eagle is the king of birds. This compound symbol indicates that Babylon was a more regal kingdom—more civilized, cultured, and sensitive—than its successors.

After Daniel beheld it a while, this lion was *transformed*—from a winged lion to a wingless lion, then to a man with a fully human heart. This represents the changing of King Nebuchadnezzar by divine chastening, which, in God's sight, changed him from a high-flying monarch to a humbled one (wingless), then to a kind of believer, with a heart soft and responsive to God's will and rule. (See Dan. 4:37; Ezek. 17:3, 12.)

No such transformation occurred in the next three animals or in the kingdoms they typified. Nebuchadnezzar was the only Gentile monarch God led to repentance. While God called the Persian monarch Cyrus his "anointed" (Isa. 45:1–4), this was only because God chose, raised, and used him as an instrument of liberation for His captive people. It does not indicate God's personal dealings with him or his response in faith and submission to God's will.

Medo-Persia

"And, behold, another beast, a second, like a bear..." (Dan. 7:5). The bear is a less regal, less intelligent, less graceful (more lumbering in its movements), and less refined animal than the lion. Hence, the Medes and Persians were a somewhat less refined or culturally inferior people than their Babylonian predecessors. The bear Daniel saw was of lop-sided stature, higher on one side of its body, because the Persians were of greater size, strength, and duration than the Medes. This bear's huge appetite for flesh is mentioned: "Arise, devour much flesh" (v. 5). Perhaps this is a reference to the excessively large numbers of soldiers and innocents killed in the Persian wars with Lydia, Babylonia, and Egypt. (Even as recently as the Iran-Iraq war of the 1980s, the Iranians, descendants of the Persians, demonstrated an extraordinary indifference toward casualties by frequently sending thousands of their soldiers to their deaths in futile infantry frontal assaults.) The "three ribs" lodged in its teeth may represent the tri-regents of Chaldea—Nabonidus, Belshazzar, Daniel—who ruled at the time the bear devoured Babylon (see Dan. 5:29–31), or it may refer to the three major internal divisions of Babylon over which the three ruled. It may also refer to perhaps both.

Greece

"After this I beheld, and, lo, another, like a leopard..."

(Dan. 7:6). This leopard, with its four wings, is obviously swifter than either a bear or a lion. It speaks of the extraordinary, almost miraculous, speed with which Alexander the Great made his military conquests and enlarged the dominion of Greece.

Specifically, the four wings and four heads each symbolize Alexander's four generals. Their able and loyal leadership helped hasten Alexander's conquests, as wings might hasten even a leopard's pace. They also assumed the governance (headship) of his kingdom after his untimely death. Hence, they first served as his "wings," then as the "heads" of his surviving empire.

Rome

"After this I saw in the night visions, and, behold, a fourth beast...and it was diverse from all the beasts that were before it" (Dan. 7:7). The fourth beast Daniel observed is "diverse" from the first three and from any Daniel had ever seen or heard of, for he found no animal with which he could compare it (see vv. 7, 19, 23). Succinctly, this kingdom is different in that it is stronger (numerically, politically), more terrifying, and more ruthless (cruel) than any previous. This is revealed in the phrases "strong exceedingly," "dreadful and terrible," and "[it] stamped the residue with its feet." Undoubtedly this beast was the Roman Empire. Rome was absolutely unique, one of a kind. Militarily, politically, territorially, and in its length of rule, it was the strongest and greatest Gentile world power to date. Its vast strength is alluded to in its name, which scholars believe was perhaps taken from the Greek word *rhome*, meaning "strong" (*National Geographic*, July 1997, p. 13).

Not accidentally, Daniel made special note of this beast's "great [large] iron teeth" (vv. 7, 19). These large iron teeth symbolize the Roman *legions*; the iron speaks of their strength and the teeth of their function.

For centuries Roman armies were as "strong [unbreakable, inflexible] as iron" (Dan. 2:40), which they used in combat perhaps more widely and effectively than any previous world power. Daniel's use of iron as the symbol for Rome agrees with

Nebuchadnezzar's vision, in which Rome is represented not by gold, silver, or bronze, but by iron. (See Dan. 2:33.) That this beast's teeth are made of iron reveals something further. Our teeth tear apart the flesh we consume. In the same way, armies are the "teeth" of nations with which they tear the flesh of opposing nations on the field of battle and "consume" them, assimilating their territory, resources, and citizenry. "Large iron teeth" bring to mind the terrible sight of a Roman phalanx methodically marching over its foes. "Stamping the residue" in "wanton destructiveness" (*The Modern Language Bible*) refers to Roman cruelty: Typically their legions left few or no survivors. Together, the words "broke. . . devoured...and stamped" (Dan. 7:7, 23) speak of *an incredibly thorough destructive force*. Without a doubt, that describes the armies of Rome.

7:2–7 The Foreknower—hence the Controller—of nations. I am impressed with the specificity of Daniel's vision. Observe the distinguishing details he gives us:

- One Gentile world leader, Babylon's King Nebuchadnezzar, will be changed, but no others.

- One kingdom, Medo-Persia, will be stronger in one of its sectors; the others will have no such imbalance.

- One kingdom, Greece, will conquer with unprecedented speed and eventually be divided into four quadrants; none of the others will experience this.

- The kingdoms will appear in this order—Babylon, Medo-Persia, Greece, Rome—not in any other.

Thus God discloses the precise order of these Gentile kingdoms and the unique features of each. Such precise foreknowledge betrays both God's omniscience and omnipotence: He foresees, prepares, releases, prospers, and terminates each of the world-ruling Gentile empires, personally controlling their courses at all times. (This does not make Him responsible for the morally abhorrent deeds that leaders and nations choose to do of their own free will, which, by divine permission, operates *within* the larger scope of God's omnipotence.) Thus, God is the great Controller of nations.

In this day of unprecedented "distress of nations, with perplexity" (Luke 21:25), it is immensely comforting to know *the nations are in His hand!* At any moment, He can draw the line over which no head of state or army or coalition of nations may pass (see Job 38:11), and He does so whenever He pleases to favor, test, or deliver His redeemed ones.

See Daniel 4:25–26; 5:18; Romans 8:28; Acts 15:18.

Lesson: *God foreknows, and hence controls, the course of all nations.*

7:1–7 A very sure prophecy of world history. Daniel says his great vision came "in the first year of Belshazzar, king of Babylon" (Dan. 7:1). *The Ryrie Study Bible* notes that this was fourteen years *before* the Babylonian kingdom fell to the Medo-Persians (p. 1321). So the reader should understand that God spoke all these things and Daniel wrote them long before they occurred. At the time God and His prophet declared them, there were no clear indications that any kingdom was a threat to overcome, and thus succeed, mighty Babylon. Its fall was humanly unforeseeable.

Both Nebuchadnezzar's and Daniel's corroborating visions (chapters 2, 7) have long since been fulfilled *exactly as prophesied*—over many centuries, through the rise and fall of many nations, and despite the military conquests of numerous vain leaders bent on world conquest—through the Roman era, and none have conquered the world since. Should we not firmly expect the remainder of Daniel's prophetic revelations to be fulfilled exactly as prophesied? The indisputable credibility of Daniel's prophecies past should render his yet-unfulfilled prophecies especially valuable in these last days. Even secular historians must admit that his (and the Bible's) prophecies have been quite remarkably fulfilled to date. Hence, they cannot intelligently attempt to discredit the portions of his prophecies that remain to be fulfilled. Indeed, as Daniel himself told Nebuchadnezzar, "The dream is certain, and the interpretation of it sure" (Dan. 2:45).

For us then, as *believers*, should we not believe them with absolute confidence? Truly, "we have also a more sure word of prophecy, unto which ye do well that ye take heed" (2 Pet. 1:19).

See Daniel 2:45; 2 Peter 1:19.

Lesson: *The undeniably precise fulfillments of Daniel's (and the Bible's) past and present-day prophecies confirm that the future also will unfold exactly as prophesied.*

7:1–7 Two men, two visions, two perspectives—one message. In the Book of Daniel, God gives two men the same prophetic message using very different symbols.

Contrasting Daniel's vision (chapter 7) with Nebuchadnezzar's (chapter 2), *The New Scofield Study Bible* notes that one represents "the imposing outward power and splendor" of the successive Gentile world powers, while the other reveals their "true character" (p. 907). Nebuchadnezzar, a worldly man of externals, sees the impressive outward appearance of these world-ruling governments that occupy the "times of the Gentiles" (see note below). Daniel, a deeply spiritual man, sees the inner spiritual realities of these kingdoms that, like wild animals, greedily attack and devour one another without mercy. Scofield further states they are "rapacious and warlike, established and maintained by force. It is remarkable that the heraldic insignia of the Gentile nations are all beasts or birds of prey" (p. 907). Despite these differences in appearance, the messages are identical in their real story—that three successive Gentile kingdoms will arise after Babylon with divine authorization to rule the world, including Israel, and their collective authority will one day suddenly end.

Seeing that the two visions end identically, *The Modern Language Bible* states, "In both, the kingdom of this world is superseded by a kingdom of celestial origin; that of

Nebuchadrezzar [alternate spelling], by 'a stone,' which becomes a great mountain filling the whole earth [2:34, 35]; that of Daniel 'like a son of man,' coming with the clouds of heaven, to whom universal and everlasting dominion are given [7:13, 14]. The visions are parallel" (p. 881). Hence, it is not the prophecies that are different but their symbols and perspectives. Daniel and Nebuchadnezzar see the same prophetic motion picture but using different casts of actors and from different vantage points in the world theater. It's not the first time God has done this.

He inspired the Gospel writers to describe four perspectives of the one Christ: Matthew sees Jesus as the ruling Lion of the tribe of Judah; Mark, as the humble, laboring ox-servant of the Lord; Luke, as the perfect Son of Man; and John, as the soaring eagle of heaven, the divine Son of God. Thus four men give us four visions from four perspectives—with one central character and message. To this day, the Holy Spirit constantly gives teachers in the Church differing perspectives—different points of truth, Scripture references, historical examples, hypothetical life-illustrations, descriptive terminologies, and, hence, unique sermons on the same doctrines and moral lessons. Just as Jesus did in the beginning of this era, the Teacher (Holy Spirit) gives every one of His ministers pieces of bread and fish with which to feed the multitudes in His Church—but always different pieces.

See "How do you see the system?" chapter 2.

Lesson: *God often gives ministers differing perspectives on the same messages, moral lessons, or doctrines.*

7:1–28 The times of the Gentiles. The "times of the Gentiles," a phrase used only once in the entire Bible—and that by Jesus (Luke 21:24)—may be defined as:

> That period of human history in which God authorizes specific Gentile nations to rule the world, including in particular permission to overrule His chosen people (Jews), their land (Palestine), and their capital (Jerusalem).

Chronologically, this period began with the Babylonian captivity of Jerusalem (586 B.C.) and will not end until Armageddon, because only then will Jerusalem never again be "trodden down by the Gentiles" (Luke 21:24) or solely under Gentile control. In the early 1970s, I heard one teacher claim rather excitedly that the times of the Gentiles had been fulfilled in 1967, when Israeli armies retook the entire city of Jerusalem. This would have been true, were it not for one coming period of time in which Jerusalem will again be ruled by Gentiles: the latter half of the tribulation. (See Rev. 11:2.)

The Book of Daniel gives two prominent prophetic visions describing the times of the Gentiles in its entirety. In chapter 7, Daniel records his vision of this period. Like Nebuchadnezzar's earlier vision (chapter 2), Daniel's stretches all the way from the Babylonian captivity to the destruction of Antichrist's kingdom by Jesus and the inauguration of Christ's millennial kingdom. One later event Daniel alone describes is the great "white throne" judgment (Dan. 7:9–10), which occurs at the end of Christ's thousand-year reign. (See Rev. 20:11–15.)

See "The times of the Gentiles: the Gentile image / smiting Stone vision," chapter 2.

See Luke 21:24.

7:1–28 Daniel's apocalypse. Daniel's great vision contains similar content to that found in John's apocalypse (Rev. 4–19). As in the Book of Revelation, Daniel 7 has three types of passages. They are those revealing:

1. AN EARTHLY STORY, depicted partly in symbolic and partly in literal language

2. A HEAVENLY STORY, giving glimpses of simultaneous heavenly activity

3. PARENTHETIC INFORMATION, supplying information pertinent to one or both of the two ongoing stories (for example, vv. 9–10 are parenthetic, looking forward to the end of the vision; v. 11 then resumes the earthly story begun in v. 8)

In Daniel 7:13–14, Daniel describes the heavenly ceremony at which Jesus is invested with His full kingdom authority and glory, which is both worldwide and everlasting; Daniel's account is strikingly similar to John's (see Rev. 5:6–12).

See Revelation 4–5, heavenly; Revelation 13, earthly; Revelation 14:13, parenthetic.

Lesson: *Like the Book of Revelation, the Book of Daniel contains apocalyptic material; hence, some of its passages are similar in style and content to those found in Revelation.*

7:1 Put it in writing! Immediately after Daniel had his dream, "he wrote the dream" (Dan. 7:1). Why? There were several good reasons for his actions:

- This enabled him to not forget and thus lose the detailed information he received.

- By writing the vision, he could more easily focus on its essential meaning. In *Disciples Indeed,* the late Bible teacher Oswald Chambers taught, "It is by thinking with your pen in hand that you will get to the heart of your subject" (p. 50). Thus the more Daniel wrote out his vision, the more clearly he understood it.

- His writings became food for his soul. It preserved his revelation for later private contemplation. Whenever he felt weak, low, or heavy, he could reread the vision and feed and restore his soul.

- His writings became spiritual food for others. Surely he shared his inspiring revelations with his fellow Jewish exiles, who in turn published them in their synagogues.

- Once written, his vision became spiritual food for the ages. For twenty-five centuries now, countless Jews and Christians have feasted and grown strong in the faith by reading his scroll.

- His writings honored God. We show respect for people by respecting their words. By carefully recording all the words God spoke (or showed him), Daniel honored

God who spoke them. By inscribing rather than ignoring the vision, Daniel treasured it—and the God who
gave it.

As a diligent and wise hunter of truth, Daniel didn't let the
vision fall to the ground unheeded and unrecorded. Rather, he
counted his prophetic "prey" precious by immediately preserv-
ing it. (See Prov. 12:27.)

We should learn to do the same. We should record every
legitimate divine communication we receive, such as (in Dan. 7)
truly inspired dreams; meaningful life impressions; instructive
or corrective experiences; inspiring sermons, pieces, and anec-
dotes; and most especially sound biblical insights. Like Daniel's
writings, our notes will help us:

- Remember our revelations more accurately

- Focus on their essential meaning more clearly

- Preserve them as food for our souls and springboards
  for study

- Have spiritual resources to share with other believers

- Have spiritual truth to give to posterity—orally or in
  print

- Honor God, whose words and insights we treasure

See Revelation 1:11, 19; Proverbs 12:27; Habakkuk 2:2;
Luke 1:1–4; Exodus 17:14; 24:4; 34:27–28; Deuteronomy 17:18;
31:9, 24; Joshua 24:26.

*Lesson: Whenever God gives you meaningful spiritual
insights, write them down—for your benefit and
the benefit of others.*

7:2–3 About the great sea. When not used in association
with a specific body of water (the Sea of Galilee, etc.), but
rather in an allegorical, prophetic, or visionary context such as
Daniel 7, the word *sea* refers to the great unsaved populace
worldwide: the vast multinational, multiracial, multicultural
body of unredeemed humanity.

Incidentally, one of the four mysteries Solomon lists as being "too wonderful" for unspiritual people to understand is "the way of a ship in the midst of the sea" (Prov. 30:19). This is a symbolic representation of the Church (ship) sailing by God's gracious guidance through the vast, rough, and deadly perils (waters) of this present "sea," or worldwide body of unbelievers.

See Isaiah 60:5; Matthew 13:47; Luke 21:25; Revelation 13:1; Proverbs 30:19.

7:7c Ten horns. Horns are the most prominent (uppermost, highly visible) features of animals. So when horns are placed on the symbols for nations they symbolize prominent leaders, or heads of state. Ten of them mean simply ten prominent leaders, or heads of state.

These ten horns correspond to the ten toes of King Nebuchadnezzar's vision (Dan. 2:34, 41–44). Again, both visions agree. Nebuchadnezzar sees the final form of Gentile rule as having ten divisions or countries and by implication ten heads of state; Daniel sees ten heads of state, who by implication rule over ten divisions or countries of the kingdom.

See Revelation 17:12–14, 16–17; 13:1.

Lesson: In apocalyptic symbolism, "horns" often refer to prominent leaders, or heads of state.

7:9–14 A series of things to come. In these parenthetic verses Daniel notes briefly three important future events.

1. THE GREAT WHITE THRONE JUDGMENT that follows the end of the millennial kingdom of Christ (Dan. 7:9–10; Rev. 20:11–15).

2. The destruction of the beast (man and system) at ARMAGEDDON (Dan. 7:11–12; Rev. 19:11–20).

3. The HEAVENLY CORONATION of Jesus in which He is invested with His full millennial authority and glory (Dan. 7:13–14; Rev. 5:1–14).

7:15–16 The prophet's personal reaction. Here, as in other references, Daniel shares with us his personal reaction to his prophetic revelations. Rarely did his messages or interpretations bring glee or celebration. Heavy words, they often brought him temporary internal distress.

He was perplexed and troubled by King Nebuchadnezzar's dream (Dan. 4:19). He was "grieved" and "troubled" by this vision of the four beasts (Dan. 7:15–16) and temporarily lost his smile (Dan. 7:28). He was physically overwhelmed—rendered sick—by his vision of the "king of fierce countenance" and all the evil he would do to the Jews (Dan. 8:23, 27). And he was weakened and rendered unconscious by his vision of Christ (Dan. 10:8–9, 15–17). Why all this stress on the prophet?

His messages had great emotional impact. Succinctly, they revealed: Yes, God would faithfully preserve the Jews in their captivity and ultimately give them victory over all their enemies and oppressors, but not until they finished walking the long and arduous road called "the times of the Gentiles," in which they must suffer cruel defeats at the hands of the Romans, Syrians, and in the final days, Antichrist. The truth be told, it was not going to be easy for the chosen nation. Nor was such news, and such a prophetic burden, easy to bear for Daniel, who loved God's people greatly. When those we love greatly suffer, we suffer greatly. If a prophet's heart does not bleed for God's people, his calling is questionable. Clearly, Daniel was deeply moved by news of the Jews' sufferings.

See 1 Samuel 8:6; 16:1; Habakkuk 1:1; Matthew 23:37; Romans 9:1–3; Jeremiah 9:1–3; 15:17–18; Amos 3:13; Revelation 1:17.

Lesson: *Sometimes a minister's messages weigh heavy on*
his heart.

7:16 A man of truth. Puzzled, Daniel asked to know "the truth of all this," meaning the interpretation of the symbolic vision he had just beheld. Daniel was a man in perpetual pursuit of truth. Whether it was pleasing or distressing, predictable or surprising, Daniel always wanted the truth.

There seem to be among us today two kinds of Christians: those who always want to hear something pleasant, whether or not it's the truth, and those who always want to hear the truth, whether or not it's pleasing. Which type are we becoming: people who love and seek truth, or those who settle for soothing religious lies?

Correspondingly, there are two general types of ministers abroad today: those who always strain to tell their people something soft and easy, with little regard for its biblical accuracy, and those who draw near God's heart by prayerfully pouring over His Word and then "preach the Word" (2 Tim. 4:2)—the truth the Spirit is telling them—whether it pleases or displeases their people. Minister, are you a true or false prophet to the people?

See John 8:31–32; 14:21, 23; 17:17; 2 Timothy 4:2–4; Psalms 25:5; 43:3; 86:11; 119:30.

Lesson: We should aspire to be seekers, lovers, obeyers, and ministers of truth.

7:3,17,23 A key to understanding the beast symbol. Daniel 7 reveals that God uses "beasts" as a dual symbol, representing both Gentile world governments and their supreme leaders. Note that in vv. 3–7 the word "beast" clearly refers to Gentile governments, with their supreme leaders depicted either as heads or horns. Then in v. 17, the word "beasts" plainly applies not to any government but to its human leaders: "These great beasts...are four *kings*, who shall arise..." (emphasis added). Again in v. 23, "beast" refers solely to a government (the final Romanesque European federation): "Thus he said, The fourth beast shall be the fourth *kingdom* upon earth..." (emphasis added). So we see in some references "beast" refers to a Gentile kingdom, while in others it symbolizes the kingdom's human leader. Why is this?

Perhaps because *the cultural values, beliefs, and typical lifestyles of these Gentile kingdoms are embodied in the men that head them.* The man at the head of the government is all that the people are (or government is) in miniature, or conversely, all that he is inwardly is expressed outwardly in the spirit, laws, and actions of the government he heads. The Clinton presidency is a case in point. Bill and Hillary Clinton embodied the secular, amoral, anti-traditional, baby-boomer culture that arose in America during the 1960s and is now a disturbingly large part of this nation's electorate. Hence, they were very accurate symbols of the changing national character.

God hinted at this in His extraordinary dealings with King Nebuchadnezzar. God took the first ruler of the "beast" system and transformed him into a beast-like state (see "Do you want to be a beast?" chapter 4; also, "Pride—a transformer," chapter 5), thus indicating in the divine mind a full identification between the beast (Gentile) governments and their leaders. Since both are like "beasts" to Him (without awareness of, or communication and fellowship with Him; unspiritual, living only for fleshly appetites and temporal ends), God uses this designation for both.

This interpretive key helps greatly in understanding Revelation 13, which is arguably the single most important chapter in the Book of Revelation concerning Antichrist and his three-and-a-half-year government. There, as in Daniel 7, "beast" represents alternately both the system and the man that heads it. Consider these usages in Daniel 7: vv. 1–7, "beast" means system; vv. 11–12, leaders; v. 19, system; v. 17, leaders. Consider these usages in Revelation 13: vv. 1–3, "beast" means system; vv. 4–16, leaders (vv. 4–10, Antichrist; vv. 11–16, false prophet).

This dual usage of the term "beast" also explains why both the system and the man called "the beast" will be slain and revived. The Roman "beast" system of government, which was "slain" when western Rome fell in A.D. 496, will be revived in the coming Romanesque European federation. The individual "beast," Antichrist, will be assassinated and then supernaturally revived by satanic power.

Lesson: *In apocalyptic symbolism, "beast" represents both Gentile nations and their leaders.*

7:9,13,22 The "Ancient of days"—first and last mention. This divine name "Ancient of days" (Dan. 7:9, 13, 22) is used only in this chapter. Nowhere else in the Bible is God called by this title.

The first two references clearly refer to God the Father, the first describing Him as heaven's ultimate Judge and placing Him on its central throne (v. 9), and the second mentioning Him as distinct from another divine being, "the Son of man," clearly a reference to Jesus (v. 13). In the third reference (v. 22), the term Ancient of days just as clearly refers to Christ. Why? How can this divine name apply both to the Father and the Son? Because in Daniel 7:22 the Ancient of days visits the earth *in the person of His Son*, Jesus, to execute judgment on Antichrist at Armageddon, just as He did in the creation (see Heb. 1:1–2) and the incarnation (see Matt. 1:23).

Hence, this designation is rightly applied to God the Father, who at times works through the agency of His Son.

See Matthew 1:23; Hebrews 1:1–2; Revelation 19:11–16.

Lesson: *The Ancient of days is a poetic name for God the Father.*

7:19–27 The tribulation period foretold. The final portion of Daniel's dream describes certain features of the tribulation period.

- Antichrist, whose stare will be steely and intimidating, will be a very blatant blasphemer of God and His people (v. 20).

- Antichrist will arise just after ten other European heads of state come to power (v. 24).

- Antichrist will quickly subvert (politically or militarily) three heads of state and assume their dominion, then becoming the strongest king in the European federation (v. 24).

- By a swift and crushing military campaign (accompanied perhaps by deceptively peaceful rhetoric and diplomacy), Antichrist will subsequently attain dominion over the entire world (v. 23).

- Antichrist will militarily attack and defeat Israel (at the mid-point) and rule its people until God's appointed time of judgment (vv. 21–22).

- Antichrist's rule over Israel will be cruelly oppressive: He will openly denounce their God and Messiah; he will change all their (public) religious observances and practices; their hopes and spirits will be worn down by his unrelentingly cruel policies, until they reach the point of utter collapse (v. 25; see Dan. 12:7b).

- After three and a half years, God will intervene through the return of His Son to take Antichrist's dominion and give it to Israel; then Christ and overcoming Jews (and Gentiles, a fact not revealed to Daniel) will rule the world permanently (v. 27).

Missing from this vision's End-Time description are two details given later in Daniel's writings:

- Antichrist's rank self-idolization (Dan. 8:25; 9:27)

- Antichrist's incredible direct military attack upon Jesus and His armies (Dan. 8:25).

All of these prophetic details agree fully with John's revelation.

Though it certainly contained some troublesome material, this prophecy that, when all was said and done, the Israelites—"the people of the saints of the Most High"—would rule the world forever was most comforting news to a people and prophet who were presently captive to their enemies.

7:23–24 Kingdoms that have never died: Rome and Greece. Note this important fact: *Only once in this chapter/*

vision does Daniel foresee the end of the fourth beast, which symbolizes Roman domination, and that is clearly a reference to Armageddon (vv. 11–12). And at three points, he describes the first and last forms of Roman dominion as one:

1. In vv. 7–8, there is no clear break between the first appearance of the beast (early Roman Empire) and its ten horns and "little horn" (features of the final European federation).

2. In vv. 19–20, the same continuity appears: v. 19 describing early Rome and v. 20 its final form.

3. In vv. 23–24, the same fluidity is present: v. 23 describes early Rome; v. 24 continues the previous thought saying, "And…out of this kingdom" ten kings shall arise, then another (clearly the Antichrist, leader of the final Roman system).

Notice too the conjunction *and* is used to connect all three references, without any mention of the beast terminating. Hence, to the Spirit who inspired this vision (or from heaven's perspective), Roman domination of the world has never really ended, nor will it, until Armageddon. How can this be?

Here's the explanation. While Rome officially fell in the fifth century A.D., its *spirit* lives on to this day. Author T. R. Reid observed that when the Roman epic poet Horace mused on his life's work, comparing his quiet literary legacy to the louder achievements of Roman builders and soldiers, he noted:

> I have erected a monument more lasting than bronze
> And taller than the regal peak of the pyramids…
> *I shall never completely die.*

Reid then goes on to conclude:

> That famous epilogue from Horace's third book of Odes ["I shall never completely die"] has been endlessly quoted as a testament to the immortality of literature. But it could also stand as a tribute to the Roman Empire and the countless Roman influences that still

flow through our daily lives some 15 centuries after the
walls of Rome came tumbling down.

(National Geographic (Aug. 1997), p. 61)

In Western law, language (Latin), government (democracy),
and many other phases of our lives (architecture, engineering,
calendar year, literature, art, sport, leisure, city life, etc.), we
are still influenced, and so to some degree "ruled," by Roman
ways.

When drafting our democratic form of government, the
American Founding Fathers used the early Roman republic as a
model, incorporating many of its basic elements. For instance,
they decided to use the Roman bicameral system of lawmaking;
hence our Congress, with its House of Representatives (our ple-
beians) and Senate (our patricians), was created. To this and
other Roman ways, they added their own eighteenth-century
initiatives, such as the equal division of power between our
three branches of government. Yet even this was largely to prevent a president from "crossing the Rubicon" and becoming
another dictatorial Caesar—one Roman error they were determined to avoid—or tyrannical king, such as those that had troubled Europe for centuries. Indeed, in many ways the Roman
republic lives on in the republic of the United States.

Similarly, in chapter 8, Daniel foresees no complete end to
the Greek domination of the Gentile world. Observe that Daniel
8:22 speaks of the division of the Greek empire after
Alexander's death, then verse 23 continues the thought without
interruption, "in the latter time of *their* kingdom," as if the
extended Grecian kingdom ruled by Alexander's four generals
does not end until "transgressors are come to the full" and the
"king of fierce countenance" arises, which are two clear references to the End Times and Antichrist respectively. Notice also
that the two verses are verbally linked, again, by the use of the
conjunction *and*, which begins verse 23. Why is there no break
between these two verses, which overleap more than two thousand years in their fulfillments? Because, as with Rome, there is

a sense in which Greece still influences, and hence to some degree rules, the world to this day. How is this? Because Rome assimilated much of Greek culture into its own. *World Book Encyclopedia* contributor Donald Kagan summarizes:

> In spite of these setbacks [military defeats to the Romans], Greek civilization continued to spread. The Romans adopted Greek culture. Greek traditions lived on not only in Greece, but also in the writings of Roman orators and poets such as Cicero, Horace, and Virgil...
>
> (*World Book Encyclopedia*, 1980, p. 368)

The Greeks were the Gentile world's first great thinkers; the Romans, its first, and perhaps greatest, doers. Thus the Greeks originated and the Romans implemented. The Romans took Greek ideals and methods and, adding their own wisdom and ways, developed their republic-turned-empire and its government into an efficient world-ruling machine (or beast). Truly the Greek deposit into Romanesque life was extensive: literature, art, architecture, government (embryonic democracy), sport and physical fitness, religion (mythological gods), etc. The resulting mix of arts, ideas, beliefs, and practices became Greco-Roman culture—without which modern Western culture would be little more than an empty shell.

So the fourth beast is Rome politically, yet Greco-Roman culturally. And since neither chapter 7 nor 8 foretells a complete end to either Roman or Greece dominance before the End Times, they will continue—as they do to this day—to influence (and so rule) the political and ideological ways of this Western-dominated Gentile world system. From the heavenly perspective, therefore, Greco-Roman ideals and ways are still very much alive...and will continue until Antichrist emerges from a final European ten-nation federation espousing Greco-Roman ways (see Dan. 7:7–8, 19–20, 23–24; 8:21–23). (Perhaps this helps explain why Russian communism, whose culture was heavily Marxist and *not* Greco-Roman, failed to achieve the world domination it so earnestly sought.)

King Nebuchadnezzar's dream (Dan. 2:31–45) agrees with this in that it, too, foresees no end of the Gentile system's fourth kingdom, Rome, until it assumes the form of ten toes, a clear reference to the Romanesque federation of the End Times. Only in this form—and hence not before—is it totally and finally destroyed. What does this imply? The *spirit* of Roman government will continue until Armageddon.

Summing up, while the *visible and direct political dominion* of both Greece and Rome terminated many centuries ago, their *spiritual influence* on Western Gentile culture and government has never died. (Admittedly, Greco-Roman influence has been almost exclusively a Western phenomenon; it has *not* dominated the East. The Middle East, India, Asia, and the vast Pacific, with the exception of Australia and New Zealand, have cultures entirely their own.) It has continued to this day and will continue to underlie and pervade this world until the one-world government of Antichrist manifests...and is shortly thereafter destroyed by Jesus' return to earth (Dan. 7:22, 26–27).

Lesson: While as visible political entities the Greek and Roman kingdoms fell long ago, they live on in Western life and government through the continuing influence of Greco-Roman culture.

7:14,22,25,27 Given from above. Four times in this chapter Daniel refers to either authority to rule or authority for military victory being "given" from heaven.

- In Daniel 7:14, Christ is "given" authority to rule the earth forever.

- In Daniel 7:25, Antichrist is "given" military and political authority over the Jews—but only for an appointed time of three and a half years (see Rev. 13:5, 7).

- In Daniel 7:22, the Jews are "given" judgment (upon Antichrist) and authority to rule the earth under Christ.

- In Daniel 7:27, again, the Jews are "given" authority to rule the earth under Christ.

This is in perfect accord with God's great revelation to King Nebuchadnezzar, that "the heavens do rule" (Dan. 4:26) and that therefore God "gives" power to rule politically or to prevail militarily to whomsoever He pleases (see various uses of "give" in 4:17, 25, 32; also Dan. 8:12–13).

That God sometimes gives power or victory to tyrants and wicked nations reveals that such conferences are not tokens of His approval (see Dan. 4:17). Rather, whenever God gives authority or victory, it is always to serve His sovereign purposes: to chasten or test His people and thus further His work in them for their eternal blessing and His eternal glory.

See Daniel 4:17, 25–26, 32; 7:14, 22, 25, 27; 8:12–13; Revelation 13:5, 7; Job 1:12; 2:6; John 3:27; Proverbs 21:31. *The New Scofield Reference Bible* notes that seven times Jesus speaks of Christians as being "given" to Him by the Father; see John 17:2, 6 (twice), 9, 11, 12, 24.

Lesson: Kings and nations cannot rule, nor can armies be victorious, unless God gives His permission. Such permission is granted only to serve God's eternal purposes.

7:21–27 The saints' ultimate test: the triumphing of the wicked. The tribulation period, as described in these verses, will be the Jewish saints' ultimate test of loyalty, faith, and endurance. Figuratively, their struggle with Antichrist portrays a message to Christians: the nature of our ultimate tests. In such trials, God lets us experience adversities similar to those the Jews will face in the tribulation. Here is how our ultimate tests unfold.

The spirit of Antichrist in sinners and apostate Christians moves them to attack spiritual Christians, or make "war with the saints" (Dan. 7:21); an all-out conflict of wills ensues. Incensed by our uncompromising practice of biblical principles and ways, they oppose and accuse us without cause; so they "speak great words" (v. 25) against us, our faith, and our God. To our utter surprise, God gives *them*, not us, the victory in our power struggle; and they "prevailed against them" (v. 21).

Using their newly won authority, they oppress us with burdensome injustices. As time passes, we become weary, or exhausted, through prolonged oppression: "and shall wear out the saints of the Most High" (v. 25). Surprisingly, God defers His judgment of our adversaries; thus our loyalty to Him, faith, importunity in prayer, and endurance are severely tested. (See Luke 18:1–8.) By their relentless "war" our enemies hope to change us and end our previously effective testimony. They bring unyielding pressure to bear to force us to abandon our uncompromising compliance with God's law (Word) and our regular times of worship; thus they try to "change the times and the laws" (Dan. 7:25).

But in His great faithfulness God allows this to continue only until His appointed time of judgment: "until a time and times and the dividing of time" (v. 25). Then He intervenes in power to judge our oppressors and deliver us: "But the judgment shall sit; and they shall take away his dominion..." (v. 26). At long last, our ultimate test ends and our ultimate triumph ensues: To our delight God reverses the triumphing of the wicked by giving us, His proven servants, the very authority He has stripped from our enemies: "And the kingdom and dominion...shall be given to the people of the saints of the Most High..." (v. 27). So in the end we prevail—and our enemies fail in their quest to end our faith and testimony.

See Luke 18:1–8; 22:53b; Job 20:4–5; Psalms 13:2; 37:7–9, 35–36; 66:8–12; Revelation 13:10c.

Lesson: *The triumphing of the wicked—when God permits evildoers to temporarily defeat us—is the ultimate test of our loyalty, faith, and endurance.*

CHAPTER EIGHT

ON ANTIOCHUS IV AND ANTICHRIST

8:1–26 THE RAM, THE HE-GOAT, AND THE LITTLE HORN: OLD VISION, NEW SYMBOLS, NEW TWIST. In this, Daniel's second vision of the coming Gentile world powers (see Dan. 7:1–14), and his book's third (see Dan. 2:31–35), Daniel relates an old message with new symbols and a new twist.

The Medo-Persian kingdom, here represented by a two-horned ram, will succeed the Babylonian (Dan. 8:1–4). Daniel's location, beside the Ulai canal in Shushan (Susa), the capital of Persia, helps him identify Persia as the ram, for in his vision the ram also stands beside the Ulai canal (see vv. 2–3). His observation that "the higher [horn] came up last," reveals that the Medes would dominate first, then the Persians, who would be greater in power and stature. After this he sees that the Medo-Persian kingdom will be succeeded by the Greeks represented as a buck goat with one large horn (Alexander the Great; see vv. 5–8). Thus far, Daniel's second vision has related old information, albeit with new symbols. Twice previously he informed us that the Greeks will supercede the Medo-Persian kingdom.

So he added some new information: After Alexander's conquest, Alexander will suddenly die in his prime and be succeeded by his four generals (v. 8). Of this division *The Ryrie Study Bible* says, "Cassender took Macedonia; Lysimachus, Thrace and much of Asia Minor; Seleucus, Syria; and Ptolemy, Egypt" (p. 1323). Through these generals and their successors, Greek rule will continue until the Romans gradually assimilate their power.

Then Daniel revealed a new twist in this old prophecy—two coming blasphemers. First, he described the second-century B.C. Syrian ruler, Antiochus IV (called Epiphanes; see vv. 9–14); second, the Antichrist, the "king of fierce countenance" (vv. 23–25) who appears in "the time of the end" (v. 17). It is an intriguing but ominous twist.

8:9–14,23–25 On Antiochus IV and Antichrist. Daniel 8 introduces the reader to King Antiochus IV (Epiphanes) of Syria, who ruled from 175 to 163 B.C. and also gives additional information concerning the Antichrist. Specifically, Antiochus IV is described in verses 9–14 (which also give distinct foreshadowings of Antichrist), while Antichrist alone is foreseen in verses 23–25. First, exactly who is King Antiochus IV?

King Antiochus IV (Dan. 8:9–14)

King Antiochus IV, or Epiphanes, was the eighth ruler of the Seleucid dynasty in Syria (175–163 B.C.). Antioch, the capital of the Seleucid rulers, was named for Antiochus IV's forebear, Antiochus I. The name *Antiochus* means "withstander," which is very fitting seeing Antiochus IV doggedly withstood God's will among the Jews. That Antiochus IV named himself *Epiphanes*, meaning "God is manifest," clearly indicates that he held himself to be divine. (He actually authorized the minting of a coin inscribed with his image and the caption, "King Antiochus... God made visible.")

Antiochus' wicked life's work lay in his diabolical passion to Hellenize the Jews, or force them to abandon their Hebrew faith, religion, and culture and adopt the beliefs, values, and practices of the Greeks. Not long after he came to power in Syria, Antiochus instituted a fervent anti-Judaism campaign in Israel, which was then under Syrian control. He passed laws forbidding observance of the Jewish law, including circumcision, prayer, observance of the Sabbath rest, and all other forms of Jewish worship. He destroyed all the copies of the Old Testament scriptures (Torah) he could obtain (apparently prompting godly Jews to hide the sacred scrolls, some of which may have been among the Dead Sea Scrolls discovered in 1947).

Some Jews, including the corrupt high priest Jason, succumbed to Hellenization and utterly abandoned their faith. Others, including the Hasmoneans (or Maccabees) and the Hasidim (the pious) resisted, refusing to worship Greek gods. Those who were caught by Syrian authorities were summarily killed.

Later, in 168 B.C., Antiochus entered Jerusalem, plundered the temple and defiled it by offering a pig on the altar to Zeus (the chief Greek deity) that he had built. (It was this blasphemous act that, along with the prevailing tyrannical oppression, sparked the priest Mattathias's resistance and the subsequent Maccabean revolt.)

Summarizing, Antiochus IV dedicated himself to the task of systematically exterminating the Jewish faith, or as one source stated, he tried his best to "extirpate Judaism."

Antiochus IV's reign of terror is briefly described in Daniel 8:9–14:

- Verse 9: He is a "little horn," yet not that described in chapter 7, because he arises from one of the four horns of the post-Alexander Grecian kingdom, not from the ten-nation federation of the End Times (see Dan. 7:7–8, 24). After coming to power, his influence grows, most notably in Palestine, "the pleasant land."

- Verse 10: Ever the aggrandizer, he grew as great as a god (heavenly being) in his own estimation, then trampled upon everything truly divine and holy, in particular the "host" and "stars" of heaven—the Jewish saints and their priests.

- Verse 11: He even defied God Himself by entering, plundering, and desecrating His holy temple and by halting the daily sacrifices God commanded; thus he left God's holy sanctuary "cast down"—dishonored, defiled, and desolate.

- Verse 12: Because of the Jews' prevailing sins (including eagerly forsaking Judaism and embracing Greek idolatry and ways), the Jewish "host" and their temple were "given" into Antiochus IV's power for an appointed time, and "the truth"—God's truth and true religion—lay slain in the dust, lifeless, while evil prospered by divine permission.

- Verses 13–14: The period of desolation, beginning with Antiochus IV's oppressive Hellenization policy and lasting throughout the temple desecration (the "transgression of desolation," or the altar to Zeus), was twenty-three hundred days, or six years and three and a half months (171–165 B.C.). (The desecration of the temple and the subsequent Maccabean revolt lasted exactly three years: 168–165 B.C.)

- Verse 14b: The sanctuary was "cleansed" when the Maccabees retook, restored, and rededicated the temple in December 165 B.C. This joyous liberation of the temple and re-genesis of God's prescribed way of worship is commemorated in the Feast of Lights, or Hanukkah (meaning "dedication" in Hebrew). So God and His people prevailed over the withstander.

By all these wicked deeds—exalting himself as a god; hating and attacking God's people and their faith; desecrating God's temple; making idolatry the state religion (thus changing the Jews' times and laws, Dan. 7:25); defeating God's people and cruelly oppressing them (Dan. 8:10, 12) and hence defying God's will for His people, temple, and worship (v. 11)—Antiochus IV proved himself a strong type of the coming Antichrist. In all these ways he foreshadowed the final man of sin.

See "The Syrian and Egyptian wars, King Antiochus IV, and Antichrist," chapter 11.

The Antichrist (Dan. 8:23–25)

The second sinister figure described in Daniel 8 is none other than the Antichrist. While he and Antiochus IV share the same anti-God, anti-Jewish spirit and perform very similar missions—to overthrow the rule, religion, and people of God to establish the rule, religion, and people of Satan—Daniel 8:23–25 contains language that applies solely to Antichrist.

- Verse 23: This king "stands up" (rising to worldly prominence and defiance of God), not to succeed one of the four horns (kings) who ruled Alexander the Great's empire (see vv. 8–9) but to rule "in the latter time of their kingdom." This refers to the terminal period of the times of the Gentiles when the *spirit* of the Greco-Roman kingdom (see "Kingdoms that have never died," chapter 7) pervades the revived fourth beast and "the transgressors are come to the full"—sin worldwide has reached its outrageous and final heights. Though Jewish apostasy was significant when Antiochus IV came to power, the *world's* sin was not yet "full," nor had the "latter time" yet been reached. Also, this verse describes a "king of fierce countenance" ["hard-faced" (*The Modern Language Bible*); "stern-faced" (New International Version)]; in another reference Daniel describes Antichrist as having a cold, demonic (Hitler-like) glare (see Dan. 7:20). History does not specify that Antiochus IV had a "fierce countenance."

- Verse 24: This king is satanically empowered: "mighty, but not by his own power"; Antichrist alone will have full and direct satanic empowerment. (See Rev. 13:4a; 2 Thess. 2:9.) This king shall "destroy wonderfully," or enjoy astonishing military success. While this is unquestionably true of Antichrist (see Rev. 6:2; 13:4b), Antiochus IV was neither an outstanding strategist nor a renowned conqueror. This great conqueror will first defeat the Jewish people, then oppress them for a season; many references attribute this to Antichrist. (See Dan. 7:21, 25; 9:27; Rev. 13:7.)

- Verse 25: A skilled deceiver, this king will conquer ("destroy") many people (including, but not limited to,

Jews) by his deceptive policies (surely a reference to his seven-year peace agreement with Israel and other nations, which he signs insincerely; Dan. 9:27; see John 5:43). He will be excessively vain, a reference to Antichrist's blatant self-deification. (See 2 Thess. 2:3–4.) He will challenge the Prince of princes (Messiah Jesus) to a military confrontation (at Armageddon; Rev. 19:19), at which battle he will be "broken without hand," or killed by a direct divine act. (Daniel 2 reveals it is the "stone...cut out without hands," or Jesus Christ, that smites the final form of the Gentile image and its final leader; Dan. 2:34; 2 Thess. 2:8; Rev. 19:11–16.) While Antiochus IV indeed "withstood" God's will, even he did not challenge God personally on the field of battle, nor was he killed by an indisputably divine act. (Antiochus died from an intestinal disease.) These facts will find complete fulfillment only in the Antichrist.

8:15–19 A vision for two End Times. Repeatedly Daniel 8 reveals that this vision describes Israel's End Times and is not intended for her immediate future. When Daniel earnestly "sought for the meaning" (Dan. 8:15) of this vision of the ram, the rough goat, and the little horn, he overheard God order the angel Gabriel to explain the whole matter for him (v. 16). Here is Gabriel's infallible interpretation:

- Gabriel pointedly says the vision is for "the time of the end": "Understand, O son of man; for at the time of the end shall be the vision" (v. 17).

- Again, he specifies that it is for "the [time of the] last end of the indignation" (v. 19).

- He places the rise of the "king of fierce countenance" as being "in the latter time of their kingdom" (v. 23), a reference not to the latter period of the reign of Alexander's successors but to the End-Time and final form of the beast system, which will be a continuation of the *spirit* of Greco-Roman culture (see note above).

- He orders Daniel to "shut thou up the vision," then adds, "for it shall be for many days" (v. 26). Thus this vision is *sealed* until the "distant future" (v. 26, AMP). This proves that it was not given for immediate fulfillment.

These statements made by God's handpicked interpreter are definitive and irrefutable. It is unthinkable that Gabriel's repeated clear references to the End Times mean anything other or less than they declare. But just what did He mean by "the time of the end" (v. 17)?

The New Scofield Study Bible describes two separate times of the end:

> Two "ends" seem to be in view here: (1) historically, the end of the third empire (Grecian) of Alexander, out of one of the divisions of which (Syria) the 'little horn' of v. 9 (Antiochus Epiphanes) arose; and (2) prophetically, the end of "the times of the Gentiles"—Daniel's final time of the end (see Dan. 12:4). (p. 911)

Accordingly, Antiochus IV (Epiphanes) arose during the first "time of the end" as described by Scofield above (see Dan. 8:9–14), nearly four hundred years, or "many days," after Daniel's vision-prophecy. And Antichrist will arise in the extreme "distant future"—the tribulation period, or last days of the fourth and final beast system (see Dan. 8:23–25).

8:13 First mention—the abomination of desolation. This is the first mention of an abomination of desolation (here rendered "transgression of desolation") in the Bible. It is also the first of five references to the desolation of the Jewish temple in the Book of Daniel. (See Dan. 9:17, 27; 11:31; 12:11.) Other references in Daniel's writing speak of the desolation of the Jews' land and of their capital city, Jerusalem (Dan. 9:18, 26). The most well-known reference to this perhaps is Christ's prophecy of the desolation of the yet-to-be-constructed temple of the tribulation period, in which He described "the abomination of desolation, spoken of by Daniel the prophet" (Matt. 24:15).

In every instance of an "abomination of desolation" in the temple three things occur:

1. The worship of God ceases.

2. The worship of an idol (idolatrous object or person) ensues.

3. The Spirit of God, grieved, departs.

Before and during the Babylonian captivity, the idol was not one but a whole host of heathen idols whom the backslidden Israelites worshiped in Solomon's temple. In the time of Antiochus IV (Epiphanes), the idol was an altar to the chief Greek god, Zeus, which Antiochus erected in the reconstructed (Zerubbabel's) temple. In Antichrist's heyday, the idol will be an image of himself placed in the temple of the tribulation period, which his assistant, the false prophet, will supernaturally animate through satanic power. (See Rev. 13:11–15.)

Why does the Spirit refer to these idols in the temple as "abomination[s] of desolation"? Because in each case, the presence of a heathen idol displaced the presence of the holy God, leaving the holy place spiritually desolate. God will not share His glory or worship with any entity (1 Cor. 1:29, 31). Hence, when we give worshipful adoration to anything or anyone else, that idol, whether material or immaterial, present or merely desired, is an abomination to God and so causes Him to withdraw His presence, leaving us desolate, or without the presence of God. Because the abomination is what causes the desolation, it is called an "abomination of [that causes] desolation." So it is when the Christian allows any sin to rest in his or her heart (inner temple).

Any sin resting in our hearts renders our personal temple desolate, or void of the peaceful, powerful presence of God. Why? Because wherever sin is, God is not; wherever sin rests, God departs. Because God is holy, whenever sin departs (through confession of sin and repentance), God can enter our hearts by faith. Conversely, when sin reenters our hearts, God departs, just as He removed His glory from Israel's tabernacle (see 1 Sam. 4:21) and later from its temple (see Ezek. 10:1–22). Amid life's many uncertainties, one fact remains rock-solid:

God will never coexist with sin—in your temple, or mine, or Israel's. This is why He withdrew from Eden in the beginning; Adam's sin was the "abomination" that caused Eden's desolation. (See Gen. 3:23–24.)

Who or what is enthroned as the true Lord of your bodily temple, the Christ or the (an) abomination?

See 1 Samuel 4:21; Ezekiel 10:4, 19; 11:23; Genesis 3:23–24; Hosea 5:6, 15; Deuteronomy 31:16–18; Matthew 23:37–39.

Lesson: Sin is an abomination to God that renders our hearts desolate, or void of His peaceful, powerful presence.

8:9 Have you ever considered this little horn? Thus far in our study of the Book of Daniel, we've considered two "little horn[s]": King Antiochus IV (Epiphanes) (Dan. 8:9–14) and the coming Antichrist (Dan. 7:8, 20–27). There is one more little horn we must consider: the little horn in us. If we walk in the pride and self-will of our old nature (the spirit of the little horn), we become near fulfillments of the final little horn prophecy. Consider these parallels between the final man of sin and the man of sin in us.

Every Christian has a "man of sin" (God-hating rebel) in his or her heart—the old sin nature. Though the power of the Spirit mortifies this man of sin as we believe and obey, something terrible happens if we rebel anew against God's revealed will: Our man of sin revives and reveals himself. Why? Because by our rebellion (the spirit of Antichrist), we have defied God's rule in our life and enthroned a new god, our self-will. This inner uprising quenches all true worship of God in our hearts and renders our bodily temples increasingly more desolate. Daily the Holy Spirit, whose life-flow we have quenched (1 Thess. 5:19), grieves over us (see Eph. 4:30) until He is finally forced to depart, leaving our inner sanctum empty.

Soon our new master (Satan, the inspirer and ruler of every

man of sin; see Rom. 6:16) moves and uses us precisely as he will yet use Antichrist. Incensed with God, we begin to oppose (make war) and oppress submissive "remnant" Christians who remain true to God's Word and ways.

Consequently, God warns us to repent. If we don't respond, He begins sending chastisements (plagues) upon us, and we experience a time of needless distress, sorrow, and loss (tribulation period). If we still refuse to surrender to God's good will and stop oppressing His remnant, one day He sends terminal judgment (a personal Armageddon). And the little horn in us is no more.

Lesson: Every Christian who rebels against God's will becomes a little Antichrist and, barring repentance, follows the tragic pattern of the little horn to come.

8:15 Seeking to understand the vision. Daniel was an unrelenting seeker of spiritual understanding. When the meaning of the vision God gave him remained obscure, Daniel could have resigned himself. God didn't give him the light, so he would just acquiesce in the darkness. But Daniel refused to settle for ignorance. Instead he went to prayer, beseeching God to remove the veil of obscurity: "I, Daniel…sought for the meaning" (Dan. 8:15). Then He waited patiently in God's presence, meditating on the vision and expecting understanding from above. And according to his faith, so God dealt with him, sending the angel Gabriel with a precise interpretation: "And I heard a man's voice…who called, and said, Gabriel, make this man to understand the vision" (v. 16). Thus, in the end, Daniel fully understood the vision.

This wasn't the only time Daniel set himself to understand revelations he considered vital to himself and his people (see Dan. 9:2–3; 10:1–3), nor was it the only time God responded to such requests. In the Book of Daniel, three times God sent angels to give special interpretations to Daniel concerning very perplexing issues, scriptures, or visions. Always they were sent in response to Daniel's earnest prayers for understanding. (See

Dan. 8:16–19; 9:21–23; 10:10–14, 21.) In these instances, Daniel's example challenges us.

We must not accept a lack of biblical understanding. Rather, we should earnestly seek the meaning of our vision—the biblical book, passage, or doctrine that puzzles us. In these last days it is especially imperative that we understand the vision of God's End-Time plan as He reveals it in the Books of Revelation, Daniel, the four Gospels, and the Epistles, especially 1 and 2 Thessalonians. If we set ourselves to "seek for the meaning," God will respond to us just as He did to Daniel. If we wait patiently and prayerfully before Him, He will send us whatever "angels" we need—teachers, mentors, tapes, books, tracts, magazines, more of His Holy Spirit, who is *the* Teacher, or literal angels—to give us the light that explains the obscure passage we're studying or makes the pieces of the jigsaw puzzle of End-Time prophecy suddenly fit together. Thus, in the end, we too fully understand the vision.

At least two factors may affect this. First, sin (any disobedience to God's revealed will) will effectively block us from receiving understanding from God, even if we fervently pray for it. Second, we need time to grow in obedience before God will grant us full understanding of the deeper truths of the Bible. Hence we should seek biblical understanding, not only with determination but with patient persistence. What God hides from us today He will disclose tomorrow, if we but continue walking with Him today.

Every time we study or read spiritual subject matter, we should ask the Lord to give us full understanding of the Bible passages and reference materials we study. Jesus promised blessings to those who ask, seek, and knock (Luke 11:9–10). King Solomon taught we would receive wisdom and knowledge, but only if we cried out for them (Prov. 2:3–6). And James plainly rebukes us for forgetting to ask: "Ye have not, because ye ask not" (James 4:2). So don't fret over your "vision"; seek to understand it. Ask God for clear understanding today.

See John 16:13; 2 Corinthians 12:8; 2 Timothy 2:7;

Proverbs 2:3–6, 11; James 4:2c; Ezra 7:10 (AMP); Matthew 17:10–13.

Lesson: *If we patiently seek to understand the Bible's reve-*
lations, especially its vision of the End Times, God
will faithfully give us the proper interpretation.

8:16 Introducing Gabriel: a first mention. This is the first mention of the angel Gabriel in the Book of Daniel and one of only four references to him by name in the entire Bible. (See Dan. 9:21; Luke 1:19, 26.)

That Gabriel stands in God's immediate presence (see Luke 1:19) and was given such important messages as Daniel's End-Time revelations (see Dan. 8:16; 9:21) and the Annunciation (news of Jesus' miraculous conception; see Luke 1:26) suggests that he is an archangel, though only Michael is explicitly assigned that status. (See Jude 9; Dan. 10:13; 12:1.)

8:9–14,23–26 The Spirit lifts up a standard. Not long after Antiochus IV desecrated the temple in Jerusalem, he sent a representative to the nearby Jewish village of Modin and ordered the priest Mattathias to offer sacrifice to a Greek god. Mattathias, a godly Jew, immediately refused. An apostate Jew then stepped forward to offer the sacrifice. Horrified and enraged by the idolatry, Mattathias killed the unfaithful Jew (and by some accounts, the Syrian representative also) and then fled to the Judean hills with his five sons. Other Jewish zealots (including the Hasidim) rallied to their side, and soon a full-scale rebellion was launched. Led first by Mattathias and later by his son Judah Maccabee (the "Hammer"), the Jews' guerilla warfare tactics won them several impressive victories over the Syrian armies. After three years of fighting, the Maccabees finally prevailed. In December 165 B.C., they retook Jerusalem and cleansed and rededicated the temple. The Maccabees, and other Jewish leaders, maintained control of Jerusalem and Palestine for most of the next one hundred years. (Rome conquered Palestine in 64 B.C.) Thus the flood of persecution was halted. Observe God's line of action in this crisis.

When Satan sent his agent to desecrate God's temple in Jerusalem, God did not sit by idly. Rather, He answered immediately by raising up a standard against the enemy in Modin—the bold resistance of the Maccabees. Thus, when the enemy came in "like a flood [suddenly, overwhelmingly]," God, ever prepared, "lift[ed] up a standard [rallying point] against him" (Isa. 59:19). And in time God's servants prevailed against the powerful satanic intrusion. (Incidentally, this was a preview of the Great Tribulation to come; see Dan. 7:21–27.)

God always takes this line. Whenever the enemy suddenly overwhelms God's faithful ones, God always sends a fresh outpouring of His Spirit to inspire and empower holy overcomers, who then raise a standard around which other believers gather and gain strength, and ultimately they prevail over their persecutors.

God has repeatedly done this throughout Israel's history. When Satan assaulted Israel through Pharaoh, God raised Moses and Aaron for Israel's defense. When Satan raised up Ahab and Jezebel, God countered their work through Elijah, Elisha and Micaiah. When Satan raised the carnal, cold Pharisees and Sadducees, God responded by raising John the Baptist and Jesus of Nazareth.

God has also done this in secular history, whenever such was necessary to help His people. For instance, when Satan sent Hitler to exterminate the Jewish race, God raised up Churchill and Eisenhower, whose joint leadership helped the Allies prevail over the Nazi menace. This victory both ensured the continuance of Christianity and the culmination of Zionism in the long-awaited reestablishment of a Jewish state in Palestine. (Note Antiochus' attack was against the Jewish *faith*, while the attempted genocides of Haman and Hitler were aimed at the more fundamental target of eliminating the Jewish *people*.)

When the enemy comes in on us like a "flood"—suddenly, viciously, overwhelmingly—do we have the faith to expect the Spirit to help us? If so, we too will prevail over every assault.

See Isaiah 59:19; Acts 12:1–11; Psalm 46:10.

Lesson: *Whenever Satan viciously attacks God's people*
or their faith, God always raises up a standard of
righteous resistance—His holy, bold servants—
whose leadership invariably causes His people to
ultimately prevail.

8:9–14,23–26 A pattern of preemptive persecution. Notice
the close proximity of Antiochus IV's "mission" to the first coming of Jesus and the pattern it presents us with—namely, of
fierce satanic opposition just before Jesus comes to bless His
people. Why? Satan was trying to preempt the coming of
Messiah and the blessing of the Jews. How could Jesus come and
bless His people if their faith, worship, and separated way of life
were destroyed?

The same thing will occur in the tribulation. Satan will
arise then through the Antichrist in a bold attempt to seize control of Jerusalem, and especially the Jewish temple, just before
Jesus' second and most glorious advent.

This pattern of spiritual action suggests that *Satan always*
persecutes God's people just before Jesus comes to bless them.
For instance, in World War II, Hitler's mad quest to exterminate
the Jews occurred just before God fully regathered them to their
ancient homeland (through the Zionist movement). Why did
the Holocaust occur at that time? To thwart the Jews' conversion to faith in Christ en masse, set to occur in Palestine just
after the Rapture of the Church (see Rom. 11:25–26). If the
Jewish race had been eliminated by Hitler's genocide sixty years
ago, how could "all Israel be saved" in the coming time, as
prophesied?

Do we understand this pattern of preemptive persecution?
If so, it shouldn't surprise us when Satan persecutes or troubles
us just before Jesus visits us with significant blessings and fulfillments of His promises. Instead, the next time we get flattened
by a surprisingly sudden wave of trouble, we should immediately look up with expectancy. Our blessing is riding the crest of
the next wave!

See "Be prepared: the preemptor will visit you," chapter 6. See Acts 11:29–12:1.

Lesson: Satan often attacks us with persecution or tribulation just before Jesus visits us with blessings or fulfillments of His promises.

8:26 Seal up the vision? God gave Daniel an amazing heavenly vision concerning His people's future; then God through His angel commanded Daniel, "Shut thou up the vision" (Dan. 8:26). *The Modern Language Bible* notes, "Daniel must for the present keep it a secret" (p. 884). How baffling! Why would God command him to hide his prophetic light under a bushel? Because the time for these truths to be known had not yet come, nor would it for "many days" (v. 26).

This points up one of God's rarer ways. Just as He gives gifted persons their spiritual gifts for specific times and seasons, so God gives truths for specific seasons of need. God gives spiritual meat, but always "in due season" (Ps. 145:15). It must have been frustrating to Daniel—surely it was a trial of patience—for God to defer the delivery, understanding, and hence reception of such a powerful and direct heavenly message. But as always, Daniel was obedient (Dan. 8:27). Are we willing to follow his footsteps in this, too?

After waiting on God to give us "tidings" (see 2 Sam. 18:19–22) for our generation, are we further willing to wait until the season of our message arrives? He may not require this but command instead, "Seal *not* the |words| of the prophecy..." (Rev. 22:10, emphasis added). But what if He should ask us to await the right moment to speak the truths He has laid upon our hearts? Are we willing to obey? Jesus prophesied He would give us wonderful truths in the darkness of private study meant to be spoken in the light of public address. (See Matt. 10:27.) God gave both Elijah and John the Baptist burning messages of reform that they could not release until the day of their showing unto Israel (God's appointed time of reformation; see

1 Kings 17:1–18:1; Luke 1:80). He kept Paul waiting a decade to share his revelations about the new thing God would do in the Christian era—that is, of two separate peoples (Jew and Gentile) forming one new body of believers worldwide! If He also seals up our vision, let us patiently await the dawn of the day for which our message has been given—and by our brook Cherith or in our Judean wilderness abide and worship and glean still more truths for the day of our showing.

Sometimes the hindrance is not the season but the state of God's people. Immature believers simply can't grasp the deeper truths of the faith. Consequently, the servant of the Lord must follow the example of Jesus, who always spoke His parables to the multitudes "as they were able to hear [understand or comprehend]" them (Mark 4:33), and of the apostle Paul, who obediently withheld his full "vision" from the Corinthian Christians due to their persisting carnality (see 1 Cor. 3:1–3).

See Ecclesiastes 3:1; Psalm 145:15; Proverbs 15:23; Matthew 10:27; Isaiah 50:4; 1 Kings 17:1–16; 18:1; Luke 3:1–3; contrast Revelation 22:10.

Lesson: *God gives truths for specific seasons of need. Hence we should endeavor to minister them always "in season."*

8:27 Overwhelmed and lonely. So astonishing and moving was the content of this vision that Daniel was overwhelmed. His emotional tranquility and physical equilibrium were disturbed, and his work was halted for "certain days" (Dan. 8:27) by an undisclosed illness. Afterward, he seems to have been smitten with the loneliness of exceptional spiritual vision: ". . . but none understood it" (v. 27c).

As wondrous as it is to see deep spiritual truths and foresee important future events, as Daniel did, it is also a very lonely way. Sometimes others simply can't see what you see so clearly: "And I, Daniel, alone saw the vision; for the men that were with me saw not the vision..." (Dan. 10:7). At other times they see but refuse to admit the validity of your message and embrace it. Hence they sometimes doubt, criticize, stay away—or mock. And the minister is left to abide as Daniel did: chosen, inspired, but lonely.

Every aspiring or ordained minister longs daily for the thrill of hearing from and speaking for God. But are we also willing to bear occasional crosses of loneliness? Daniel accepted such periods of loneliness as part of his high and holy calling. Ever spiritually minded, the apostle Paul saw his distresses for Christ's sake as divine opportunities to increase his personal spiritual strength and the effectiveness of his ministry (see 2 Cor. 12:9–10). Do we have eyes to see what Paul saw, namely that every cross we accept imparts more resurrection power?

See "The prophet's personal reaction," chapter 7.

See 1 Kings 17:3–6; 19:4–5; 2 Chronicles 18:7, 26.

Lesson: Sometimes ministers with exceptional spiritual insight are overwhelmed and lonely for days on end. But accepting the cross of loneliness brings more of the power of Christ upon us.

CHAPTER NINE

A MODEL PRAYER—
AND ISRAEL'S
"SEVENTY WEEKS"

9:1–2 THE TIME OF EXILE. Daniel learned the exact time of
Israel's exile by studying the writings of Jeremiah (Dan. 9:1–2),
in which God declared that the land of Israel would be "a desolation" and the Jews would "serve the king of Babylon for seventy years." (Jer. 25:11). Furthermore, they would serve King
Nebuchadnezzar, not in their own homeland but in his (Jer.
29:10–11). This prophecy was fulfilled in two separate ways.

First, the *land* was desolate (and God's people captive) seventy years. The first deportation occurred in 605 B.C. (the second and third deportations following in 597 and 586 B.C.
respectively), and the first return of captives from Babylon
occurred in 538 B.C. Thus for roughly seventy years the homeland of Israel suffered depopulation and its people exile.

Second, the *temple* was desolate (and its worship halted) seventy years. Solomon's temple was destroyed by the Babylonians in
586 B.C. and was not rebuilt until 516 B.C. (See Ezra 6:13–15.) So
for exactly seventy years Israel had no central sanctuary, no ral-
lying point for its faithful, no national house of worship.

See Jeremiah 25:11–12; 29:10–11; desolation of temple, see 2 Chronicles 36:19 and Ezra 6:13–15; desolation of land and people, see Daniel 1:1–2 and Ezra 1:1–3.

9:1–2 You do the crime, you do the time. When perusing Jeremiah's writings, Daniel discovered that God set an *appointed time* for Israel's punishment. No matter what their subsequent experience, problems, or prayers, due to their previous persistent rebellion they would not be released until God's set time—seventy years—had expired. Why? It was a judicial sentence ordered by the Judge of all the earth, similar in composition to those issued by earthly justices. Israel had committed a major crime against heaven's law. They had rejected God, ignored His Word, and worshiped other gods. And, adding sin to sin, they had viciously rejected and mistreated the long line of prophets God sent to graciously call them to repentance. Because their offense was great, their punishment had to be severe. So it was off to prison for them—and for a long, long time. Israel had done the crime; now they would do the time. The penitentiary the Judge chose was Babylon.

The Jewish captivity speaks to Christians today. If we persistently rebel against God's Word, call, and counselors, as the Jews did, eventually God will plunge us into a time of spiritual captivity—a fixed period in which God sets us aside from His purpose and instruction and comforting presence (though not His provision) and permits us to live in a dry, frustrating captivity to the things of the world (Babylon) and its prince (King Nebuchadnezzar, a type of Satan; see Rom. 6:16). Why is this? Because we have stubbornly broken heaven's law (the collective teachings of God's Word), its Judge must deal with us sternly. Over time and with repeated premeditation we have committed the crime; now we must do the time (see Matt. 5:26).

The Scriptures reveal God setting many such appointed times of punishment:

- God set King Nebuchadnezzar's sentence at seven years (Dan. 4:16, 25, 32, 34).

- Though forgiven, Miriam was "imprisoned" seven days for her offense (Num. 12:14–15).

- Though spared death by Moses' intercession, the Jews of the Exodus were confined to the wilderness for forty years (Num. 14:32–34).

- Jacob did "hard labor" under Laban, the "warden" of Paddan-aram, for twenty years (Gen. 31:36–42).

- For disbelieving God's joyful answer to his prayers, Zacharias was confined to silence for nine months— until the time of John the Baptist's birth (Luke 1:19–20).

- For marrying Hagar and fathering Ishmael without God's approval, Abraham was placed in "solitary confinement," where he was unable to hear from heaven for thirteen years (Gen. 16:15–17:3).

Though strictly inflexible once ordered, God's set times of punishment are corrective rather than penal. By them He hopes to change, not consume, us. His plan is that by the end of our time of punishment, we will be so hungry for life and liberty that we will emerge eager to fear and obey the Lord *ad infinitim*. In Jeremiah 29:10–11, God reveals this, His good plan to release and restore His chastened people as soon as their "set time" (Ps. 102:13) arrives.

See Daniel 4:16, 25, 32; Numbers 12:14; 14:32–34; Genesis 16:16–17:1; 31:38; Matthew 5:26; Hebrews 10:26–31; Luke 1:20.

Lesson: *For the crime of persistent rebellion against Him, His Word, and His counselors, God puts disobedient Christians into fixed times of captivity to sin and its author, Satan. Though inflexible, such periods of punishment are corrective, not penal.*

9:2 Revelation...by books. Though we often think of Daniel as a visionary, he was more than that. In telling us how he discovered God's time limit on the Babylonian captivity, Daniel betrays his less well known scholarship: "I, Daniel, understood *by books*..." (Dan. 9:2, emphasis added). Like Ezra, Daniel was a man given to the study of God's Word (Ezra 7:6, 10).

Every Christian disciple and minister should follow Daniel's example. In the New Testament era, God reveals many anointed ministers who were Bible scholars: Paul, Apollos, John, and even Peter were all either well read or well taught in the holy Scriptures (see Acts 22:3; 18:24–28; 2:15–21, 25–28; John 19:23–24, 31–37). Are you studying to show yourself approved unto God—and to receive comforting revelations from Him?

See 2 Timothy 2:15; 1 Timothy 4:13–15; Ezra 7:6, 10; Joshua 1:8; Psalms 1:1–3; 119:18; Proverbs 2:1–9; Isaiah 34:16; Ezekiel 2:9–3:4; John 14:21; Acts 18:24–28; 22:3; 2:15–21, 25–28.

Lesson: *As Daniel did, we should study God's Word to discover God's truth.*

9:2 Inspiration for a closer walk. *The New Scofield Study Bible* notes:

> Daniel's prayer…arose from the study of the prophetic Scriptures (v. 2; cp. Jer. 25)…Prophetic study is intended to lead to a deeper spiritual life. (p. 912)

Indeed, after Daniel studied Jeremiah's prophecies (see Jer. 25:11–12; 29:10–11), he immediately drew near the Lord in prayer.

In thought and practice, do we separate study from prayer or join the two as one? Obviously, Daniel prayed, not only before he studied but *as* he studied. So should we. Here is an axiom for every serious Bible student or minister: What unspiritual academics miss, prayerful lovers of the Word find—always.

Daniel also sought the Lord *after* he studied. Apparently, he felt that prophetic (and all biblical) revelation was given not merely to satisfy intellectual curiosity but to induce personal spiritual preparation. Observe that when he learned God's time limit for the exile was seventy years (Dan. 9:2) and realized he had already spent some sixty-six to sixty-seven years in Babylon (605–538 B.C.), Daniel knew deliverance was close at hand. Immediately, he began praying for himself and his people so they would be prepared for their approaching deliverance: "And [so, with this revelation fresh on my mind,] I set my face unto the Lord God, to seek by prayer..." (9:3; see vv. 4–19).

Has it ever struck us that *prophetic revelation is for personal preparation*? If so, we will no longer be content merely to know what the Bible says about End-Times events; we will be driven to prepare for them...by walking ever more closely with God. What good is the knowledge of the coming flood without a fully constructed ark? What good is the knowledge of the Rapture and the Tribulation that follows without a sanctified life, proven faith, and very close fellowship with the Lord of the Rapture?

Lesson: *God gives prophetic revelation to inspire personal spiritual preparation. Studying prophecy should inspire us to draw closer to God.*

9:2 Revelation...by prayers, dreams, books. Daniel was a three-dimensional man of God: a seeker, a seer, and a scholar. Apparently, he didn't care *how* he heard truth from God—only that he heard it! Hence, he availed himself of every possible means of receiving sound communication from heaven. In his writings we find him hearing from God in three ways:

1. Through prayer, as a seeker (Dan. 2:17–20; 8:15–16; 10:12, 14; 12:8)

2. Through dreams, as a seer (Dan. 7:1–14; 8:1–14; see Num. 12:6)

3. Through books (chiefly Scripture), as a scholar (Dan. 9:2; see "Revelation...by books," chapter 9)

Similarly, God has various means of revealing truth to our hearts today. We should, therefore, avail ourselves of every biblical channel of revelation the Spirit uses. We should ask for understanding in prayer; we should heed dreams that prove to be from God; and, most importantly, we should study the books of the Bible diligently. (See 2 Tim. 2:15; 3:15–17; Luke 10:42.)

Then we too will become three-dimensional servants of God: seekers, seers, and scholars.

Sadly, too many of us are one- or two- but not three-dimensional saints. The reason for this is often the unspoken philosophy that prevails in our quarter of Christendom. Some Christian groups teach that the Bible is the only way God can speak to us and deny the legitimacy of other forms of divine communication, including those clearly authorized by the Bible! While the Bible is the prime and only infallible channel for divine communication and the one sure standard by which all other spiritual revelations must be judged, we limit God by saying the Word is the only way He speaks. Indeed He has and uses secondary means of communication. Other groups, while affirming the inspiration of the Bible, seem a bit preoccupied with seeking divine revelation through every *other* conceivable means. If God chooses to speak to these through prophecy, visions or by His "still small voice" in prayer, they will acknowledge His voice. But they're really not that interested in the Bible. God save us from the narrow limitations of our prejudiced points of view!

If we would be as well rounded as Daniel, we should seek truth from God first in His infallible Word, then add to that whatever communications He sends through secondary channels (which, of course, agree with, complement, and conform to the inerrant pattern, principles, substance, and spirit of the written Word).

Lesson: *God has different means of revealing truth to our hearts: by His Word, by prayer, by dreams, by prophecy. Consequently, we should aspire to be seekers, seers, and scholars of God.*

9:3–19 A model prayer for restoration. Daniel's prayers were as exemplary as his character and lifestyle. His prayer here (Dan. 9:3–19) for the restoration of Israel—perhaps the most famous prayer of confession in the Bible—is a model prayer, the pattern of which we do well to follow when seeking restoration from God for ourselves, our churches, our nation, or our generation.

Daniel's prayer consists of eight essential elements:

1. DETERMINATION (Dan. 9:3; see Dan. 10:2–3, 12; Gen. 32:26)

2. CONCENTRATION or fervency (Dan. 9:3; see Dan. 10:2–3, 12; James 5:16)

3. A sense of GODLY SORROW (Dan. 9:3; see Ezra 9:3–5; Neh. 1:4; 9:1)

4. WORSHIP (Dan. 9:4; see Ps. 100:4; Matt. 6:9)

5. CONFESSION OF SIN, personal and corporate (Dan. 9:5–15; see 1 John 1:9; Prov. 28:13)

6. PETITIONS for help (Dan. 9:16–17; see Phil. 4:6–7; James 4:2)

7. SUPPLICATION (pleading, reasoning, begging) (Dan. 9:18–19; see Phil. 4:6; Eph. 6:18; Acts 1:14; 1 Tim. 2:1)

8. FAITH in God's unchanging faithful character and unfailing Word (Dan. 9:4, 9, 12)

Most important, however, is the *spirit* of Daniel's prayer. It was a thoroughly humble and brutally truthful prayer. It contained no claims of merit on his or his people's part and no finding of fault with God's dealings. The Jews alone are condemned and God alone is justified (Dan. 9:14, 16). Daniel explicitly stated the Jews had "sinned" three times (see vv. 5, 11, 15) and alluded to their sins, iniquities, and rebellion, and hence their guilt, in nearly every verse. More than his technique, the spirit of Daniel's prayer got God's attention.

God's response was swift and sure. He subsequently moved upon the Persian king Cyrus to issue a decree authorizing the return of the Jews en masse to Jerusalem. (Obviously, Cyrus' decree was not issued before Daniel prayed, for he would not have asked God to turn from His wrath and restore favor if Cyrus' decree—an obvious token of divine favor—had already been published.) If we want Daniel's answer, we should simply pray His prayer—in spirit as well as substance.

Any one of us can do this, if we will. Why, even Shimei showed himself capable of praying a thoroughly humble and brutally truthful prayer. (See 2 Sam. 19:18–20.) So did wicked King Manasseh, whose response from God was truly astounding, considering the seriousness and extent of Manasseh's past sins. (See 2 Chron. 33:1–13.)

Without this thorough humility and complete truthfulness, our prayers for restoration will go unanswered. No matter how long or loud our petitions, how deep and sacrificial our fastings, and how numerous and zealous the petitioners who agree with us, the Restorer will not come to us. His unmistakably clear directions in 2 Chronicles 7:14 are proof enough of that. Truth and humility and repentance where it counts—these things alone move the God of truth to restore a sinful people.

Are we willing to pray Daniel's prayer and pay his price?

For other prayers of confession and restoration see Ezra 9:5–15; Nehemiah 1:4–11; 9:1–37.

See Daniel 10:2–3, 12; James 5:16; Psalm 100:4; Matthew 6:9; 1 John 1:9; Proverbs 28:13; Philippians 4:6–7; James 4:2; Ephesians 6:18; Acts 1:14; 1 Timothy 2:1.

Lesson: *Prayers for spiritual restoration should consist of determination, concentration, godly sorrow, worship, confession, petition, supplication, and faith. Above all else, their spirit must be one of brutal truthfulness and thorough humility. Such prayers will always elicit a favorable response from God.*

9:4–19 Identifying intercessors. In praying for his people's restoration, Daniel fully identified with them and their sin. *The Ryrie Study Bible* finds he "associated himself with the sins of the people 32 times" (p. 1325). Why did a man of Daniel's extraordinary uprightness and devotion include himself so repeatedly when describing the sin of his people? Was he depressed, as Elijah was when he fled from Jezebel (see 1 Kings 19:4)? Was he temporarily confused by a false view of himself arising from inverted religious pride? No; two things account for

Daniel's repeated identifications with his fallen brethren.

First, he was acknowledging the spiritual oneness—the indivisible unity—of the body of Israel. Even though Daniel was personally a very upright member of Israel's corporate body (see Ezek. 14:14, 20), even greatly beloved by God (see Dan. 9:23b; 10:11, 19), he was still in the body, and the body had sinned badly for many years (see Dan. 9:11). Hence, when the body sins and suffers, every member—even those personally innocent—suffer with it. (See 1 Cor. 12:26.) Other examples of innocent members of a body suffering along with guilty members are:

- Thirty-six innocent Israelite soldiers died at Ai because of Achan's sin at Jericho (Josh. 7:1, 11; 6:18).

- Miriam and Aaron's sin delayed Israel's national progress one week (Num. 12:15b).

- The prophet Jeremiah had to endure the one-and-a-half-year siege of Jerusalem, though it was caused by the sins of the nation (Jer. 28:3–8).

- The overcomers Joshua and Caleb had to wait forty years to receive their inheritances in Canaan due to the unbelief and rebellion of their brethren (Josh. 14:6–10).

So to acknowledge this oneness of the Jewish body, Daniel repeatedly prayed, "We..."

Second, Daniel, like every other Israelite then and Christian now, still possessed a sin nature (see 1 John 1:8). Hence, he was blameless, yet not without sin. Though none of his sins or failings are recorded in Scripture, he too had committed acts of sin at some point(s) in his walk with God (see Dan. 9:20, "*my sin* and the sin of my people," emphasis added; also Rom. 3:23; 7:18a; 1 John 1:10), though obviously he sought and obtained forgiveness and did not walk consistently in any sin. Observe that God placed Noah in the same high spiritual rank with Daniel in Ezekiel 14:14, 20, yet we know Noah, while very righteous, was not absolutely sinless (see Gen. 9:20–21). Similarly, Daniel was spiritually perfect (mature, full-orbed), yet not sinlessly perfect. So four times he humbly prayed, "We have sinned…" (Dan. 9:5, 8, 11, 15).

Has it sunk in on us that when the body of Christ fails, we fail with it? Do we realize that no matter how advanced our sanctification, we are still sinners saved by grace? Remembering these things will cause us to pray with greater earnestness, compassion, and faith for the church—and purging our self-righteousness will create in us an attitude to which God is much more likely to respond (see John 9:31; Ps. 66:18).

Ezra and Nehemiah were also identifying intercessors (Ezra 9:5–15; Neh. 1:4–11).

See Daniel 9:4–19 (TLB); 1 Corinthians 5:1–7; 12:12–14, 26; 1 John 5:16; Joshua 7:1, 11; Numbers 12:15b; Romans 3:23.

Lesson: *Remembering that we are united with all Christians in the body of Christ and that we still possess a sin nature, we should become identifying intercessors, humbly identifying with the Christians for whom we pray.*

9:7–8 Confusion of face. The expression "confusion of face," translated "shamefacedness" in *The Modern Language Bible* and paraphrased "shamefaced with sin" in *The Living Bible*, speaks of the shame and guilt of sin when exposed by obvious divine judgment. God's fierce judgment on Israel and Judah—a calamity Daniel describes as unprecedented in history (Dan. 9:12)—exposed the Jews' sinfulness, and God's undeniable anger with them, before all the world (vv. 7–8). Thus the Israelis' faces reflected the shame and confusion of their souls.

In other Bible references, confusion arises from sins themselves, such as:

- Trusting in human help (Isa. 30:3)
- Idolatry (Isa. 41:29)
- Fear of man (Jer. 1:17)
- Persistence in self-will (Gen. 11:1–9)
- Pride (James 4:6)
- Envy (James 3:16)
- Strife (contention, argument) (James 3:16)

● Indecision (Dan. 4:19a; James 1:8)

In his prayer, Daniel adds the qualifying phrase "of face" to point to and emphasize not the confusion of sin so much as the humiliating embarrassment that arises from its exposure.

In contrast, "confusion of face" sometimes refers to the awkwardness uncompromisingly obedient believers experience when their adversaries heap strong reproach upon them without cause (Ps. 44:15). We mustn't mistake this for the confusion that arises, as noted above, from the fear of man when we allow ourselves to be intimidated by such reproach (Ps. 71:1).

See Ezra 9:6–7; Jeremiah 7:19.

Lesson: *Sin invariably brings divine punishment and embarrassing "confusion of face."*

9:9 Hope for the hopelessly guilty. God's enduring character and mercy provided Israel with an enduring hope.

Though they had changed for the worse, falling from God's favor due to many sins over many years, God's beautiful character, specifically His great mercy, remain perfectly unchanged. Ever perceptive, Daniel remembered this and reminded God that Israel's evil behavior had not changed God's immutable character: "To the Lord, our God, belong mercies and forgivenesses, though we have rebelled against him" (Dan. 9:9). Suddenly light appeared in Israel's black tunnel of captivity. Though they were hopelessly guilty, they still had one ray of hope. Though all had been lost, all was not unrecoverable. Though captive, the Jews could have God's blessing again, if they were willing to do one thing: Seek restoration on God's abiding terms of truth, humility, and penitent obedience.

Kings Ahab and Manasseh are two striking examples of this: the hope of the hopelessly guilty. Both were extraordinarily wicked sinners who were shown extraordinary grace due to genuine penitence: Ahab received a temporary reprieve (see 1 Kings 21:27–29), while Manasseh received a full pardon and surprisingly complete restoration (see 2 Chron. 33:11–19).

Post-exilic Israel, King Ahab, and King Manasseh—these teach us that even when sin is great, there is yet hope for the truly penitent because of God's enduring mercies. Do we remember this when we intercede for or counsel backsliders?

See 2 Chronicles 33:11–19; 1 Kings 21:27–29; Lamentations 3:22–23; Psalm 51:17b; Proverbs 28:13; 1 John 1:9.

Lesson: *God offers hope even to hopelessly guilty ones, provided they seek help on His terms of truth, humility, and penitent obedience.*

9:12 Punished according to the Word. "And he hath confirmed his words..." (Dan. 9:12)—by inspiring these precise words in Daniel's prayer, God confirms to us that He indeed fulfills (executes, carries out) *all* His Word (see Mark 14:49; Luke 24:25–26). Not only His promises are reliable, but His threats are also. He punishes as He prospers, according to His Word. Daniel specified that Israel was punished "as it is written in the law of Moses" (Dan. 9:13; see v. 11). In Daniel 9:10–14, he clearly referred to Deuteronomy 28 by repeatedly stating that the Jews had not "hearkened" to God's "voice" (a key condition for blessing and/or cause of cursing given in Deut. 28:1, 13, 15, 45) and citing this as the reason "the curse" of the law (see Deut. 28:15–68) had been poured upon them.

See Mark 14:49; Luke 24:25–26; Numbers 23:19.

Lesson: *God keeps all His Word; He not only prospers, but He also punishes according to His Word.*

9:12 God punishes His own...sometimes *worse!* Daniel pointed out that God had punished His people in a sensational way: "Bringing upon us a great evil; for *under the whole heaven* hath not been done as hath been done upon Jerusalem" (Dan. 9:12, emphasis added). "Never in all history" (Dan. 9:12, TLB) had any city suffered the kind of destruction that befell Jerusalem and its temple and people.

That God did this and is "the same yesterday, and today,

and forever" (Heb. 13:8) shatters the illusion of divine permissiveness that pervades the Church today—namely, that because God loves His people with a special love He won't and can't punish them. To the contrary, it suggests that, once stirred, God's wrath upon the "[His own] children of disobedience" is even worse than what He metes out to the unredeemed. (Ananias and Sapphira were Christians; see Acts 5:1–11. And more recently, one would have to look hard and long to find a more embarrassing and far-reaching public spectacle than the demise of Jim Bakker, whose severe punishment produced a truly changed man and message.) Of whom much is given, much is required (see Luke 12:48b), and when much grace is spurned and abused, much anger is stirred. Hence, more grace means not more license to sin but more responsibility to obey—and if we rebel, greater judgment. (See Luke 12:47–48; Heb. 10:28–29.)

Have we ever realized that God's wrath is as awesome as His love? (See Heb. 10:31.) We need a revival of the healthy, purifying, confidence-restoring fear of God (Prov. 14:26).

See Hebrews 10:26–31; 12:25, 29; Luke 12:4–5; Ephesians 5:5–7; Colossians 3:5–6; Acts 5:1–11; 1 Peter 4:17.

Lesson: *Contrary to popular theology, God punishes Christians who persistently rebel and sin, sometimes even more severely than He punishes sinners.*

9:13 Amazing indifference. Despite the awesome judgment of the captivity, the Jews remained amazingly indifferent: Daniel stated, "Yet made we not our prayer...that we might turn from our iniquities..." (Dan. 9:13). After more than sixty-five years of exile, they still were not ready to stop sinning, humbly confess their guilt before God, justify Him, and prayerfully beg for restoration on His terms. Theirs was an incredibly deep spiritual sleep.

We relive their amazing indifference any time we continue practicing any sin despite our knowledge of:

- His righteous judgments revealed in His Word

- His repeated warnings and chastisements of us personally
- His punishments of fellow Christians whose sins we share
- His judgments of Christian predecessors

This is the most dangerous kind of indifference...the sleep of unjudged sin. Our awakenings often come through the unwanted rebukes, protests, or prayers of uncompromising, wide-awake servants of God, such as Ezra (Ezra 9:10–15), Nehemiah (Neh. 13:17–18, 25–27), or Daniel (Dan. 9:4–19).

How much will God have to shake us before we're fully awake to our true spiritual state before Him? And once awake, are we willing to pray, rebuke, and protest until other sleeping saints are aroused to righteousness?

See "Retracing the path of apostasy," chapter 9.

See Romans 13:11–13; Matthew 25:5; Ephesians 5:14; Judges 16:3, 14, 19, 20; Jonah 1:5b–6; Ezra 9:10–15; Nehemiah 13:17–18, 25–27.

Lesson: Despite many examples, warnings, and chastisements, sometimes we remain amazingly indifferent—spiritually asleep—toward our sins.

9:14 Justifying the Judge of all the earth. Daniel carefully and repeatedly justifies God for His decision to put Israel into captivity: "For the LORD, our God, is righteous in all his works ..." (Dan. 9:14). The Jews didn't keep their law (vv. 5, 11), obey God's voice (vv. 10–11, 14), or obey their prophets (vv. 6, 10), so God had no alternative but to bring upon them the curses specified in His law: destruction, dispersion, and captivity (vv. 11–13). Everything He did was righteous, fair, just, legal...and merciful, because God patiently withheld judgment for many years hoping the Jews would repent. So Daniel concludes that in every way his people were guilty and in every way God was just (see Rev. 16:5–7).

Note that Daniel *verbalized* this justification in audible

words. Why? Because he knew it was the truth and that righteous judges—including the Judge of all the earth—always desire and respond to petitions of truth (see Ps. 51:6; Prov. 28:13; 1 John 1:9). So Daniel simply reiterated the theme Abraham spoke when he interceded successfully for Lot's deliverance: The God of all the earth always does right. (See Gen. 18:25.)

Have we learned to justify God in prayer? Do we first tell Him how fair, patient, and good He has been toward us and others, then ask Him to intervene and help? Such praying leaves no room for self-pity or offense at God. And it opens wide the windows of heaven through which the Judge, freshly justified and blessed, quickly responds. Daniel's response was immediate: "And while I was speaking…yea, while I was speaking in prayer …the man, Gabriel…being caused to fly swiftly, touched me" (Dan. 9:20–21).

See Revelation 16:5–7; Genesis 18:25; Leviticus 10:3; 1 Chronicles 15:13; Ezra 9:7, 13.

Lesson: *In prayer, we should always justify God for all His actions.*

9:15 Reminding the Judge. A good attorney will search case law to find a case similar to his current one whose decision parallels the one he hopes to win. He will then remind the judge of such precedents and often read him the decision in hopes of swaying the judge to act in the best interests of his client.

As a good legal representative of the Jewish people, Daniel reminded God of the glorious Exodus precedent, the Jews' earlier trial in which God delivered them from bitter captivity in Egypt and won great fame for His name among all nations: "O Lord, our God, who hast brought thy people forth out of the land of Egypt with a mighty hand, and hast gotten thee renown" (Dan. 9:15). Then he bid God deliver them from their present Babylonian captivity in the same manner and restore their land and capital city, Jerusalem: "I beseech thee, let thine anger and thy fury be turned away from thy city, Jerusalem…" (v. 16).

Daniel's appeal was very, very simple: "Lord, You delivered Israel from captivity before, to glorify Your name; please do it again, for the same reason" (see v. 19).

When appealing to God in prayer, do we remind Him of His past acts of deliverance and the laws (written promises) upon which He based them, and then simply petition Him to follow His own precedent in our similar situation? It's time we learn to be good attorneys.

See Isaiah 43:26; Nehemiah 1:8–11.

Lesson: *When petitioning God for help, we should ask Him to act according to similar precedents and Bible promises.*

9:18–19 The greatest of reasons. Wisely, Daniel saved his best argument for the last. After presenting his core petitions— that God quench His anger and restore His favor (Dan. 9:16–17)— Daniel begs a quick response for the greatest of reasons: God's own great name. "Thy city and thy people," says Israel's prayer lawyer, "are called by thy name" (v. 19). Daniel was merely pointing out that God's name and His people and their capital city were forever linked, for honor or dishonor. When Jerusalem was dishonored, God was dishonored; when it was honored, He was honored. Therefore, God should restore Jerusalem and the people of Judah, Daniel reasons, not because the people were worthy but to restore honor to His great name, which had been so shamefully dishonored by Judah's long sin and captivity. How could Israel's Judge deny such a request? How could He be against any prayer-proposal that was framed to glorify His own name?

Are we mindful that we and our works, churches, ministries, and families bear Jesus' great name? If we are defeated in life, Christ will be reproached; and if we successfully do God's will, the name of Jesus will be honored. If we petition God on the grounds that His compliance will result in more honor for His great name, He will surely respond. And quickly—note again how quickly God responded to Daniel's greatest reason (see vv. 20–21).

See Ezekiel 36:21–23; Psalms 74:10; 79:9; John 12:28; 17:1.

Lesson: *The greatest reason we can give God as to why He should answer our petitions is simply... to honor His name.*

9:5 A true leader. Like the renowned sons of Issachar, true leaders understand their times and what God's people ought to do. (See 1 Chron. 12:32.) Consequently, they focus on the most vital needs of the hour and pursue them.

Daniel showed himself a true leader by promptly taking action according to the highest priority he recognized. Daniel 9 fell in an hour of apostasy, specifically the final days of that time. Hence, the most expeditious thing Daniel or any Israelite could do to hasten the deliverance and restoration of God's people was to pray sincere prayers of confession and repentance. As shown above, only by thoroughly humble and brutally truthful prayer could God's favor be restored and His intervention gained, without which no Jew would be released to return and rebuild their homeland and faith. So Daniel took the Spirit's lead and prayed. Do note that he didn't poll the Babylonian populace, or see what other prophets were saying, or listen for the rumblings of the Jews. He just did what the Spirit showed him was most needful at the moment. Thus, as a true leader, he took the initiative with and for God and set a clear example for the Jews to follow.

True Christian leaders will follow Daniel's example, too. Knowing the times and what Christians ought to do, they will simply step up and do it, whether other leaders fall in or break ranks. Do we have the vision and courage to focus only on what the Spirit is saying to the church and not what the media, the masses, and even the ministry clamor for?

See 1 Chronicles 12:32; 2 Chronicles 18:13; Revelation 2:7, 11, 17, 29; 3:6, 13, 22.

Lesson: *True Christian leaders focus on what the Spirit shows them is most needful at the time and simply step up and do it, with or without popular support.*

9:4–13 Retracing the path of apostasy. In his model prayer, Daniel retraces the steps of Israel's apostasy, beginning with their most basic error—departure from God's written Word—and ending with their being in the worst possible spiritual condition: God-forsaken, cursed, and indifferent. Here are the tragic steps He identifies:

1. FORSAKING God's Word (Dan. 9:5, 11)

2. REJECTING corrective counselors (Dan. 9:6; see 2 Chron. 36:15–16)

3. PUNISHED by divinely authorized foreign invasion and captivity (Dan. 9:11–13)

4. SMITTEN with confusion of face (Dan. 9:7–8; see Ezra 9:6–7)

5. ASLEEP with indifference (Dan. 9:13; Rom. 13:11–14; Eph. 5:14–17)

Observe that Daniel's words were spoken in the context of his prayer of confession.

Accordingly, we too should retrace the steps of our apostasy when praying prayers of confession to God for ourselves or for others. We should walk through our past, telling God when and where we rebelled against Him, what scriptures and teachers we rejected, and which counselors we spurned. Furthermore, we should acknowledge that we have lived in well-deserved confusion, that He was just to punish us according to His biblical warnings, and that we are also responsible for elongating our sufferings by our slowness to make confession to Him. We will find such confessionals to be as effective in restoring God's favor in our lives as they were in Daniel's, whose prayers helped initiate Cyrus' famous decree releasing the Jews from their captivity (Ezra 1).

While learning the vital spiritual discipline of self-examination, we may need to practice this on a daily basis. Whenever we sin in thought, word, or deed, we should simply retrace the steps of our sin before the Holy Spirit, identifying to Him the precise moment—by wrong thought, motive, emotion, word, or deed—when we turned from the light (1 John 1:9).

Why is this necessary? Because "the truth shall make you free...free indeed" (John 8:32, 36).

See 1 John 1:9; Proverbs 28:13; Jeremiah 3:13; Hosea 14:1–2; Luke 15:18–19, 21.

Lesson: *The Lord is pleased with, and we are liberated by, prayers of confession that humbly and accurately retrace the steps of our apostasy.*

9:20–23 Caution: Angels at work. Wherever construction crews are laboring to build roads or buildings, signs are placed at all the various approaches reading, "Caution: Men at work." Similarly, wherever abiding, obedient, overcoming Christians pray, they should place signs near their prayer closets that read, "Caution: Angels at work." Why?

Because the Book of Daniel reveals that whenever overcomers (like Daniel) pray according to God's will, in humility, truth, and uprightness, God immediately commands answers and dispatches angels to bring those answers (see Heb. 1:14). (While angels are the messengers, Christ is the one Mediator, or "ladder," by which they travel between heaven and earth; see John 1:51; Gen. 28:12; 1 Tim. 2:5). In this case, the angel Gabriel brought Daniel prophetic skill and understanding (Dan. 9:22).

Notice the similarities and contrasts between this answer to prayer (vv. 20–23) and that described in Daniel 10:10–14. There Daniel's prayer is answered immediately, but its manifestation is delayed three weeks due to demonic resistance. In chapter 9, it is answered *and* manifested immediately, even before Daniel finished praying! Hence, one of two things occurred:

1. Inexplicably, there was little or no demonic resistance to this prayer.

2. God sovereignly disallowed any delay by sending "overwhelming force" with Gabriel.

To believers there is a vital lesson here. If we walk uprightly and pray in faith, truth, and humility according to God's will (as Daniel), God immediately answers our prayers and dispatches angels to bring us His answers. Sometimes these answers manifest quickly, and sometimes they do not. If we see them quickly, of course, no further intercession is necessary; but if they are delayed, we should—we must—simply importune, or keep praying, till they arrive. (See Dan. 10:2–3; Luke 11:5–10; 18:1–8.) The only other option, acquiescence in failure, is totally unacceptable to overcomers.

See "Angels for the innocent," chapter 6; also "Supporting kings," chapter 11.

See Hebrews 1:14; Daniel 8:15–16; 10:12; Acts 12:5, 7–11; 2 Chronicles 32:20–21; John 1:51; Genesis 28:12; 18:23–33; 19:1, 22.

Lesson: *When humble, upright, overcoming Christians pray in faith according to God's will, angels immediately go into action, answering prayer.*

9:23 Greatly beloved by God. While the Old Testament reveals throughout that Jehovah loved all the Jews, the Book of Daniel reveals three times that Daniel was "greatly beloved" by Him (Dan. 9:23; 10:11; 10:19). Furthermore, it contains other irrefutable evidence that Daniel was a man specially approved of God. Note these:

- Daniel's extraordinary spiritual gifts of interpretation, wisdom, and administration (Dan. 1:17, 19–20; 2:48; 6:3–4)

- Daniel's miraculous deliverances from potentially and actually deadly trials (Dan. 1:14–16; 2:12–13, 19–23; 6:16–23)

- Daniel's remarkably clear and swift answers to prayer (Dan. 2:17–23; 9:20–23; 10:2–3, 12–14)

- Daniel's great favor with great men (Dan. 1:9, 19–20; 2:46–48; 4:8–9; 5:10–16; 6:2–3, 14, 16, 19, 25–28)

- Daniel's public acclaim and regal honors (Dan. 2:46–47; 5:10–12, 29; 6:25–27)

- Daniel's frequent promotions (Dan. 1:19; 2:48; 5:29; 6:1–2, 28)

- Daniel's deep and far-reaching prophecies and interpretations (chapters 2, 4, 7–9, 12)

To this, other books of the Bible add their inspired witness that, indeed, God had an exceptionally high regard for Daniel. (See Ezek. 14:14, 20; 28:3.)

If "God is no respecter of persons" (Acts 10:34), why did He hold such special favor for Daniel? Because while God is no respecter of persons, He is a respecter of excellent characters. Here are Daniel's "beloved qualities"—the character traits that made him beloved of God. Daniel was:

- Uncompromisingly loyal to God's Word (Dan. 1:8)

- Childlike yet strong in faith in God (Dan. 2:17–18; 6:10, 23)

- Humble and truthful in prayer (Dan. 9:3–19)

- Disciplined (regular) in devotion (Dan. 6:10, 16)

- Given to worship, especially thanksgiving (Dan. 2:19–23; 6:10)

- Unworldly in heart and lifestyle (in Babylon but not of it) (Dan. 1:8, 16; 6:5, 10)

- Holy, consistently innocent of and without sin and separate from sinners (Dan. 1:8, 16)

- Discreet with kings and commoners (Dan. 2:14, 16; 4:19, 27)

- Courageous in trial (willing to take necessary risks to please God; Dan. 1:11–14; 6:10)

- Humble in victory and promotion—and on "the shelf" (Dan. 2:27–30; 5:13)

- Gracious toward friends (Dan. 2:49)

- A compassionate exhorter (Dan. 4:27)

- Driven by love for God's people (Dan. 9:1–19; 10:14)

- Not covetous (Dan. 5:17)

- Not a man-pleaser (Dan. 1:8; 5:17; 6:10)

- Faithful and thorough in execution of secular duties (Dan. 6:4)

- Faithful and thorough in execution of spiritual duties (Dan. 6:10, 16, 20)

- A seeker of scriptural truth (Dan. 9:2; 10:21)

- A seeker of prophetic understanding (Dan. 7:16; 8:15; 10:12; 12:8)

We do well to study Daniel's character qualities—and even better to emulate them. While Jesus loves all people (see John 3:16), and particularly Christians (see Eph. 5:25), He explicitly promised us that He and His Father would love those who diligently seek and obey His Word with a special love (see John 14:21, 23). But what's a promise without a desire to have it?

Do we really want to be "greatly beloved" of Jesus? We can be, if we will just set our hearts and guide our steps as Daniel did.

See Daniel 1:8; 6:10; 9:3; 10:11–12, 19; Ezekiel 14:14, 20; 28:3; John 14:21, 23.

Lesson: *While God loves all Christians, those who seek to become and live like Daniel are "greatly beloved" by Him.*

9:24–27 A prophecy of Israel's "seventy weeks." In Daniel 9:24–27, we find yet another variation (or viewpoint) on the central prophetic theme of the Book of Daniel—the times of the Gentiles.

Unlike Daniel's previously recorded visions, the focal point of this prophecy is not on the succession of Gentile nations (chapters 2, 7, 8). Rather it fixes on five things vital to Hebrew interests:

1. The chosen people, the Jews (Dan. 9:24)

2. Their eternal capital city, Jerusalem (Dan. 9:24)

3. Their center of worship, the temple (Dan. 9:24, 26–27)

4. Their coming Savior-King, the anointed one, "Messiah, the Prince" (Dan. 9:25–26)

5. Their coming worst enemy, the "prince that shall come," Antichrist (Dan. 9:26–27)

Like Daniel's previously recorded visions, however, the chronological scope of this prophecy is vast, reaching from Daniel's time all the way to the millennium, or Day of the Lord, which is referred to as the time in which God brings in everlasting righteousness, fulfills all prophecies, and anoints the "most holy" (place and Person), a reference to both the dedication of Jesus' millennial temple and His coronation as King of kings (see Dan. 9:24).

Gabriel expressly states that this vision is "determined" (v. 24), or divinely predetermined (predestined). Hence, irrevocable and absolutely sure to occur, it serves as a rock-solid foundation for our faith in the End-Time events.

The Ryrie Study Bible note provides an excellent interpretation of the six key phrases found in Daniel 9:24 (pp. 1326–1327):

- *To finish the transgression*: To end the apostasy of the Jews

- *To make an end of sin*: To atone for sin...

- *To make atonement for iniquity*: Refers to the death of Christ on the cross, which is the basis for Israel's [and the world's] future forgiveness (Zech. 12:10; Rom. 11:26–27)

- *To bring in everlasting righteousness*: In the millennial kingdom of Messiah (Jer. 23:5–6)

- *To seal up the vision and prophecy*: To set God's seal of fulfillment on all the prophecies concerning the Jewish people and Jerusalem

- *To anoint the most holy place*: The anointing of the Holy of Holies in the millennial temple

Important Information (Dan. 9:24–27)

This brief prophetic passage unveils some important information concerning Israel's post-exilic period and its yet-unfulfilled tribulation drama. It reveals:

- Daniel 9:24: God sets a time limit on His remaining dealings with Israel. "Weeks" refers to weeks of years; "seventy weeks" represent 490 years. (For other use of weeks of years, see Gen. 29:27–28; also "Prophetic time," chapter 9.)

- Daniel 9:25: The Gentiles will authorize the reconstruction of Jerusalem. This was comforting news to Daniel and a direct answer to his earnest prayer (see v. 17).

- Daniel 9:25: Jerusalem's reconstruction will occur during "troublous times" (amid Jewish despair and Samaritan resistance) and only forty-nine years (seven weeks of seven years each) after the command to reconstruct Jerusalem (King Artaxerxes' decree, 445 B.C.; see Neh. 2:5–6).

- Daniel 9:25–26: The time of Christ's (first coming and) rejection is fixed. "Messiah, the Prince" will come and be "cut off" sixty-nine (seven plus sixty-two) weeks of (360-day) years (483 years) after the command authorizing the rebuilding of Jerusalem; or in approximately 30 A.D.

- Daniel 9:25–26a: Christ's rejection is described. He will be "cut off"—denied His rightful, glorious throne and killed—not due to any fault of His own but unjustly. This alludes to Jesus' unjust persecution and execution by envious national religious leaders.

- Daniel 9:26b–27: Jerusalem and its rebuilt temple will *again* be destroyed. Partially fulfilled by the Roman general Titus (70 A.D.), the ultimate fulfillment awaits the coming of the forces of Antichrist, the "prince that shall come."

- Daniel 9:26b–27: The coming of Antichrist ("the prince that shall come") is partially described and contrasted with the coming of Christ ("Messiah, the Prince").

Unlike Christ, who was distrusted and "cut off" (violently rejected) by the leaders of the Jewish people (v. 26a), Antichrist will come and *not* be "cut off." Instead the Jewish nation will receive him with full trust; Jesus foretold this in John 5:43. Then Antichrist will either initiate or renew a seven-year peace treaty with Israel (Dan. 9:27a). This seven years is the seventieth and final week of years predetermined by God for Israel's dealings with the Gentiles. After three and a half years ("in the midst of the week"), Antichrist will break this agreement and wage war with Israel, destroying Jerusalem and part of its temple (specifically its courts; see Dan. 9:26 and Rev. 11:2), halting all Jewish worship (as did Antiochus IV), and defiling the Most Holy place by "the overspreading of abominations" (his blasphemous throne and image; see 2 Thess. 2:4; Rev. 13:14–15; Matt. 24:15). This three-and-a-half-year "war" (period of treachery, military aggression, and oppression) against Israel will bring both desolation to the temple and a flood of judgments (trumpet and bowl judgments of Rev. 8–11, 16) upon the "desolator" (Dan. 9:27, literal translation), Antichrist.

- Daniel 9:26b–27: The wicked will be judged. Despite Antichrist's three-and-half-year reign of terror, "that determined" (God's predetermined judgments) will be "poured upon" the desolator at God's appointed time (see Dan. 7:22, 26)—liberating the people, city, and temple of God! Here is assurance for all oppressed believers (see Luke 18:7–8).

Summarizing, verses 24 and 25 refer primarily to Israel's history from the exile to the first coming of Christ (weeks 1–69), while verses 26 and 27 refer primarily to Israel's final struggle with Antichrist during the Great Tribulation (week 70).

9:24 A Hanukkah yet to come! By the Spirit, Daniel foresees the dedication of the millennial temple: "…and to anoint [dedicate] the most Holy [place, or temple]" (9:24).

More accurately, this will be a *re*dedication, marking the purging and reopening of the yet to be constructed Jewish temple of the tribulation after its horrible and ultimate sacrilege—the universal worship of Antichrist's image in Christ's universal temple. This coming rededication will be reminiscent of the purging and rededication of the temple by the Maccabees, only on a much grander scale. Its foretelling here by Daniel gives Hanukkah, the eight-day Jewish Festival of Dedication (or Festival of Lights) commemorating the Maccabean victory, a whole new meaning. Hanukkah is now not only a memorial but also a prophetic festival; it not only looks back to God's great victory over Antiochus IV; more importantly it looks forward to His (and our) greater victory over Antichrist, when the temple's worst day will suddenly becomes its best—the thousand-year reign and worship of Christ.

Every December, then, while for eight days the Jews worldwide look back, remember to also look forward: There's another, greater Festival of Dedication yet to come!

Lesson: Hanukkah anticipates the purging and rededication of the millennial temple of Jesus Christ.

9:24–25 Prophetic time. The beginning of Israel's seventy weeks of years is very clearly revealed by God: "From the going forth of the commandment to restore and to build Jerusalem" (Dan. 9:25). This was fulfilled in 445 B.C., when the Persian king Artaxerxes issued a decree authorizing Nehemiah's mission to rebuild the city and walls of Jerusalem (Neh. 2:5–8). That weeks of *years* are used here (instead of weeks of days) is confirmed by Daniel's next use of the term "weeks" in Daniel 10:2. On that reference *The New Scofield Study Bible* notes: "The Hebrew text reads 'weeks of days' so as to distinguish these weeks from the weeks of years in ch. 9:24–27 (p. 914)."

Most important is that sixty-nine of these weeks of years will expire before Messiah comes and is rejected by His people. *The New Scofield Study Bible* further explains that "These years… are each 360 days long." For confirmation, observe that both Revelation 11:3 and 12:6 use 1,260 days to describe the latter half of the Great Tribulation period, which is also the last half of Daniel's seventieth week of years. Doing the math, 1,260 total days divided by 3½ equals 360 days, or 3½ 360-day years. So this confirms that throughout *this* parallel prophetic passage in the Book of Daniel, 360-day years are used.

Calculating the years of Daniel's prophecy, then, 69 weeks times 7 years for each week equals 483 total years from Artaxerxes decree (445 B.C.) until Christ's rejection. Using our present 365-day calendar years, this would put Christ's cruci-fixion at A.D. 38. When, however, we subtract the difference of 5 days per year for the 483-year period, this reduces the total years by about 7 (483 x 5 days = 2,415 days; 2,415 days / 360 days = 6.7, or approximately 7 years). So when we reduce the 483 by 7, we total 476 years. Measuring from 445 B.C., this brings us to approximately A.D. 31—very, very close to the exact year of fulfillment (A.D. 30) in which Jesus was officially "cut off" by Israel.

The curious student may wonder, Why the discrepancy? Apparently because God considered this timing sufficiently close! On this *The New Scofield Study Bible* states:

> It should be remembered that, in the grand sweep of prophecy, prophetic time is invariably so near as to give full warning, so indeterminate as to give no satisfaction to mere curiosity (cp. Matt. 24:36; Acts 1:7). (p. 913)

When God declares the times in which He will execute spe-cific events in the earth, His purpose is to alert us to prepare ourselves spiritually for whatever is coming (see Heb. 11:7; Matt. 25:6–7), not to prove to skeptics that He, the omniscient One, can predict events precisely.

Lesson: *God always fulfills prophecy according to the times stated in His Word, yet sometimes prophetic time is approximate and not exact.*

9:26–27 The Church: A grand parenthesis. Though Daniel's prophecies speak of the conditions present at the end of this age (see Daniel 12:4) and the tribulation period that fol-lows, there is not a single direct reference to the Church. Why is this? Because God didn't reveal it to him. Daniel's revelations concerned Hebrew matters only: the Jews, their nation, their capital, their temple, and their relationship to the Gentile nations. This is why the apostle Paul described his revelations of the Church as a "mystery"—a previously undisclosed divine revelation.

If it were to be mentioned in this context of Israel's seventy weeks, the Church Age would be described midway through Daniel 9:26, after Messiah is cut off but before the arrival of "the prince that shall come" in the tribulation period. The entire Church Age occurs between the end of Israel's sixty-ninth week and the beginning of its seventieth week. So from Daniel's exclusively Jewish viewpoint, the Church—a gathering of predominantly Gentile redeemed ones—is just a parenthesis in Israel's long and storied history. Thus Daniel humbles us by putting us in the parenthesis when we prefer to think of ourselves as the main story!

But we need not be dejected. Remember divine mathematics: God plus nothing equals greatness! And God will yet make this ecclesiastical parenthesis great, holy, gracious, and gloriously worthy of His Son! (See Eph. 5:25–27; 4:11–16; Rev. 19:7–9.)

Lesson: *From the Jewish perspective, the Church is but a parenthesis in Israel's long and storied history. But God will yet make us a grand parenthesis indeed!*

CHAPTER TEN

"BECAUSE OF YOUR WORDS"

10:1–12:13 THE FINAL VISION. The final three chapters of the Book of Daniel reveal Daniel's final vision, which he received in answer to prayer (Dan. 10:1–3) as he was in Persia by the Tigris River (v. 4; Dan. 12:5–7).

10:1–4 Stay where God puts you. Here Daniel states that two years after Cyrus' decree releasing the Jews to return to Palestine ("in the third year of Cyrus," Dan. 10:1), he was still in Babylon (now in the Persian Empire), specifically "by the side of the great river, which is Hiddekel (Tigris)" (v. 4). So although he prayed fervently for the release of his people (Dan. 9:3–19), Daniel did not accompany them to Jerusalem. Why not? Because his calling and work were in Babylon; God wanted him there, not in Jerusalem. Unaware of his character, some may misinterpret Daniel's remaining behind as evidence of lukewarmness or even hypocrisy. But, far from that, it was still more evidence of his uncompromising obedience to God.

Daniel's actions here reveal his military mind-set. Above all else, Daniel saw himself as a good soldier in God's army. Always, then, he was obedient to current orders till further orders were given. He never initiated his own orders. He did not blindly follow trends, even good ones, nor jump on every bandwagon, even when God Himself built them and started them rolling. Nor did he run with tidings merely because he saw others doing so. (See 2 Sam. 18:21–23.) Wisely, Daniel understood *the sovereign individuality of the call of God*—that God calls each of us strictly as it pleases Him, and so each must do whatever He leads, irrespective of what others are doing. Hence, with beautiful discipline Daniel lived by this military code.

Observe how the General of Heaven's armies issued differing orders to His post-exilic soldiers. He led Mordecai, Esther, and Ezra to remain in foreign lands and blessed them for doing so, yet He ordered Zerubbabel, Joshua, and Nehemiah to return and rebuild Jerusalem's temple and walls. Sometime later, he changed Ezra's orders and sent him back to Palestine to stir the backslidden remnant to repentance (Ezra 7–10). Centuries earlier, He ordered King Saul and all the men of Israel, including David's older brothers, to go fight the Philistines, yet ordered David to remain behind and care for his father's sheep (1 Sam. 17). Obediently, David remained behind. A few days later, to David's surprise, Jesse sent him to the war camp to bring his brothers some food. So, obediently, David went to the camp—not because his brothers had done this but because he was called to do it. There he met and conquered Goliath. In all these instances, God's soldiers respected the sovereign individuality of His call. With military discipline, each did what they were told to do, without considering what others were doing. And as good soldiers, they stayed where God put them, doing what He told them to do, until they received further orders. Their mindsets were quite the opposite of the "herding" seen too often today among Christians.

Herding occurs whenever believers gather with other believers and blindly follow their path. Invariably, those who herd do so because they lack personal spiritual assurance. They have not cultivated their own ear to hear God by much fellow-ship with Him, so they must rely on other Christians for guid-ance—a very dangerous thing to do. Lacking the sharp eyesight of a lynx, most sheep don't know the difference between a safe path and a deadly cliff, but the Good Shepherd does and will always advise His sheep perfectly if they will only abide very close to Him and His Word. Nevertheless, herding remains a very strong and dangerous tendency among Christians. But we may become like Daniel.

In deciding where we will go and live and work and wor-ship, we must remember Daniel's military discipline. As it was for him, the question for us is not what are other believers doing, or where is the Spirit moving, or what is the Lord leading our close friends to do, but rather, "Lord, what wilt thou have *me* to do?" (Acts 9:6, emphasis added). The answer to this ques-tion alone constitutes our "orders."

Are we becoming good soldiers of Jesus Christ? Are we herding, or are we hearing God's voice? Are we just going where others go or learning to stay where God puts us—until further orders?

See John 2:5; 21:20–22; 1 Kings 17:2–24; 18:1–2; Acts 9:6; 26:19; Matthew 20:15; Romans 9:20–21; 2 Timothy 2:3–4.

Lesson: *God's call is an individual matter; with military discipline, we must each go where He calls, do what He commands, and stay where He puts us—until further orders.*

10:3 On anointing with oil. Daniel states that during his three-week fast he did not anoint himself. This was typical of persons in mourning in that day and culture. Why was he mourning? Despite the beginning of the Jews' return to Palestine some two years earlier, Daniel was still mourning for the yet-unrestored state of Israel. On the practice of anointing with oil, *The Zondervan Pictorial Bible Dictionary* states:

> To apply oil to a person or thing [was] a practice com-
> mon in the East. Anointing was of three kinds: ordi-
> nary, sacred, and medical. Ordinary anointing with
> scented oils was a common toilet [washing] opera-
> tion... It was discontinued during a time of mourn-
> ing... (p.46)

Orientals typically anointed themselves by rubbing in oil
(scented or unscented) on their bodies or faces after bathing (see
Ruth 3:3; 2 Sam. 12:20); thus cleaned and refreshed, their faces
"shined" with radiant health and beauty (see Ps. 104:15). This
shouldn't seem strange to us. Even as recent as the first half of the
twentieth century, most men "anointed" their hair with an oil or
grooming cream before combing. To this day, most men still put
on a touch of aftershave or cologne, thus "anointing" themselves
as they finish their daily ritual of cleansing. Ancient athletes and
posts (message runners) as well as others involved in strenuous
physical labors anointed their bodies before exerting themselves
to prevent excessive perspiration. A guest's head was often
anointed as a gesture of respect and hospitality. (See Matt. 26:7;
Luke 7:46.) Also, the bodies of the dead were anointed before
burial. (See Mark 14:8.)

Other uses, as stated by Zondervan, were for sacred or medic-
inal purposes. Holy persons (priests) and things (tabernacle, altar,
etc.) were anointed to signify complete consecration to God, while
wounds were anointed to mollify them. (See Luke 10:34.)

Anointing oil, one of the most often used biblical symbols
of the Holy Spirit, speaks to every Christian today. Do we realize what happens when God anoints us with the oil of heaven,
the Holy Spirit, in His marvelous fullness? By doing so, God:

- SIGNIFIES we are thoroughly washed in Jesus' blood—
  and saved

- INSPIRES us with joy so our faces shine daily with the
  radiant beauty of Jesus

- RUBS the fragrance of Jesus' life upon us so that sinners,
  delighted and attracted, will be drawn to Him

- STRENGTHENS AND INSULATES us to run the race set
  before us and bear God's messages without exhaustion

- HONORS us as Christ's guests, personally invited to His
  marriage supper and kingdom

- CONFIRMS that we are dead to sin—and alive unto
  Christ forevermore

- ORDAINS us as holy, New Testament believer-priests,
  fully authorized to offer effective intercession and
  pleasing worship daily

- PROVIDES us with a balm of comforting supernatural
  grace that softens and heals every heart wound we
  receive—if we but accept and trust and obey

That Daniel feels it necessary to tell us he did *not* anoint
himself for twenty-one days implies that normally he anointed
himself daily. David, who was anointed as king three times during his lifetime, also wrote of his glad anticipation of receiving
ongoing fresh anointings of the Spirit: "Thou anoint*est* my
head with oil" (Ps. 23:5, emphasis added; Ps. 92:10).

Like Daniel and David, we too need fresh anointings of the
Holy Spirit daily. We "anoint ourselves" by drawing near the
Lord in Bible meditation, prayer, and worship. There He endows
us with fresh supplies of His Spirit. Have you anointed yourself
today?

See Ephesians 5:18–20.

Lesson: *We need fresh anointings of the Holy Spirit every
day.*

10:5–7 A "vision-tation" of God. In Daniel 10:5–7, Daniel
describes the second visitation of God recorded in this book, the
first being described in Daniel 3:25. Unlike the first visitation,
however, this second visitation is also a vision: "And I, Daniel,
alone saw the *vision*..." (Dan. 10:7, emphasis added). It is therefore a "vision-tation," a vision *and* a visitation of God combined.

That this vision is of the glory of Jesus Christ and not
merely of an angel is seen in:

1. Its similarities to the vision of the apostle John (Rev. 1:13–16), the Transfiguration (Matt. 17:2–3), and the vision of Saul of Tarsus (Acts 9:1–9; cp. Dan. 10:7 & Acts 22:9), all of which we know to be visions or visitations of Jesus in His full glory.

2. Daniel's description. Daniel, who saw angels on several occasions (Dan. 7:16; 8:16; 9:21–23; 10:13, 21), described the event as "this great vision" (Dan. 10:8), clearly indicating he considered it something far grander than the sighting of an angel.

The other "one like the appearance of a man" (vv. 10–15, 18–21) was an angel, who, as on earlier occasions, was present to interpret to Daniel what he was seeing and hearing (see Dan. 7:16; 8:16; 9:21–23; 10:14, 21).

Hence, this is also a *theophany*, or "a pre-incarnation manifestation of God in human form" (see Gen. 18; Dan. 3:25). *The Zondervan Pictorial Bible Dictionary* notes:

> There is good reason to think that theophanies before the incarnation of Christ were visible manifestations of the pre-incarnate Son of God. It is to be noticed that theophanies ceased with the incarnation of our Lord. (p. 846)

10:5–7 The conditions for visitation. Most interesting are the circumstances of this visitation: Daniel was mourning, not merrymaking; he was grieving over the "unfinished business" of Israel's full repentance and restoration (see Dan. 9:3–19), not glorying over the limited progress that had been made. (Cyrus' decree had been issued approximately two years earlier, and the first expedition under Zerubbabel had already returned to Jerusalem.)

Gifted twentieth-century writer and prophet A. W. Tozer wrote a piece and a book entitled *God Tells the Man Who Cares*. Here we see God doing just that—visiting a man who cared greatly about God's will and people to inform him of things to come (see Dan. 10:14). By relating this to us in this chapter, the

Holy Spirit subtly intimates that God will do this again if He can find Christians with humble, truthful, broken hearts like Daniel's.

This is a challenge to us in this Laodicean generation. If we really want a visitation in these last days, we'll quit boasting of our material prosperity, numbers of converts, and institutional growth, and we will face our spiritual bankruptcy. (See Rev. 3:17.) We'll stop howling at Christian comedians and begin facing the stark reality of our besetting sins and crippling moral compromise. (See Rev. 3:14–16.) (I have a healthy sense of humor and know well "a merry heart doeth good like a medicine," but there's no place for unchecked frivolity in the pulpit or in God's house, especially in these perilous times of imminent worldwide judgment.) Jesus has promised to visit us if we will show Him we care (Rev. 3:20). Ecclesiastes declares it is better to experience godly mourning than ungodly mirth (Eccles. 7:2–6). If we want to receive a "vision-tation"—a new vision of and visitation by Christ—we can have it, but only if we follow Daniel's example, not by indulging in self-complacent pride and thoughtless religious merriment but by mourning over our selfish sins and stubborn refusal to do God's will and all the trouble and confusion they have caused.

Everywhere Christians are praying for a visitation; where are those who are meeting the conditions?

See 2 Chronicles 7:14; Revelation 3:20; Ecclesiastes 7:2–6.

Lesson: *Jesus will visit us as He did Daniel—not when we're rolling with laughter but when we're grieving over our sins and lukewarmness and praying earnestly for mercy.*

10:10–21 God answers prayer from the first day...but keep praying! Here Daniel is touched by an angel, who informs him that his prayers (Dan. 10:2–3) have been answered. The angel's speech reveals some vital secrets about prayer. They are:

- Earnest, believing prayer offered according to God's

will and accompanied by fasting is heard immediately in heaven (Dan. 10:12; see Mark 11:24; 1 John 5:14–15).

- God responds immediately—literally "from the first day" (Dan. 10:12)—by dispatching angels with His answers (Dan. 10:12; 9:23; Heb. 1:14). Other Bible references reveal this counterbalancing truth: Sometimes God purposely delays the execution of these divine orders because He has sovereignly fixed an appointed or "set" time to act (see Ps. 102:13; Dan. 7:21–22).

- Demons often, perhaps always, resist the angels who bring the answers to our prayers (Dan. 10:13a).

- In such cases, continued prayer and fasting stirs God to send overwhelming angelic intervention, resulting in a spiritual breakthrough (Dan. 10:2, 13b–14).

- Implied is that if we "faint" (Luke 18:1), or quit believing, praying, and waiting patiently for God's answer, we will not *receive* the answer God has already granted and sent (see 2 Kings 7:1–2; James 1:6–7; Num. 14:28–30).

So we see the imperative of importunity and the true nature of the prayer of faith. Some teach if we truly believe we have received our petitions (Mark 11:24), we should never again pray about them. Yet if Daniel had done this, he never would have received his answer. Why? Because it was his twenty-one-day continuance in importunity that caused the heavenly breakthrough. (See Dan. 10:2, 13b–14.) We too must learn to persist in both belief and prayer. At its core, the true prayer of faith is a matter, not of believing we have received *or* continuing to pray, but of believing we have received *and* continuing to pray. The message of Daniel 10 is this: God answers prayer literally "from the first day" it is offered, but since demons resist the arrival of our answers, we must believe we have received *and* continue praying until our answers arrive (holding and confessing confidence that we *have* been heard; 1 John 5:14–15).

As no other portion of sacred Scripture does, this account

explains what happens as we continue praying: *Our prayers carry forward an invisible but real heavenly conflict.* It is a perfect illustration of the New Testament revelation given in Ephesians 6:10–18. When his prayer wasn't answered speedily, Daniel stood fast, "strong in the Lord, and in the power of his might." Fully clad in "the whole armor of God," he kept "praying always with all prayer and supplication in the Spirit." As he thus withstood, holy angels kept fighting for his cause with ever more effectiveness against "the rulers of the darkness of this world" and "spiritual wickedness in high places." Eventually—in this case twenty-one days later—a breakthrough came. Hence Daniel was a true prayer warrior—a believer whose steadfast prayers caused and controlled a heavenly angelic "holy war" that weakened the kingdom of darkness and strengthened and blessed the children of light. Wisely, Daniel understood that the weapons of his warfare were not carnal but mighty through God to pull down strongholds. (See 2 Cor. 10:4.) Personally, he couldn't overpower or control the evil angels that opposed his answer, but he could do one thing: keep praying in faith! So he used the weapon of prayer. The good news is that this was enough!

Has it ever hit you, that by standing in God's armor and praying in the Spirit according to God's will, you too can prevail over all the power of the enemy? Are you fainting or standing, giving up the good fight or seeking your breakthrough?

See "Caution: Angels at work," chapter 9.

See Luke 11:1–10; 18:1–8; Matthew 15:21–28; Mark 10:46–52; 1 Kings 18:42–45; Acts 12:5, 12; 2 Corinthians 10:3–5; Ephesians 6:10–18.

Lesson: *God answers prayer from the first day it is offered. But since demons resist the arrival of His answers, we should both believe we have received our answers and continue praying until they arrive.*

10:12 Have we come to the "first day"? The angel explicitly says God answered Daniel's prayers "from the first day" (Dan. 10:12). But he doesn't stop there. Rather he goes on to describe that "first day" of prayer by revealing more fully Daniel's attitude and actions. On that "first day," Daniel was:

1. DETERMINED to get an answer. He "set thine [his] heart" to hear from God (Dan. 10:12; see Dan. 9:3). So he was not indifferent.

2. SELF-DISCIPLINED. Humbly, he put himself on a partial fast to assure God's answer (Dan. 10:12, 2–3). So he was not indulgent.

We must understand that God didn't respond the first day Daniel merely prayed; He responded the first day he prayed *and* did the other things mentioned: setting his heart and disciplining himself. Thus God reveals that, to Him, not only the right requests but the right attitude and actions are vital to the success of our prayers.

So Daniel sets for us an example that both reassures and rebukes us. If we are becoming zealous prayer warriors, Daniel's spiritual success reassures us that we too will succeed, but if our petitions are usually spiritless and apathetic and our daily lives are undisciplined, Daniel is a rebuke to us. We're not praying as he prayed. Why not? Sadly, some Christians live their whole lives without reaching Daniel's "first day." They dutifully pray the right petitions but fail to possess Daniel's accompanying attitude and actions.

What about us? Do we make the right requests but fail to fix our hearts or discipline our lives? Then we cannot hope for the success Daniel enjoyed in prayer—but we can change. This is the day the Lord has made; why not make it your "first day"?

See James 5:16b–18; 1 Kings 18:42–45; 2 Corinthians 11:27; Mark 9:29.

Lesson: *God will answer our prayers the first day we pray with humble, determined hearts and self-disciplined lives.*

10:12 "Because of your words." The angel also explicitly told Daniel he had been sent "because of your words" (Dan. 10:12, NKJV). Other translations read: "in response to your words" (NAS); "in response to your prayers" (MODERN LANGUAGE BIBLE); "as a consequence of...your words" (AMP). All these renderings point out that God listens very carefully to the humble, fervent prayers of His redeemed ones. His decisions and responsive actions spring from the exact "words" they speak.

Have we ever realized that "our words"—the very things we say, the precise requests we make, the situations and persons we choose to focus on—make a difference? If we speak no words in prayer, nothing happens. But if our words address certain problems, needs, and desires, things happen in those very areas "because of our words." Though small, this is a very inspiring insight. Faith that God actually sends angels in response to *our words* (not Daniel's, Noah's, or Moses') puts fresh life and meaning into our prayers. It makes us realize that our prayer time really counts, that our private talks with God do make a difference. If God acts *because of our words*—and the Book of Daniel reveals He does—our seemingly mundane conversations with Him in the secret place are anything but mundane. They are vitally important to us and others.

So before you pray, stop and think: What you say really matters. God will be issuing orders, angels will be flying swiftly, demons will be resisting, revelations will be forthcoming, you will be touched and strengthened, circumstances will be changed and lives permanently altered, all "because of your words."

See Matthew 6:6, 8, 32–33; Luke 1:13; Genesis 24:12–14, 19; Numbers 14:19–20; Judges 6:36–40; 1 Kings 3:12; 2 Chronicles 30:20; Psalms 20:1–5; 21:2; 37:4; Daniel 2:18–19, 23; Mark 11:24; Hebrews 1:14; Philemon 22; John 9:31b; 1 Peter 3:12a; Acts 12:5–11.

Lesson: *The specific words we speak in our prayer petitions are very important; God sends angels to fulfill them.*

10:21 Michael—Israel's keeper. Daniel's angelic visitor furthermore identifies Michael as Israel's designated guardian angel: "Michael, your [Israel's] prince" (Dan. 10:21). Accordingly, the Bible reveals Michael acting in Israel's defense, opposing evil angels who sought to hinder Israel's prophets (Dan. 10:13) and opposing Antichrist and his anti-Israeli campaign of terror (Dan. 12:1).

While Michael is the only angel specifically identified as an archangel in the Bible (see Jude 9), the totality of biblical evidence seems to indicate he is one of three original and two remaining archangels, the others being Gabriel and Lucifer. Though this is clearly debatable, I believe Bible evidence supports the position that *originally* the archangels were:

1. Lucifer, the highest cherub and closest to God (see Ezek. 28:14)

2. Michael, the special guardian of Israel (see Dan. 12:1; Jude 9; Rev. 12:7)

3. Gabriel, who stands in God's presence and delivers His most important messages (see Dan. 8:16; 9:21; Luke 1:19, 26).

Since Lucifer's rebellion, of course, only Michael and Gabriel have retained their original position; hence, their vital appearances to help the righteous in the ongoing drama of human history.

See "Introducing Gabriel: a first mention," chapter 8; also "There shall be a time of great trouble," and "Michael shall 'stand up,'" chapter 12.

Lesson: Michael is an archangel and the designated guardian of Israel.

10:7–9,11,15,17 The rigors of revelation. Daniel paid a high price for the final lofty revelation he received (chapters 10–12). In Daniel 10 he records seven personal distresses:

1. LONELINESS. Daniel's companions didn't see, and so couldn't share, his vision; then they abandoned him (v. 7).

2. CONVICTION OF SIN. After seeing God, Daniel's human goodness seemed but "corruption"; hence he grieved over his innate sinfulness (vv. 8, 16; see Isa. 6:5; Rom. 7:18).

3. COMPLETE EXHAUSTION. Drained by the sheer excitement of the vision, he "retained no strength" (vv. 8, 16–17).

4. UNCONSCIOUSNESS. He was rendered unconscious, "in a deep sleep" (v. 9; see Acts 10:10).

5. INVOLUNTARY PROSTRATION. Spontaneously he found himself "on my face" (v. 9).

6. SPEECHLESSNESS. He was temporarily stricken "dumb" (v. 15; see Ezek. 3:26).

7. BREATHLESSNESS. His heavy spiritual burden made breathing difficult (v. 17).

In addition to these, Daniel had other distresses to bear during his prophetic tenure. For instance, anguishing decisions (chapter 1), sudden, deadly troubles (chapter 2), unpleasant interpretations to evil and volatile kings (chapters 4 and 5), cruel persecution from his enemies (chapter 6), and his own self-imposed spiritual disciplines, such as the twenty-one days of partial fasting and grief noted in this chapter (Dan. 10:2–4). Ah, but such is the life of a prophet!

Now who is in a hurry to be a prophet or prophetess? Let him or her understand that along with the inestimable privileges of access to God, hearing His voice and speaking for Him, come the inescapable rigors of revelation. Why does God reveal them? To check our headlong rush into the ministry with the sobering truth that a degree of personal distress always accompanies heavenly messages. To comfort God's people, ministers must periodically endure discomforts. This was Daniel's experience.

That it is also true of every messenger of God is a test.

Do we love Jesus and His people enough to bear the rigors of revelation?

See "Overwhelmed and lonely," chapter 8; also "The prophet's personal reaction," chapter 7.

See Daniel 7:15–16; 8:27; Exodus 3:6; Ezekiel 1:28; 3:23, 26; Isaiah 6:5; Jeremiah 9:1; Amos 2:13; Mark 9:5–6; Revelation 1:17.

Lesson: *To bring comforting messages to God's people, ministers must periodically endure discomfort.*

CHAPTER ELEVEN

MORE ON ANTIOCHUS IV— AND ANTICHRIST

11:1 SUPPORTING KINGS. As Daniel 11 opens, Daniel's angelic visitor testifies that two years earlier God sent him "to confirm and to strengthen" King Darius the Mede during what was then the first year of his rule in Babylon (see Dan. 5:30–6:3). This he did no doubt by various means, such as:

- Giving Darius personal strength, judicial wisdom, administrative skill, and acumen

- Giving Darius wise counselors and able administrators, such as Daniel (see Dan. 6:1–3)

- Giving Darius favor with influential regional leaders, who in turn helped him establish his administration in their region

- Frustrating Darius's secret enemies, who tried to ruin him or his helpers surreptitiously (see Dan. 6:24)

- Driving away or terminating all who made open claims to Darius's throne (see 1 Kings 2:12–46)

- Establishing stability in Darius's kingdom by fostering

economic prosperity, health, and goodwill among the king's newly conquered subjects

- Establishing peace by restraining military aggression by foreign nations

- Supernaturally shielding the kingdom from any other potentially ruinous occurrences—natural disasters, crop failures, plagues, drought, etc.

Taken together, these and perhaps other measures taken by the angel gave Darius confidence in rulership during his first year, a period when any monarch was most susceptible to failure due to self-doubt, death plots, or rebellion. But why did God's angel support Darius, a heathen king?

Though not stated in chapter 11, clear reasons for this divine support by angelic (and human) agency are found elsewhere in the Book of Daniel. Succinctly, they are:

- Darius favored God's favored prophet, Daniel (Dan. 6:1–3, 14, 16, 18, 19, 23).

- Darius favored God's favored people, the Jews (Dan. 6:24).

- Darius had greatly honored God (Dan. 6:25–27).

So God blessed the king who honored Him, blessed His prophet, and blessed His people. Two universal and perpetual fundamental spiritual principles were at work here: Genesis 12:3 and 1 Samuel 2:30. Always, God blesses those who bless His people. Always, He honors those who honor Him.

He does the same to this day. God supports heads of state (even if, as Darius, they are not believers) who favor Christians, the Christian faith, the Church, and the state of Israel by assigning angels "to confirm and to strengthen" them, particularly in the first crucial months and years of their service. Thus we see yet another function of angels: to render special assistance to leaders who in any way honor God or bless His covenant people. The implications to the contrary seem obvious.

Namely, this implies that God also sends angels to frustrate and oppose the works of heads of state who dishonor Him or oppose His people and plan in the earth. Biblical history repeatedly confirms this. Joseph was, in a sense, an angel to the Pharaoh who so highly favored him and his father's family, for it was through Joseph that Pharaoh was confirmed and strengthened during the great famine, surely the worst period of his reign (see Gen. 41–50). Conversely, God sent evil angels (including the death angel) to plague and frustrate the Pharaoh of the Exodus for his cruel mistreatment of His people and obstinate opposition to His revealed will.

What about your King Darius? If the leader of your nation promotes policies that honor God and bless His people, pray for angels to support him. If he doesn't, pray for his repentance. And meanwhile, remember who is frustrating him and why.

See "Caution: Angels at work," chapter 9.

See Genesis 12:3; 1 Kings 2:12–46; Isaiah 45:1–4.

Lesson: *God sends angels to support heads of state who honor Him by favoring His people and plan in the world, and He also sends angels to frustrate those who don't.*

11:2–45 The Syrian and Egyptian wars, King Antiochus IV, and Antichrist. After leaping forward to describe the tribulation period (chapter 9) and then informing us of the very difficult prayer-battle by which Daniel received his angelic interpreter (chapter 10), the spirit of prophecy next described what the angel revealed. That inspired foretelling began with the near future, specifically the duration of the Persian Empire and four of its remaining prominent kings (Dan. 11:2). They were:

1. Cyrus II (550–530 B.C.)

2. Cambyses (529–522 B.C.)

3. Darius I Hystaspes (521–486 B.C.)

4. Xerxes (486–465 B.C.) or Artaxerxes (465–424 B.C.)

Daniel's interpreter then described the Greek dominion and influence that would follow, first under "a mighty king" (Alexander the Great, Dan. 11:3), then under the four generals who succeeded him, none of whom would be his children or rule a territory as vast as his (Dan. 11:4). With this, we come to the period of the Syrian and Egyptian wars.

The Syrian and Egyptian wars (Daniel 11:5–20).

As noted in chapter 8, Alexander the Great's four generals succeeded him after his untimely death. In chapter 11, the spirit of prophecy focused on two of the dynasties that ruled in the former Alexandrian empire: the Seleucids (or Seleucidae) of Syria (kings of the north) and the Ptolemies of Egypt (kings of the south). Each of these ruling families came to power in 323 B.C., after Alexander's death, and held sway until the Romans conquered them in 65 B.C. (Seleucidae) and 30 B.C. (Ptolemies) respectively.

Important points disclosed in this prophetic passage are:

- Daniel 11:6: The two dynasties made a marriage alliance; Berenice, the daughter of Ptolemy II Philadelphus (the king of the south) married the Syrian ruler (the king of the north). But this treaty failed and war ensued.

- Daniel 11:7–9: The first conflict occurred when the armies of the king of Egypt (Ptolemy III Euergetes), who was closely related to Queen Berenice of Syria (v. 8), invaded and conquered Syria, taking great spoil with him back to Egypt (v. 8).

- Daniel 11:10–12: Stirred by vengeance, the Syrian king's two sons (Seleucus III Ceraunus and Antiochus III the Great) formed a large army and attacked the Egyptians, albeit unsuccessfully (vv. 10–11). After the Egyptian forces withstood their Syrian invaders, their king, Ptolemy V, was enlarged with pride, but his kingdom did not grow larger (v. 12).

- Daniel 11:13–14: Not to be denied, the Syrians again attacked, this time under the leadership of King

Antiochus III the Great, whose even larger armies included many non-Syrian soldiers ("many," v. 14a), among them Jewish zealots who had tried unsuccessfully to drive the Egyptians from Palestine and reestablish "the vision" of Jewish autonomy (v. 14b).

- Daniel 11:15: This time the Syrian coalition prevailed, besieging and taking Egypt's strongest cities and defeating its best warriors (v. 15).

- Daniel 11:16: In the same campaign, Syrian forces took control of Palestine, "the glorious land."

- Daniel 11:17–19: Victorious, Antiochus III the Great made another marriage alliance with the Ptolemies, which, like the first, failed to establish lasting peace (v. 17). Afterward he conducted other military campaigns in Asia Minor and Greece. *The Ryrie Study Bible* says of his eventual demise: He was "defeated by the Romans at Magnesia in 190 B.C., was forced to pay tribute, and soon died (v. 19)" (p. 1330).

- Daniel 11:20: Antiochus III's successor was Seleucus IV Philopator. A "raiser of taxes" in the glorious kingdom (Israel), he laid a heavy tribute on the Jews before his death.

This brings us to the next and most notorious of the Seleucidae, Antiochus IV.

More on King Antiochus IV (Epiphanes) (Daniel 11:21–35)

Continuing in the spirit of prophecy, Daniel's interpreter gives us more vital information about King Antiochus IV (Epiphanes) and his reign of terror in Israel.

- Daniel 11:21: Though of royal descent, Antiochus IV gained the Syrian throne not by right but by craft. *The Living Bible* notes, "When his brother Seleucus was assassinated, [he] ingratiated himself with the Romans and took over" (p. 913).

- Daniel 11:22–24: His early reign was marked by military success. He repelled invading armies and forced them to make peace with him (v. 22). But he did not honor his peace agreements, using them instead as political fronts behind which he plotted further military actions against unsuspecting kings and nations (v. 23a). Forming a strong army from a comparatively small population (v. 23b), he proved more successful at war and plunder than any of his Seleucid predecessors (v. 24)— but only "for a time" (v. 24); this is, until his predestined time of judgment (as will later be the case with Antichrist).

- Daniel 11:25–28: He invaded Egypt, whose king was betrayed by his trusted associates (vv. 25c–26), and after defeating the huge Egyptian army, forced the "king of the south" to accept a peace treaty that greatly enriched Antiochus IV (vv. 27–28a). While returning to Syria through Palestine, Antiochus IV received his wicked inspiration to destroy the Jewish religion, his "final solution" to the Jewish problem (v. 28).

- Daniel 11:29–30: Later he attempted to invade and spoil Egypt again (v. 29) but was repulsed by the intervention of Roman naval forces based in (or sailing from) Cyprus ("Kittim"; v. 30). Enraged by this defeat, he turned on the Jews by first plotting (v. 30b, c), then launching, a violent and cruel anti-Judaism campaign throughout Israel (vv. 31–35).

- Daniel 11:31: By military force, he entered Jerusalem, stopped all Jewish worship, erected an idol-altar to Zeus ("the abomination that maketh desolate"), and profaned the temple by sacrificing a pig on its altar (v. 31). Thus, strangely, Satan's servant triumphed over God's people. But, again, only until "the time appointed" for judgment (v. 27b).

- Daniel 11:32–35: This *triumphing of the wicked* forced a spiritual polarization among the Jews. All apostates came together in support of Antiochus IV, who influenced and misled their leaders with flatteries (vv. 30c, 32a); some apostates later feigned true faith and loyalty to Jehovah when this was to their advantage (v. 34b). Simultaneously, all godly Jews (the right-

eous remnant) banded together under the leadership of
the Maccabees. These uncompromisingly righteous
believers (of the same stock as Daniel and his three
friends) boldly resisted the Syrian armies (v. 32b) and
taught many Jews God's Word, despite forbiddance by
Syrian law (v. 33a). In retaliation, "some" of them were
taken captive by the Syrians, who burned their homes
and sacked their cities (v. 33b). During this time, these
suffering zealots received limited help from disloyal
Jews, who, despite their open betrayal of Jehovah,
hoped to retain the favor of His true servants (v. 34).
Antiochus IV's cruel intentions aside, God had a good
purpose in allowing this long and bitter war: It was an
ultimate test, sent to "test" the Jews' faith, loyalty, and
patience, to "purge" their hearts of sin and their congregations of apostates, and to make them "white" with
righteous acts in the first "time of the end," or final
years of the post-exilic period (v. 35). Thus He prepared them for the coming of their Messiah (see Mal.
3:3–4; 4:1–3).

See "On Antiochus IV and Antichrist," chapter 8.

More on Antichrist—the "willful king" (Daniel 11:36–45)

As if leaping a great valley (the Church Age) lying between
the first "time of the end" (Dan. 11:35), which occurred just
before Jesus' first coming, and the second "time of the end,"
which will immediately precede His second coming to earth, the
remainder of chapter 11 (vv. 36–45) gives us further vital information about Antichrist, the prime character in the tribulation
drama. That this latter "time of the end" (Dan. 11:35, 40; 12:4,
9) is in fact the tribulation period is proven in Daniel 12:1,
where the Spirit speaking through Daniel's angelic interpreter
begins, "And at that time…" By his careful use of the conjunction and, the preceding passage (Dan. 11:36–45) is solidly
linked to that which follows it (chapter 12), which unmistakably
describes Michael's intervention on Israel's behalf during the
tribulation period. The strong language used in Daniel 12—"a

time of trouble, such as never was since there was a nation" (Dan. 12:1)—precludes its application to any other time.

Clearly, then, the time of Antichrist is foreseen in Daniel 11:36–45, with only limited or near fulfillments occurring in the life and times of Antiochus IV. This willful king:

- SERVES HIS—NOT GOD'S OR MAN'S—WILL. With utter disdain for the will of God or man, this "king" (head of state) will do "according to his will" (Dan. 11:36). Shockingly, God gives him "carte blanche"—though only for a limited amount of time, "till the indignation be accomplished" (Dan. 11:36; see Rev. 13:5; Dan. 7:22, 25).

- CLAIMS DEITY. He "shall exalt himself, and magnify himself above every god" (Dan. 11:36). Purporting to be the consummation of all religions incarnate, he naturally disregards all religions and gods except himself. And this, his great lie, will be believed by the masses: "And [he] shall prosper [in his false claims]" (Dan. 11:36; see 2 Thess. 2:4; Rev. 13:14–15).

- REVERES WAR, CLAIMS TO BE THE "GOD OF WAR." "The god of forces (lit. *fortresses*)" (Dan. 11:38) may refer to a religious cult that he founds at the first of the seven-year tribulation. This religion idolizes war in general and himself in particular as the "god of war" incarnate. Antichrist worships war. In his and his followers' eyes, war is life's most noble pursuit and military heroism its highest achievement. As history's most successful warrior (heading its most imposing military "beast" ever), he must be greater than all conquerors—or their gods (see Rev. 13:4; 6:2; Dan. 8:24). Hence, his divine claims and the creation of an image to honor himself, the "god of war," and hence the worship of those who share his fanatical devotion to warfare. (Antichrist will be militarily irresistible from the start of the seven-year period [see Rev. 6:2]; the masses worship his miraculous success at war; see Rev. 13:4.) This—himself, the "god of war" and his image—is the god "whom his fathers knew not" (Dan. 11:38) and whom he calls all to worship.

- REWARDS HIS WORSHIPERS. Those who show reverence

for Antichrist and his "divine image" will be rewarded, some with high political empowerment: "He shall cause them to rule over many, and shall divide the land for gain" (Dan. 11:39). His most ardent worshipers will become his ten lieutenant-kings, whose fanatical, to-the-death devotion to the "god of war" leads them to just that: death in war with Antichrist. (See Rev. 17:12–14; 19:19–21.) In this and the previous point, Hitler was an amazingly accurate type of antichrist.

- OPENLY SLANDERS GOD. A skilled orator, his recurring theme will be deriding God, which he will do with unprecedented openness and vehemence: "[He shall] speak marvelous ["monstrous," NAS; "astonishing," AMP; "unheard-of," NIV] things against the God of gods" (Dan. 11:36; see Dan. 7:20, 25; Rev. 13:5–6). This begins with his furious reaction to the shocking but undeniable Rapture of the Church, yet undisclosed to Daniel.

- ENJOYS UNPRECEDENTED POLITICAL AND MILITARY SUCCESS. The consummate politician and military commander, he will succeed at everything he undertakes, politically and militarily, "and shall prosper" (Dan. 11:36). But this lasts only until his course and God's plagues are finished: "till the indignation be accomplished" (Dan. 11:36; see Job 20:4–5).

- INVADES, CONQUERS, AND RULES ISRAEL. He "shall enter also into the glorious land..." (Dan. 11:41), a reference to his successful military campaign against Israel at the mid-point of the tribulation (see Rev. 13:7a; Dan. 8:24; 7:21, 25). Then Israel is ruled three and a half years under "his hand [control]" (Dan. 11:41–42).

- CONQUERS AND RULES MANY NATIONS. Not only Israel, but "many countries shall be overthrown [by the willful king]...He shall stretch forth his hand also upon the [many] countries [to rule them]" (Dan. 11:41–42). Revelation specifies that his domain will in fact be *all* nations (divine authorization for, if not actual governance; see Rev. 13:7b).

- FAVORS AND SPARES SELECT ARAB STATES. Antichrist's inbred hatred of everything Jewish will make him an enthusiastic sympathizer with the "Palestinian cause." So when he invades the Middle East, he will spare the Arab nations that have long hated and vexed Israel: "But these shall escape out of his hand, even [the people descended from] Edom, and Moab, and the chief of the children of Ammon" (Dan. 11:41b). After crushing Israel, it is only natural that he reward her most current and vicious enemies among the Arab peoples and states—Syria, Iraq, Iran, Lebanon, Jordan, Saudi Arabia, and the so-called Palestinian refugees.

- CONTROLS WORLD MONETARY SYSTEM. Reference is made here to Antichrist gaining control ("have power," Dan. 11:43) over not only the wealth and monetary systems of natural Egypt but also those of spiritual Egypt—the whole world (see Rev. 13:16–17).

- WILL FACE REBELLION. The ageless, universal law of sowing and reaping will at last overtake even Antichrist. In his final days, the arch-rebel will have to take his own medicine—rebellion, as insurrection brews in both the Far East and Europe: "But tidings [bad news] out of the east and out of the north shall trouble him…" (Dan. 11:44). To preserve his throne, therefore, the "god of war" will leave Jerusalem, his seat of power, and "go forth with great fury to destroy, and utterly to |sweep| away [his] many [challengers]" (Dan. 11:44). By divine providence, he will gather his vast military forces between Jerusalem and the Mediterranean (Dan. 11:45a) in a place called *Armageddon* (the mountain of Megiddo; see Rev. 16:16).

- LIKE HIS RISE, HIS FALL IS DIVINELY FOREORDAINED AND IMMUTABLE. God declares this willful king shall come on the scene and "shall do" (Dan. 11:36) various evils; thus, God predestines his entrance in Israel's future. But God also declares he will prosper only "till the indignation [God's wrathful trumpet and bowl judgments] be accomplished…which is [divinely pre-]determined" (Dan. 11:36); hence, God also predestines his exit. "Yet he shall come to his end…" (Dan. 11:45; see Dan. 7:24, 26; 9:24, 26–27; 8:23, 25; Acts 15:18). So Antichrist's rise and fall are divinely foreordained and immutable—

neither earthly nor heavenly forces can change them. "For that which is [pre-]determined shall be done" (Dan. 11:36c).

See "The tribulation period foretold," chapter 7; "On Antiochus IV and Antichrist," chapter 8; "A prophecy of Israel's seventy weeks," chapter 9.

11:37–38 The desire of women. "Neither shall he regard... the desire of women" (Dan. 11:37). The popular idea taken from this verse, that Antichrist will not have a natural desire for women, is erroneous. To the contrary, this states that he will have no respect for Tammuz, the idol god (purported husband of Ashtoreth [Ishtar]) whom many women of Daniel's (and Ezekiel's) day desired with foolish and idolatrous passion. The prophet Ezekiel describes seeing Hebrew women mourning for Tammuz at the very gate of the Jewish temple (Ezek. 8:14).

The context in verses 37 and 38—the various religions and gods of history—is the key to interpreting the "desire of women." It has nothing to do with sexuality and everything to do with worship. The thought here is that Antichrist will neither worship nor respect *any idol-god*, whether those preferred by men ("the gods of his fathers") or those worshiped by women ("the desire of women"). In no way does this text state Antichrist will be void of a natural sex drive and thus be either asexual, homosexual, or bisexual in behavior. Remember, Hitler, who was a strong Antichrist type, was strongly heterosexual, carrying on well-documented affairs with his teenage niece, Geli Raubal, and later with his longtime mistress Eva Von Braun, whom he married on April 29, 1945, the day before they both committed suicide.

11:44–45 At the end of the end...more trouble! While Antichrist is given authority to rule all nations for three and a half years (see Rev. 13:5), his reign is not trouble-free. These verses describe the troubling military insurrections (prompted by the horrific devastations of the trumpet and bowl judgments) that arise within his worldwide kingdom in its final months as his evil utopia begins falling apart. Why will this happen?

First, because it is the judgment of God. Antichrist has sown rebellion, so he must reap it; he has plotted and overthrown others, so his overthrow must be plotted (see Rev. 13:9–10). Second, severe pressure from outside a kingdom typically prompts rebellion within it. When wars go badly, heads of state always risk rebellion from their people. (Remember, Hitler became the object of several death plots, one of which almost succeeded, in the final year [July 1944] of his crumbling Third Reich. Also, Pharaoh's counselors severely criticized him when his stubborn resistance to God's will resulted in the near-dismantlement of Egypt; see Exod. 10:7.) So in the final months and days of the Great Tribulation (thirteen months, one day, one hour; see Rev. 9:15), with the world's institutions, economies, and very ecosystems on the brink of utter and irrecoverable collapse, certain nations and leaders—the largest of which will be China—will have had enough of Antichrist and will decide to take military action against him. (See Rev. 9:13–19; 16:12.)

But while they plan their mammoth coup, another even greater problem presents itself: It becomes clear that Jesus will soon return to earth to liberate Israel and assume control of the nations. The persistent messages of God's final, faithful prophets, the two witnesses, will make this terrifying prospect inescapably clear to these world leaders. So despite their lust to unseat Antichrist, they will all agree on one thing: They must first fight Jesus and His heavenly armies when they appear—or there will be no dominion left to fight over! So they gather in Palestine to defeat the King of kings! (See Rev. 19:19; 17:14; Dan. 8:25c.) It will be a military base like this world has never seen!

Heads of state and their armies from the north and south and east of Palestine will converge with Antichrist's forces at Armageddon ("between the seas in the glorious holy mountain," Dan. 11:45) with two mingled yet clear motives: to stop the return of Christ *and* to overthrow Antichrist. Only their former objective will be addressed, however, because Jesus will annihilate them at Armageddon before they attempt to unseat Antichrist.

Thus God permits Antichrist to be rejected and conspired against but not overthrown. That great honor is reserved for Jesus and the saints. (See Ps. 149:7–9; Zech. 14:5d.)

11:45 Seeing the end from the beginning. "Yet he [Antichrist] shall come to his end..." (Dan. 11:45). With these words, Daniel points to the end of the times of the Gentiles. That Daniel lived and began prophesying of the times of the Gentiles at their beginning, and yet so vividly described their end, reaffirms to every Bible reader that God knows the end of everything from its beginning—including the history of the world, the Church, our entire lives, and our tests of faith.

This is why the wisest man who ever lived wrote that we should "trust in the Lord with all thine heart" (Prov. 3:5–6). Are you trusting Him fully now? Or are you worried that Omniscience may overlook something or Omnipotence somehow fail you?

See "Revealing the end from the beginning," Introduction. See Isaiah 46:10; Acts 15:18.

Lesson: Because God knows the end of all things—world and church history, our lives, our tests—from their beginning, we should trust Him with all our hearts.

CHAPTER TWELVE

A TIME OF GREAT TROUBLE—AND GREAT TRIUMPH

12:1 THERE SHALL BE A TIME OF GREAT TROUBLE. Daniel plainly foretells the coming of a special time of unprecedented worldwide trouble:

> There shall be a time of trouble, such as never was since there was a nation even to that same time...
>
> —DANIEL 12:1

This dark prediction is not the only such one found in holy writ. Three confirmed prophets—Jeremiah (Jer. 30:4–7), Jesus (Matt. 24:15–28), and the apostle John (Rev. 12:1–17)—corroborate Daniel's ominous report. Each declares that, indeed, a time of unparalleled distress and suffering is coming to the whole world, but especially to Israel.

There are striking similarities between the information given in Daniel 12:1 and that found in Jeremiah 30:4–7, Matthew 24:15–28, and Revelation 6:1–8; 12:1–17. Jointly these passages reveal three key truths:

1. A time of unprecedented worldwide trouble is coming.

Daniel calls this period of sorrow "a time of trouble, such as never was since there was a nation" (Dan. 12:1). Jeremiah adds, "That day is great, so that none is like it" (Jer. 30:7). Jesus says further, "For then shall be great tribulation, such as was not since the beginning of the world to this time, no, nor ever shall be" (Matt. 24:21; see Mark 13:14–19). And John foresees a time when the Lamb of God opens the heavenly seals to a book of judgment that release upon earth war, famine, and death (Rev. 6:1–8; 9:15) with such devastating force that ultimately approximately half the world's population will die (if Rev. 6:8 and 9:15 are fulfilled sequentially)—a severe depopulation never before seen in the post-flood world.

There has been an undeniably obvious buildup of *worldwide* catastrophic wars and threats over just this last century: World War I, World War II, the Cold War (threatening universal nuclear destruction). Each one of these times of worldwide travail was unprecedented. The next—the tribulation period—will also be unmatched and final because it will terminate the times of the Gentiles. This final travail of the present world system will bring forth two very ugly children:

- World War III (see Rev. 6:2–8)
- Holocaust II (see Rev. 6:9–11; 12:11; 13:15; 15:2–4; 20:4)

2. That time will particularly concern Israel.

Daniel predicts this time will require special intervention by the archangel Michael to save the Jews from utter annihilation: "Michael [shall] stand up, the great prince who standeth for the children of thy people" (Dan. 12:1). Israel must be in very great trouble if Michael is called into action ("stand up") to deliver them. Accordingly, Jeremiah called it "the time of *Jacob's* [Israel's] trouble" (Jer. 30:7, emphasis added), not that of any other individual nation; hence he implied Israel will be the epicenter of the crisis. Jesus agreed, foreseeing an abominable idol standing in the "holy place" and advising His followers in that day to flee to the hills of "Judea," and pray that they not violate the "Sabbath" in their flight. (See Matt. 24:15–21.) By use of these distinctively Jewish terms, Jesus obviously addresses converted Jews in great trouble in Palestine, not Gentiles dispersed throughout the world. In inspired allegory, the apostle John foretells a time of great trouble for Israel (see Rev. 12:1–17), in which she will "travail" (the same metaphor Jeremiah used; see Jer. 30:6–7) in a desperate struggle against relentless lethal assaults from the "dragon" (Satan in Antichrist). He too says that Michael will fight, or as Daniel says, "stand up," for Israel during this epic struggle. (See Rev. 12:7.)

So we see the distinctive *Jewishness* of the tribulation period. It is not a Church test but rather a Jewish test, a time sent primarily to try "Jacob's" children (Jer. 30:7). Here we find further evidence that the true Church will be translated before the tribulation. (See 1 Thess. 5:9–10.) Nowhere does the Bible predict a special time (dispensation, epoch, era) of testing for the Church! (Its prime apocalyptic books—Daniel and Revelation— omit any mention of the ecclesiastical body, an unthinkable error if the times they describe were meant for the body of Christ; note this omission in Rev. 4–19.) Rather, the New Testament teaches throughout its Gospels, Epistles, and the Book of Acts that believers' tests (our times of tribulation and persecution) arise *now in this time*, anytime, anywhere, and with anyone who uncompromisingly believes, obeys, or ministers God's Word. (See Matt. 13:21; James 1:2–4; 1 Pet. 1:6–7; 4:12.) Church history, replete with the testing of Christians (not Jews), only further confirms that the true Church is being tested now, daily.

3. God will deliver all believing Jews.

Despite the Jews' extreme trouble, Daniel foresees their deliverance. He prophesied, "At that time thy people shall be delivered," adding the qualifying phrase, "every one that shall be found written in the [Lamb's] book [of life]" (Dan. 12:1). By his reference to the book of life, we know he is speaking of converted or "completed" Jews, not those who still reject their Messiah.

Jeremiah agreed, writing, "He [the people of Jacob] shall be saved out of it" (Jer. 30:7). Jesus further assured believing Jews of ultimate deliverance by revealing that God will "shorten the days" of the great tribulation (latter three and a half years) solely to save Israel's oppressed but faithful remnant (Matt. 24:22). The apostle John foresaw Israel's salvation from its tribulation in two phases: 1) her miraculous preservation from the "flood" of trouble that will assail her (Rev. 12:6, 14–16); and 2) her final deliverance by divine intervention, when the King of kings crushes her cruel oppressor, Antichrist (Rev. 19:11–20). Elsewhere John notes that other believing Jews will be saved, not by being hidden and later liberated but by translation just before the mid-point of the tribulation (Rev. 12:5; 7:9–17; 14:1–5). Still other Jews will be released from Antichrist's tyranny by suffering martyrdom rather than worship Antichrist's image (see Rev. 12:11b; 6:9–11; 13:15; 15:2–4; 20:4); this will be "Holocaust II," as noted above.

Thus four consummately credible, divinely chosen runners—Daniel, Jeremiah, Jesus, and John—have come racing to us from the past bearing the same excited tidings concerning the future:

- There shall be a time of unparalleled worldwide trouble.

- Israel will be its epicenter.

- All believing Jews will be delivered out of it—by translation, martyrdom, or hiding and liberation.

Do we believe our witnesses? Are we preparing now to "escape all these things that shall come to pass" (Luke 21:36) by watching and praying and being uncompromisingly righteous in our manner of life? Remember, only overcomers in action will be taken. (See Rev. 3:10; Luke 21:34–36.)

12:1 Michael will "stand up." Michael is the archangel (Jude 9) whose specific assignment is to watch over, assist, and defend the people of Israel. Daniel says that during the tribulation period Michael will "stand up," or *rise and act in defense of* Israel (Dan. 12:1).

As Michael will do for Israel during the tribulation, so angels do for us now in this time. When we are under special attack from demons and call on God for help, God sends angels to fight our invisible and visible enemies and liberate us. (See Acts 12:5–11.) Hence, they rise and act in our defense in times of trouble.

See "Michael—Israel's keeper," chapter 10.

See Daniel 10:13, 21; Psalm 91:10–12; Acts 12:5–11; Hebrews 1:14; Revelation 12:7; Jude 9.

Lesson: *Angels rise and act in our defense in times of great trouble.*

12:2 Sleeping *bodies.* At first glance, this text may seem to teach that redeemed Jews are sleeping in their graves. But this is not the case. "Those who sleep in the dust of the earth" (Dan. 12:2) may be paraphrased, "those whose *bodies* sleep in the dust of the earth." (For another instance of this usage, see Matthew 27:52.) Other biblical references reveal repeatedly and irrefutably that at the moment of physical death redeemed souls go immediately to the presence of God. (See Luke 23:43; 24:5–6; 2 Corinthians 5:8, 1–4). At the Rapture, Christ will bring their *souls* with Him when He appears (1 Thess. 4:14), reunite them with their resurrected, glorified *bodies*, and then catch away every living overcoming Christian (1 Thess. 4:15–18)—all in one miraculous millisecond (1 Cor. 15:51–52).

See Luke 23:43; 24:5–6; 1 Corinthians 15:6; 2 Corinthians 5:8; Matthew 27:52–53; 1 Thessalonians 4:14–18.

Lesson: *When believers die, their bodies fall asleep in Jesus but their souls go immediately to the presence of the Lord. At the Rapture, their souls will be reunited with their raised, glorified bodies and gathered with translated living believers to forever be with the Lord.*

12:2 The resurrections. The first and second resurrections are succinctly described in this verse.

The "many" (Dan. 12:2) who awake to everlasting life are the righteous Jews of all ages, including the tribulation period, who are raised after Armageddon for participation in the millennium kingdom of Christ. This is the *second part* of the first resurrection (see Rev. 20:4–6), the first part being the resurrection of Christians at the Rapture (see 1 Thess. 4:13–18). The others whom Daniel foresees rising "to shame and everlasting contempt" (Dan. 12:2) are the wicked dead raised at the end of the millennium. These are raised after the destruction of the heavens and earth (v. 2b) for participation in the great "white throne" judgment. (See Rev. 20:11–15.)

As in numerous other Bible references, this verse reveals that both the righteous and unrighteous will one day be resurrected and give account to God. Are we ordering our daily thoughts, decisions, and actions with this in mind?

See "The message of the last day," chapter 5; also, "The last word: judgment," chapter 12.

See Daniel 12:13; Ecclesiastes 12:13–14; Acts 17:31; Romans 2:5–16; 14:10–12; 2 Corinthians 5:10; Revelation 20:11–15.

Lesson: *All people—believers and unbelievers—will one day be resurrected and give account to God.*

12:3 Wise ones and reformers will shine. Daniel says in the End Times two groups of persons will "shine...forever and ever" (Dan. 12:3). Naturally, this unusual symbolism prompts certain questions.

Who are these perpetually shining ones? First, they are the "wise," meaning godly teachers, or those who are both God-fearing *and* filled with divine wisdom from God's Word. Various translations support this interpretation: "those who have insight" (NAS); "those who are teachers" (MODERN LANGUAGE BIBLE); and "the teachers and those who are wise" (AMP). Second, they are "they that turn many to righteousness," or uncompromisingly righteous reformers; this includes godly ministers, such as evangelists and prophets, and also any other believer who exhorts others to turn to God in repentance and faith. These turn both sinners and backslidden saints to righteousness (right relationship with and right living before God).

The Book of Revelation specifically identifies two groups of these shining ones. First, the 144,000 Jewish male evangelists (see Rev. 7:1–8) who will lead the great reformation/revival in Israel during the first half of the tribulation culminating in the great mid-tribulation translation. (See Revelation 7:9–17; 14:1–5.) Their ministry will be "as the stars," or worldwide in scope, and very effective, as they will turn "many" to righteousness (Dan. 12:3, 10). Second, the two witnesses, who will be God's only surviving *public* spokesmen during the last half of the tribulation (or Great Tribulation). (See Rev. 11:4–14.) Though not as visibly successful as the 144,000, the two witnesses' ministry will be just as wide and effective: Their words will help sustain the hidden remnant, convert many Gentiles who sympathize with the Jews (see Matt. 25:34–40), and usher in the second coming of Christ.

Why are these said to "shine"? Because, being filled with the light of the knowledge of God, they dispense that light throughout this sin-darkened world by word and deed. (See Matt. 5:14–16; Acts 26:18.)

When will they shine? Primarily, these will shine "as the stars" (Dan. 12:3), which appear most clearly in the night sky. Hence, godly teachers and reformers will shine forth with the light of God's Word just before, during, and after the long, black night of the tribulation period, which will be appallingly dark with the fullness of sin and spiritual delusion. Secondarily, these wise ones and exhorters will then continue shining throughout the thousand-year Day of the Lord and the endless Day of God that follows. Their spiritual radiance combined with that of the reigning Light of the world will result in an unprecedented profusion of spiritual light, a perpetual state in which "the earth shall be filled with the knowledge of the glory of the LORD, as the waters cover the sea" (Hab. 2:14).

The scriptures describe shining ones in earlier times. For instance, Elijah and Micaiah shone during the dark apostasy of Israel. Daniel, Mordecai, Ezra, and Nehemiah shone during the depressing and still-backslidden days after the exile. And John the Baptist and Jesus shone in the days when Pharisaism and Sadduceeism covered Israel like a dark cloud. Church history also describes Martin Luther, who shone with unmistakable brilliance in the Middle Ages when the Church was darkened by clerical corruption, erroneous tradition, and widespread ignorance of God's Word.

Where are God's shining ones in these present, sin-darkened times? They are not hard to identify. Invariably, light-bearers do the following:

- Fill their souls with the light of God's Word. (See Ps. 1:1–3; John 8:31–32; 2 Tim. 2:15; 1 Tim. 4:13–15.)

- Walk in the light of God's will. (See James 1:22–25; 1 John 1:5–10.)

- Share the light freely. (See Matt. 10:27, 8; 2 Tim. 2:2.)

- Hate darkness, shunning sin and separating from unrepentant sinners. (See Job 1:1, 8; Prov. 8:13; 1 Cor. 5:1–13; 15:33; 2 Cor. 6:14–7:1; 2 Tim. 2:19–21.)

- Suffer hatred from those who practice darkness. (See John 3:20; 15:18–19; 2 Chron. 18:7.)

- Exhort those who turn aside to darkness. (See Heb. 3:13; Rev. 3:19; Prov. 27:5–6; 28:23; Gal. 2:11–14.)

Are we in process of becoming a shining one? Why not? See Luke 1:16–17; 2 Chronicles 19:4; Romans 11:26–27; Revelation 7:1–8.

Lesson: *Uncompromisingly righteous teachers and reformers will have wide and effective ministries in these last days of the Church Age, in the tribulation period, and in the Day of the Lord.*

12:3–4,9–10 More signs of "the time of the end." Twice in chapter 12 Daniel referred to "the time of the end" (Dan. 12:4, 9). While he gave other details about this terminal period of the times of the Gentiles in previous chapters, he revealed *six* more signs of its buildup in this final chapter.

In this context, "the time of the end" has a twofold meaning. Primarily, it refers to Israel's seventieth week of years, known as the tribulation period (see "A prophecy of Israel's seventy weeks," chapter 9). Secondarily, it refers to the Church's final years on earth. Because the Church's last days immediately precede Israel's last days and these two sequentially fulfilled periods are so brief, their characteristics naturally overlap somewhat. Once the following six signs of the End Times begin, they will lead up to and extend through Israel's final seven years. So these signs tell us that both the Church's final days on earth and Israel's final days of Gentile oppression are at hand.

The six signs Daniel foresaw are:

1. Unprecedented growth of human knowledge (Dan. 12:4b)

Daniel foresaw a time in which "knowledge shall be increased" (Dan. 12:4b). For twenty-five centuries, no dramatically sudden increase of human knowledge occurred. But the amazing twentieth century changed this in an unmistakable way. Over the last one hundred years, human knowledge has increased greatly. In the last fifty years, it has grown at such an increasingly frenetic pace that it is now almost impossible to keep track of what mankind knows, especially in the areas of science and technology.

2. Unprecedented speed, scope, and volume of transportation (Dan. 12:4b)

Daniel also envisioned a time when many people will "run to and fro" (Dan. 12:4b). As with human knowledge, human transportation has also taken a quantum leap forward over the last one hundred years. At the close of the nineteenth century, millions lived their entire lives in their own locality, traveling rarely and slowly, by foot, horseback, carriage, or steamship.

Remote continents were virtually shut off to the outside world. And the only creatures that flew had feathers. Today millions commute to work or travel for business or pleasure, running "to and fro" on and between every continent by automobile, high-speed train, and airliner. We are literally a world of people in constant motion, twenty-four hours a day, seven days a week. No other century since Daniel's has experienced such a notable change in the speed, scope, and volume of its transportation.

3. Unprecedented distress of nations worldwide, especially in Israel (Dan. 12:1)

As stated in an earlier entry, Daniel described the coming of a time of unprecedented worldwide trouble that particularly involves Israel: "There shall be a time of trouble, such as never was since there was a nation…and at that time thy people [Israel] shall be delivered" (Dan. 12:1). Wars, revolutions, plagues, and famines have visited every century from Daniel's to the present. But no century has witnessed such distress of nations as the twentieth century. Its unique resumé of adversities includes massive destruction and death due to two world wars; the invention and use of atomic, chemical, and biological weapons; waves of moral, social, and political revolution; wearying international anxieties due to decades of nuclear proliferation, rival ideologies (capitalism vs. communism), and unresolved religiously based claims (Middle East); the advent of potential worldwide thermonuclear annihilation; the proliferation of weapons of mass destruction with intercontinental delivery systems among rogue nations; random suicide bombings and other acts of destruction by fanatical terrorists. This ever-increasing buffeting of nations is no accident but rather the gradual buildup to the full and final "distress of nations, with perplexity" (Luke 21:25) of which Jesus prophesied.

Yet quietly, as the twentieth century wore on, the world's attention became increasingly focused on the survival of one seemingly unimportant, small, newly reformed Middle Eastern nation: Israel. And increasingly this nation's troubles have commanded the attention, resources, diplomacy, and military intervention of all others, East and West. Why? Because God is fulfilling His plan as set forth in the Book of Daniel.

4. End-Time prophecies will be clearly and widely understood (Dan. 12:9–10)

The angelic interpreter said Daniel's End-Time prophecies were "closed up and sealed till the time of the end" (Dan. 12:9, 4). That is, they will not be opened, and so released and fully understood, until the time of the end arrives. The angel goes on to assure Daniel that in that future period, "the wise shall understand [these and all prophecies with unprecedented clarity]" (v. 10).

In the latter half of the twentieth century, understanding of and emphasis upon Bible prophecy has increased dramatically. After Israel's widely celebrated reestablishment in Palestine (1948), and especially her retaking of the entire city of Jerusalem (1967), the Holy Spirit began unsealing the End-Time prophecies for all to behold and believe. All the scattered pieces of the grand mosaic of prophecy began coming together for Spirit-filled teachers, whose lectures and writings then began to form the complete End-Time picture for God's people to view. Now, after decades of widespread publishing of prophetic teaching, any wise (God-fearing) one may understand every jot and tittle of Bible prophecy, including Daniel's visions. Consequently, End-Time prophecy is more clearly and widely understood today than every before. On every continent believers are regularly informed and inspired by prophetic instruction through every conceivable media: print, radio, television, audio and video cassette, and Internet. Hence, *spiritual* knowledge has now increased almost as dramatically as human knowledge (see v. 4b).

5. The "understanding gap" will increase (Dan. 12:10b)

Daniel's interpreter observed that in the time of the end, evildoers will not understand their times or what God is doing in the earth: "None of the wicked shall understand" (Dan. 12:10b). Why? Because their enthusiastic devotion to idolatry and sin will have utterly destroyed their capacity to perceive the will and workings of a holy God. Notice the accompanying reference to their evil deeds: "The wicked shall do wickedly" (v. 10a), as if to imply that, like everything else in their time, their sins will also be unprecedented in number and wickedness. (See Rev. 9:20–21.) Meanwhile, God-fearing ones will understand exactly what God is doing and why: "But the wise shall understand." Hence, there will be a huge mental hiatus between the viewpoint of saints and sinners. Saints will say Antichrist is the devil incarnate; sinners will believe he is God incarnate. Saints will affirm that Israel is the chosen nation; sinners will accuse Jews of being the scourge of the earth. Saints will glory in Jesus as their Savior, Lord, and coming King; sinners will mock everything associated with Him and persecute everyone who serves Him. Saints will claim God is holy and hates the prevailing idolatry and sinfulness; sinners will claim they are just expressing themselves and exercising their God-given rights. Thus the "understanding gap" will be wider than in any previous period in history.

This understanding gap is present today—and widening by the minute. Just open your eyes and notice how utterly irreconcilable the basic views are of those who believe and obey Scripture and those who reject it. Pick any controversial religious or moral issue—the Palestinian issue, abortion, the new birth or homosexuality—and you will see that right now "none of the wicked shall understand, but the wise shall understand." Why? Because we're already living in the last days of the Church Age.

6. God will raise up many overcomers (Dan. 12:3, 10)

Daniel foresaw the time of the end as a period in which "many" would be saved: "they that [shall] turn many to righteousness…" (Dan. 12:3). But that's not all. These many saved ones will go on to become true overcomers, fully sanctified and thoroughly tested: "Many shall be purified, and made white, and |tested|" (v. 10). Thus God will not only save but completely conform them to the character image of Christ. His will be a complete work of grace. And perhaps even more surprisingly, these End-Time converts will not only "just believe" but will let God do whatever He wants in and with them, submitting to His instruction, conviction, and correction, and to the sufferings of the cross. Theirs will be a total commitment, and their time, one marked by deep Christianity.

Presently, *shallow* is the word that most accurately describes Christianity in this Laodicean period. (Christ's message to the Laodicean Christians, who represent prophetically believers in these last days of the Church, definitely confirms this [Rev. 3:14–22].) But in these last days God will change that. He will so work by His Spirit that "many" Christians will no longer be content with shallow Christianity. They will desire to be all God wants them to be and do all He wants them to do. God will take these willing hearts through the fires of testing where their souls will be purged of carnality and their faith and loyalty to Christ proven. Their fiery trials will foreshadow the "Babylonian furnace" of the tribulation, which Daniel's three friends experienced (Dan. 3) and he foresaw in this final chapter. (See Dan. 12:10; Mal. 3:1–4.) So in the Church's and Israel's respective "times of the end," God's heart desire will finally be realized: He will raise up many overcomers, forged in the fires of testing and henceforth fit for His full fellowship and use in His kingdom.

Do we really realize what these signs mean? Today we stand on the doorstep of Daniel's "time of the end."

12:5–13 "How long?" Daniel overhears one angel asking another the question of the hour: "How long" will it be until the end of these "wonders" (Dan. 12:6), or awesome earthly signs and times of trouble, and the beginning of the kingdom of Messiah and His people? During the tribulation, this twofold question will captivate the attention of everyone: saints in heaven, survivors on earth, Israel's hidden remnant, and perhaps the angels, too.

Question #1: "How long" until the end of the Great Tribulation?

The angel's answer is that the end of the tribulation period ("time of trouble," Dan. 12:1) may be measured in two ways. They are:

1. CHRONOLOGICALLY. It will last until three and a half years expire, here described as "times [two years], time [one year], and a half [half year]" (Dan. 12:7a; see Dan. 7:25b; Rev. 12:6, 14). To further assure us, the same period is described elsewhere in Scripture in months and days (forty-two months or 1,260 days; see Rev. 11:2–3; 13:5).

2. CONDITIONALLY. It will last until the condition of the Jewish people (hidden remnant) deteriorates: "When he [Antichrist] shall have accomplished |the breaking up of| the power of the holy people, all these things shall be finished" (Dan. 12:7b; see Dan. 7:25a). After three and a half years of oppression, the hidden remnant's psychological and physical strength will be utterly expended. So God will intervene and end their captivity. Hence, His people will be *at their breaking point* when Jesus returns to earth to destroy their oppressor, Antichrist. (See Deut. 32:36.) Thus He will faithfully shorten the days of their captivity to save them from utter collapse. (See Matt. 24:21–22).

Question #2: "How long" until the kingdom of Christ appears?

The full manifestation of Christ's millennial kingdom will not appear immediately after He returns at the end of 1,260 days (three and a half years). That wondrous epoch of blessing, which will be begun by a grand coronation ceremony to "anoint the most Holy [place and person]" (Dan. 9:24), will be delayed an additional seventy-five days. Notice the angel explicitly states that 1,335 days will pass from the time the "abomination that maketh desolate" is set up (the mid-point of the tribulation) until the full blessing (the kingdom of Christ) appears (Dan. 12:11–12).

So while Jesus returns after 1,260 days, His kingdom isn't fully manifested until the end of 1,335 days—or seventy-five days later. Those who wait patiently for that time are described as fully blessed: *"Blessed [fully blessed] is he* that waiteth, and cometh to the thousand three hundred and five and thirty days" (v. 12, emphasis added).

Why will tribulation survivors have to wait seventy-five days after Antichrist's defeat to receive the full blessing of Christ's kingdom? These days will be needed to:

1. RECKON WITH SURVIVORS. After defeating Antichrist at Armageddon, Jesus will judge the tribulation survivors to determine who will be permitted to live on in His kingdom. After gathering them, He will divide the "sheep" from the "goats," just as He described in His prophetic parable (Matt. 25:31–46). Those who harmed or refused to aid the Jewish remnant will be slain and banished to hell, while those who aided them will receive the blessing of life in His kingdom: "Come, ye blessed of my Father, inherit the kingdom prepared for you..." (Matt. 25:34).

2. RESTORE THE EARTH. After the cataclysmic worldwide plagues of the Great Tribulation, which will utterly dismantle the earth's basic life systems and spoil its beauty (see Rev. 8, 9, 16), the whole earth will need to be restored. The most basic cycles and systems of nature (water cycle, food chain, marine life, animal life, agriculture, etc.) will have to be reestablished before humankind may again live and flourish on earth. This will be reminiscent of the reestablishment of normal life after the Flood. (See Gen. 9.)

3. REBUILD JERUSALEM AND THE TEMPLE AND REESTABLISH ITS WORSHIP. This time will further serve to cleanse the Jewish temple and begin rebuilding Jerusalem, both of which will have suffered severe damage and defilement during the Great Tribulation. Also, it will allow time for new priests to be selected and dedicated for

service, who will then reestablish temple worship according to God's law. This will be reminiscent of the Maccabean cleansing and rededication of the temple after the desecrations of Antiochus IV. (See "A Hanukkah yet to come," chapter 9.)

4. READY CHRIST'S ADMINISTRATION AND BEGIN REBUILDING THE WORLD. As incoming world ruler, Jesus will need time to select which overcomers will serve in His new administration and instruct them sufficiently on their new duties. They will then begin physically rebuilding and reorganizing the cities, towns, provinces, and nations destroyed by the wars and plagues of the tribulation period. Although on a much grander scale, this will be reminiscent of the physical and governmental rebuilding of Europe and Japan after World War II.

Incidentally, in the present American system of democracy, it takes about seventy-five days for the orderly transfer of power from one presidential administration to the next. Typically, Nov. 1–7 is Election Day, and Jan. 20 is Inauguration Day. Similarly, the seventy-five-day period following Christ's return will allow for an *orderly transition of power* between the administrations of Antichrist and Christ.

12:3,10 A time of great triumph. These verses give us a small glimpse of the least recognized yet most important phase of the tribulation period. While it is widely known as a time of great trouble (see "There shall be a time of great trouble," chapter 12), the tribulation will also be a time of great triumph from God's perspective. Why?

Because while the grim reaper is taking many in death (see Rev. 6:8; 14:17–20), simultaneously the Great Reaper will be redeeming many and bringing them into His heavenly garner (see Rev. 14:14–16). Oh, how sufficient His grace will be! Despite the unprecedented prevalence of sin worldwide, the horrific plagues of judgment throughout the earth, the cruel ravages of war, and severe depopulation caused by epidemic diseases, starvation, and murder, God will accomplish a *great work of salvation and sanctification in many*. In the ultimate demonstration of Him working all things together for His people's good, God will use the awesome forces He unleashes to help expedite His age-old purpose, namely, to save many people and transform them (by intensive teaching and testing) into sanctified, proven overcomers in action, similar in character to Daniel, Shadrach, Meshach, Abednego, the Maccabees, and most importantly, Christ. Hence, they will be "conformed to the image of His Son" (Rom. 8:28–29). That this divine triumph, won largely by the ministries of the 144,000 Jewish witnesses, will occur in large and not small numbers of people is proven by the interpreter's repeated use of the word "many." Clearly, he intimates a greater divine work amid the great diabolical deception: "They shall turn *many* to righteousness...*Many* shall be purified, and made white, and |tested|" (Dan. 12:3, 10, emphasis added). This perspective changes our whole view of the tribulation: Its sad judgments will be swallowed up by its joyous victories. Finally, God's perfect will will be fulfilled in "many!" Many will be saved; many will be transformed; many will become overcomers; many will bear the character image of God's Son!

For Israel, this will also be a time of great national triumph. Her most furious troubles will usher in her finest hour. Finally, the long and burdensome "times of the Gentiles" will end and the long-awaited kingdom of Messiah will be established in Palestine! (See Dan. 9:24, 27; 8:25; 7:26–27; 2:44–45, 34–35). And every weary Jew will be "like them that dream" (Ps. 126:1).

Lesson: *Besides being a time of great trouble, the tribulation will be one of great triumph for God and His people. Amid its terrible judgments, "many" will be saved, sanctified, tested, and transformed into overcomers in action, conformed to the image of Christ. Then will come endless victory—the kingdom of Christ on this earth!*

12:1,10 More trouble, more triumph. The principle seen in the foregoing entry is this: By increasing the pressure, God hastens His work in the world, the Church, or the individual believer. Tribulation constrains obedience to God; persisting tribulation constrains consistent obedience to God; and consistent obedience to God hastens sanctification and establishes godly character. So holy pressure expedites God's work in our souls. Think of all the work He did in the three Jews in a very short time by thrusting them into Nebuchadnezzar's furnace. (See Dan. 3.) Thus the more trouble God permitted to touch His people, the more His work triumphed in them—provided they yielded to His will in the fires!

Joseph is another case in point. By permitting many adversities to try Joseph in his early years, God developed in him a spiritual maturity far beyond his years. Joseph's graces could not have been duplicated in an untried or lightly tried peer.

Shouldn't this give us a new perspective on our trials? James thinks so:

> When all kinds of trials and temptations crowd into your lives, my brothers, don't resent them as intruders, but welcome them as friends! Realize that they come to test your faith and to produce in you the quality of endurance. But let the process go on until that endurance is fully developed, and you will find you have become men of mature character, men of integrity with no weak spots.
>
> —James 1:2–4, PHILLIPS

See "Trial by fire—deadly but beneficial," chapter 3; and "Trial by fire—the goal," chapter 3.

See Exodus 1:12; 1 Peter 1:6–7; 2 Corinthians 1:5.

Lesson: By increasing the pressure of our trials, God hastens His work in our souls.

12:13 The last word: Judgment. The angel ended Daniel's question-and-answer session by informing him that he was to finish out his life, die, and then await the "time of the end," when he will rise and stand before God to be judged along with his generation: "But go thou thy way till the [time of the] end be; for thou shalt rest [in death], and [after resurrection] stand in thy lot at the end of the days [or time of the end]" (Dan. 12:13). Specifically, Daniel will be raised in the second part of the first resurrection described in Daniel 12:2a.

Thus, fittingly, Daniel's great writing ends just as the Book of Ecclesiastes (Eccles. 12:13–14) and the Bible itself (Rev. 20:11–15) does, with the single most important issue facing every prophet and every person—the judgment of God. All souls, redeemed and unredeemed, will one day be resurrected bodily to give account of their lives to God. All will be judged according to their works: the redeemed, to determine their rewards, honors, and service in God's eternal kingdom (see 1 Cor. 3:12–15; 2 Cor. 5:10–11); and the unredeemed, to determine their degree of punishment in the lake of fire (see Rev. 20:12–13, 15).

If even Daniel needed to be reminded of coming judgment, so should we. No matter what your experience in life, never lose touch with this "weightier matter" (Matt. 23:23). Like a true keel, it will keep you sailing upright and on course for glory, not shame.

See "The message of the last day," chapter 5.

See 1 Peter 4:17; Matthew 23:23; Daniel 12:2; Ecclesiastes 12:13–14.

Lesson: *At the last, every person will be raised from death and judged by God.*

Without application to our lives, biblical information is interesting but impertinent. You now have a significant amount of data about the man Daniel and his message. For the duration, it's there, saved in your cerebral computer. You can recall it, talk about it, preach it, and teach it. But here's the most pertinent question: Will you live it? All the information in this book is much ado about nothing if it fails to produce godly changes in your lifestyle and character. God doesn't want you just to preach Daniel's character; He wants you to possess it. Demonstration is far better than mere dissertation. Revelation (biblical prophecy) is given for preparation and information for transformation—always. If the study of this book leaves you informed but untransformed and enlightened but unprepared, it has failed its purpose. And, sadly, so have you.

Of the prophet Samuel the Bible says, "The Lord...did let none of his words *fall to the ground*" (1 Sam. 3:19, emphasis added). This means that Samuel's counsels and prophecies never went unheeded by men or unfulfilled by God. Whenever Samuel spoke, God's people always listened; after Samuel spoke, God always acted. Thus God's word through Samuel never returned to God "void"—empty, or without causing God's desired results. (See Isa. 55:11.) Will the same be true of us after our study of the life and Book of Daniel? Will we let the Word live and work and create in us God's desired results? Will these divine principles be "made flesh" (John 1:14) in us or made futile? Will we let Daniel's utterances—these mighty revelations of a master prophet—fall to the ground, unheeded by us and unfulfilled in us? Or will we wisely apply them to our lives and works, so they

294

become the seeds of more spiritual life and fruit in us and more glory for God?

The Bible informs us that the Holy Spirit wants to transform us into the image of God's Son. (See Rom. 8:29.) I am absolutely convinced that part of this transformation process is making us—you, me, and every believer living in these last days—like the "faithful four" so clearly showcased in the Book of Daniel. Every one of us is called to become *overcomers in action*. Christ's inspired messages to the Church Age only confirm, and never contradict, this conviction. (See Revelation chapters 2–3.) And this exposition of the Book of Daniel is given primarily to facilitate this paramount divine objective.

So do God's will. Prayerfully ponder Daniel's prophetic revelations until they inspire you. Let them fill you with heavenly certainty in these increasingly uncertain times and fully prepare you for what lies ahead for this unprepared world and sleeping church. Prayerfully study the faithful four's experiences till they challenge you to change wherever necessary. Then go forth and walk in the ways of Daniel and his three friends...

- Be uncompromisingly loyal to God's words and ways...

- Be faithful, never seeking power or prosperity by compromising the truth...

- Expect and endure your own trial by fire...

- Share bravely and humbly whatever God shows you to whomever He sends you...

- Be prepared, always living ready for divine service at a moment's notice...

- And whatever life brings—preferment, promotion, or persecution—remain uncompromisingly loyal to your God, His words, and His ways...

...until you become like them.

Then God's purpose in giving the Book of Daniel will be fulfilled in you: Its revelations will have prepared you, and its information will have transformed you. To God be the glory!

BIBLIOGRAPHY

The Amplified Bible. Grand Rapids, Mich.: Zondervan. 1965.

The New Analytical Bible. Chicago: Dickson Publishing. 1973.

The Living Bible. Wheaton, Ill: Tyndale House. 1971.

The Modern Language Bible (New Berkley Version in Modern English). Grand Rapids, Mich.: Zondervan. 1969.

Phillips, J. B. *The New Testament in Modern English*. New York: MacMillan. 1972.

The Open Bible. Nashville, Tenn.: Nelson Publishers. 1975.

Ryrie, Charles C. *The Ryrie Study Bible*. Chicago: Moody Press. 1978.

The New Scofield Study Bible. New York: Oxford University Press. 1967.

The Spirit-Filled Life Bible. Nashville, Tenn.: Nelson Publishers. 1991.

Wycliffe Bible Encyclopedia. 2 vols. Chicago: Moody Press. 1975.

Tenney, Merrill C., ed. *The Zondervan Pictorial Bible Dictionary*. Grand Rapids, Mich.: Zondervan. 1967.

Tozer, A. W. *The Best of A. W. Tozer*. Camp Hill, Pa.: Christian Publications. 1978.

————. *Paths to Power*. Camp Hill, Pa.: Christian Publications.

Vos, Howard F. *Exploring Church History*. Nashville, Tenn.: Nelson Publishers. 1994.

ABOUT THIS MINISTRY...

Mission Statement

GREG HINNANT MINISTRIES exists to train believers to walk in New Testament discipleship by teaching the timeless, priceless, and unfailing principles of the Word of God. By doing so we are helping prepare the body of Christ worldwide for the appearing of our Lord Jesus Christ.

> Prepare ye the way of the Lord.
>
> —ISAIAH 40:3

Ministries Available

We offer a *monthly Bible message* (hard copy or e-mail) to interested believers. Pastors and others in Christian ministry are particularly encouraged to take advantage of this mailing. Foreign readers are also served, preferably by e-mail.

We presently offer for sale three additional *books* (see below) and numerous *audio cassette tapes* of Bro. Greg's messages. Current price lists are available upon request.

Visit us at our website: www.GregHinnantMinistries.org

To Contact This Ministry

Mail: Greg Hinnant Ministries
        P. O. Box 788
        High Point, NC 27261
Tel.:   (336) 882-1645
Fax: (336) 886-7227
E-mail: rghinnant@aol.com or rghministries@aol.com
(area codes and e-mail address subject to change)

Other Books by the Author

Walking in His Ways (Creation House Press). This twenty-four-chapter work sets forth the essential principles for true biblical discipleship, guiding the reader through the successive stages of spiritual development, from spiritual infancy to spiritual maturity. It is the textbook for Bro. Greg's course on Biblical Discipleship (Christian Life School of Theology,

Columbus, Ga.). Every serious-minded believer is sure to find timely instruction or confirmation in this book.

Walking on Water (Creation House Press). This twenty-chapter study on the Christian testing process identifies many tried and true biblical principles that enable us to walk on—rather than sink beneath—the turbulent waters of life. It offers aspiring overcomers tested truths for these trying times.

Spiritual Truths for Overcoming Adversity (Greg Hinnant Ministries). This twenty-six-chapter, plainly written book offers strong meat for strongly tried believers and ministers. Its numerous biblical principles help frustrated, overwhelmed Christians drop carnal attitudes and grasp new spiritual attitudes that enable them to endure and grow in any adversity.